# The Story of C

Cecil Headlam

**Alpha Editions**

This edition published in 2024

ISBN : 9789362923509

Design and Setting By
**Alpha Editions**
www.alphaedis.com
Email - info@alphaedis.com

As per information held with us this book is in Public Domain.
This book is a reproduction of an important historical work. Alpha Editions uses the best technology to reproduce historical work in the same manner it was first published to preserve its original nature. Any marks or number seen are left intentionally to preserve its true form.

# Contents

CHAPTER I  Druids and Romans: The Crypt ................................................................. - 1 -

CHAPTER II  Saints and Barbarians ..................................... - 19 -

CHAPTER III  Theobald-the-Trickster and Fulbert the Bishop ................................................ - 31 -

CHAPTER IV  S. Ives and the Crusades ............................... - 48 -

CHAPTER V  The Cathedral and Its Builders .................................................................... - 66 -

CHAPTER VI  Mediæval Glass and Mediæval Guilds ............................................................ - 91 -

CHAPTER VII  *The Cathedral* .............................................. - 114 -

CHAPTER VIII  The Birth of the Bourgeoisie and the English Occupation ..................... - 147 -

CHAPTER IX  The Siege and the Breach, 1568 ................................................................... - 164 -

CHAPTER X  Mathurin Regnier and the Renaissance at Chartres ....................................... - 178 -

CHAPTER XI  The Coronation of Henri Quatre ................................................................. - 189 -

CHAPTER XII  The Revolution—S. Père ......................... - 201 -

CHAPTER XIII  The Prussians at Chartres ................................................................................- 215 -

CHAPTER XIV  Itinerary and Expeditions ........................................................................- 218 -

FOOTNOTES: ....................................................................- 220 -

# CHAPTER I

## Druids and Romans: The Crypt

BUILT half on the slope and half on the strath in a depression of calcareous soil, Chartres lies along the banks of the gliding Eure, breaking the long levels of La Beauce.

La Beauce, indeed, is still the waterless, shadeless, woodless plain that the Bishop of Poitiers described in the sixth century, but it is now also one immense field of corn in which man has planted a few scattered farms and pleasure houses.[1] It is the granary of France. *Le blé c'est la Beauce et la Beauce c'est Chartres.*[2]

And on every side of it, spread out in the summer time like a many-coloured carpet under the great dome of the sky, stretch the cornfields, cut by the black lines of the railway, or by the straight, disheartening lengths of roads which run beyond the distant horizon of monotonous level, to Dreux, to Orléans, to Paris. The twin spires of Chartres are the only landmark. The sole beauty in this country must be found in its fecundity; in the fields of standing corn, which the passing breezes curve into travelling waves, and in the endless perspective of sameness which inspires the same emotions of mingled pleasure and sadness as the sight of the vast and melancholy ocean. And, like a ship for ever a-sail in the distance, everywhere the great Church of Chartres is visible, with the passing light or shadow upon its grey, weather-beaten surfaces, or, as it seemed to Lowell:—

'Silent and grey as forest-leaguered cliff
Left inland by the ocean's slow retreat.'

Chartres is no place for an Atheist.[3] The exclamation of Napoleon on first entering the Cathedral of Notre-Dame is the keynote and summary of the town. For from the earliest dawn of its history down to the present day Chartres has preserved, almost unbroken, the tradition of a religious centre. Other notes have indeed been struck here and died away in the distance of ages. There have been discords in the score of her worldly history. The armies of Cæsar and of Hastings have come and gone; the armies of England, of France, of Germany, have marched through the narrow, tortuous streets of this ancient city and left scarce a trace behind. Mediævalism with all its charm and all its vileness has disappeared before the excesses of that Revolution which sowed the seed of modern French civilisation. The thick forests which were once the glory of the Druids have vanished and given place to innumerable acres of tillage, whilst the sound of the woodman's axe has been replaced by the swish of the scythe and the hum of the threshing machine. But through all these changes Chartres has remained true to her heritage. She has been always the first town of Our Lady, the chosen citadel of the Virgin. The friars of the Middle Ages, who obtained the right of coining money, stamped on their coins the legend *Prima Sedes Francie*, and Charles-le-Chauve, when he presented to the town the Veil of the Blessed Mary, chose the Church of Chartres as the earliest and most august sanctuary of the cult of the Virgin. And even before the Christian era it was so. For, by a strange coincidence, in which there has been found something more than a coincidence, or nothing more than a reflection of Isis worship, or, again, merely a monkish invention, but by a strange coincidence, at any rate, the grotto, above which, in after years, the mediæval masons were to rear the superb superstructure of their Cathedral, was dedicated by the ancient Druids: 'To the Virgin who shall bear a son'—*Virgini Pariituræ*.—There, upon the very spot in the dim vast crypt which is to-day the most famous and the most frequented shrine in the world, they worshipped an image which was the forerunner of the statue of Notre-Dame-de-Sous-Terre.

Were they moved by some echo of those most ancient Eastern rites which include the cult of a virgin mother and child, or had they heard, these wise and inscrutable priests, some echo of Isaiah's prophecy: *A virgin shall conceive and bear a son?* Possibly. At any rate, we know that a hundred years before the coming of Christ the Messianic idea had grown familiar to the Gentile world. The works of Greek and Roman writers are eloquent of this fact. Plato, in a passage which seems to echo the very words of Scripture, had long ago foretold what would be the fate of the perfectly just man upon earth; and Vergil, voicing the prevailing belief that the world's great age was soon to begin anew, and referring to an oracle of the Sybil, prayed for the speedy coming of the promised Saviour in language strikingly like that in which the prophets of the Old Testament speak of the Messiah. The Magi, the wise men and watchful astrologers of the East, waited impatiently for the coming of God upon earth, till they beheld a new star which rose over Bethlehem and announced His Nativity. And these ancient Druids also gave expression to the yearning of all Creation. *Virgini Pariituræ*—To the Virgin who shall bear a son, they dedicated a wooden statue in the mysterious sanctuary hidden in the depths of their sacred forest, beneath the shade of which was the meeting-place of the Carnutes.

Thus it comes about that with the dawn of history we see, through the mist of the ages as it were, a solemn procession winding amongst the trees of the primeval forest.

At the head are two white bulls and the sacrificial priests, and in their train follow bards and novices chanting anthems, and a herald clad in white. The Druids follow. One of them is carrying bread, another a vase full of water, the third an ivory hand, the emblem of Justice. The high priest closes the procession, and about him cluster the other priests of the Oak and the chiefs of the local tribes. For the oak, Pliny tells us in his *Natural History*, is the Druid's sacred tree, and the mistletoe that grows thereon they regard as sent from Heaven and as the sign of a tree chosen by God. This golden bough of mistletoe, which they call All-Heal, the high priest is now about to cull from the chosen oak with his golden hook. As it falls, the sacred plant is caught beneath in a white mantle; the victims are slain, and the mistletoe is distributed whilst God is besought to prosper His gift to them unto whom He has vouchsafed it.

Such rites, so it may appear to the least imaginative of us as we behold to-day the pilgrims crowding to the shrine of Our Lady, or the long processions of priests and choristers winding their way from the sculptured portals of the Cathedral to visit the Abbey of S. Père, or the Chapel of Notre-Dame-de-la-Brèche, or through the crypt to the shrine of Notre-Dame-de-Sous-Terre,[4] are curiously prophetic of the history of the place. So thinking, we shall look at the western towers and note, like Gaston Latour, the bigness of the actual stones of the masonry, contrary to the usual Gothic manner, as if in reminiscence of those old Druidic piles amid which the Virgin of Chartres had been adored, long before the birth of Christ, by a mystic race, possessed of some prophetic sense of the grace in store for them.

Who then were these Druids and who the Carnutes? From the Carnutes the modern name of this their town is derived, and philologists assure us that the root of the name is to be found in the word for oak, which, in Celtic, bears some resemblance to the Latin *quercus*. Similarly Évreux is derived from the word *ebvre* = forest. All Central Gaul in those days was covered with oak forests as with a garment. Hence, it is suggested, the name of Carnutes was applied as a generic term to the dwellers in those forests, and was specialised as the title of the Chartrains *par excellence* on account of the choice of this spot by the Druids for their deliberations and their sacrifices. It may be so. Philology is one of the most amusing diversions. It is quite as intellectual as most other parlour games, and often much more entertaining. Human as heraldry and more profitable than pedigree hunting it certainly is, but somehow it is less convincing. Therefore if anyone prefer to derive this word Carnutes from *cairn*—the stone which formed the Druidical altar and equally with oaks seems to have played an important part in their ceremonies, he may be as much right as anybody else.

The condition of the Gauls at the time of the Roman conquest has been described by their conqueror. Cæsar in his *Commentaries* states that the Gauls were divided into three classes—priests, nobles and nobodies. The priests, who enjoyed complete immunity from military service, insisted on oral tradition in the teaching of their tenets. Their object in so doing, as Cæsar conjectured, was to prevent the memory from being weakened and their doctrines from being vulgarised; but the result has been that, apart from the few facts I shall mention and a vast superstructure of theory and legend which has been built upon them, they have faded from the ken of mankind. Chief among their tenets Cæsar mentions the belief in the immortality and the transmigration of the soul. The Druids were properly the highest of three orders of priests—Bards, Soothsayers and Druids, the latter being philosophers who, to the natural science studied by the soothsayers, added the study of ethics. There would seem to have been much of the Pythagorean and something also of the Brahman in these philosophers, whose teaching was once expounded by the Arch-Druid Divitiacus, in Rome, to the sympathetic ears of Marcus Tullius Cicero and his brother Quintus.

That teaching, alas! has not been enshrined in Cicero's sonorous page, but Lucan in his *Pharsalia* corroborates Cæsar:—

'The Druids now, while arms are heard no more,
Old mysteries and barbarous rites restore:
A tribe who singular religion love,
And haunt the lonely coverts of the grove.
If dying mortals' doom they sing aright
No ghosts descend to dwell in dreadful night,
No parting souls to grisly Pluto go,
Nor seek the dreary silent shades below:
But forth they fly immortal in their kind
And other bodies in new worlds they find.
Thus life forever runs its endless race,
And like a line death but divides the space.
A stop which can but for a moment last,
A point between the future and the past.
Thrice happy they beneath their northern skies
Who that worst fear, the fear of death, despise!'

In another passage the same poet describes in dark colours the gloomy rites of the barbarous priests; their rude, misshapen images, and the scene of their ritual in the sacred wood, smeared with human blood.

But of their ritual we really know nothing, apart from the fact of human sacrifices, which, in extreme cases, they justified by the dogma that 'unless for the life of a man man's life be rendered the wrath of the immortal gods cannot be appeased,' and excepting their veneration for the mistletoe.[5]

The power of this priesthood was not confined to things spiritual. The Druids acted as a court of public arbitration, and the most important private suits, especially cases of murder and homicide, were submitted to their judgment. Now Britain was the headquarters of Druidism, but once a year, it is recorded by Cæsar, a general assembly of the order was held within the territories of the Carnutes, and there the sacred rites were celebrated, the young priests, after a prolonged course of training, initiated, and the Arch-Druid annually elected. It is probable that these ceremonies took place at Chartres—although it is possible that the claim of Dreux, of Senantes, of Alluyes, or of other neighbouring places which can boast Druidical remains, may be as well grounded.

But, at least, it is evident that the *Pays Chartrain* was a stronghold of priests rather than of fighters, and, perhaps, it was for this reason that in the early years of the Gallic War, the Carnutes, who among the Celtic Gauls were subject to the Remi (Reims), took but little part in the active resistance to Cæsar's arms. They had, in fact, welcomed rather than resisted the Proconsul, regarding him as their champion and liberator from the invasion of the Helvetii and the threatened dominion of the Germans. But when he began to meddle with their institutions they grew restive, and determined to throw off the Roman yoke. For, before

Cæsar's time, there had been, apparently, a general movement against monarchical government throughout Gaul, with the result that most of the tribes were free, but with a constitution decidedly aristocratic or theocratic. Thus at Chartres—*Autricum* was its Latin name—fifty years before the coming of the Romans, Priscus had been reigning.

A pious legend recounts that, during the lifetime of this King the son of one of the great chieftains was drawn lifeless from a deep well into which he had fallen. The father took in his arms the body of his child, already cold in death, mounted his charger, and, riding at a gallop for twenty leagues, approached the altar of the Virgin, whom the Druids worshipped, and laid the boy at her feet. Then life came back to the lad, he opened his eyes and smiled at the sacred statue. King Priscus, the legend adds, on hearing of this miracle, summoned a great assembly of priests and nobles, and appointed the Lady of Miracles his heiress and the Queen of his realms.

Thus legend. In fact we know that after the days of Priscus monarchy no longer obtained among the Carnutes.

But there was a certain Tasgetius, a descendant of the old royal house of the Carnutes. As a reward for his services to the Romans Cæsar restored him to his hereditary throne. The theocracy felt itself attacked; the Druids roused the republican spirit of the people. The doubtful success of Cæsar's second expedition to Britain seemed to offer a good opportunity for successful revolt. The people rose and assassinated their King, who was also the Roman nominee. Cæsar immediately ordered a legion under Lucius Plancus to advance upon Chartres, punish the conspirators, and take up its winter quarters there.

When the railway was being constructed in 1846, it was necessary to remove a vast mound which lay to the west of the town between the Portes des Épars and Porte Chastelet. Many Roman, Gallic and Carlovingian coins[6] were found in it, and it is supposed that this mound represented in part the material dug out when the foundations of the crypt and of the Cathedral were sunk, and in part the remains of the camp of Plancus.

The threatening aspect of affairs in Gaul called for prompt action on the part of Cæsar. Before the end of the winter (53 B.C.) he made a dash into the country of the Nervii, and then in the early spring held his usual Council of Gaul, probably at Amiens. The Carnutes, Senones and Treveri, omitted to send their representatives. Cæsar took this as a declaration of war. He immediately broke up the Council and ordered it to meet again at Paris, which was a convenient point for operating against the Senones at Sens, and thereafter against their neighbours the Carnutes at Chartres. The brilliant rapidity of his movements terrified these tribes. Acco, the leader of the conspiracy, summoned his supporters to the towns. But whilst they were endeavouring to obey the summons, news came that the Romans were already in their midst. Through the Ædui and Remi, who acted as mediators, the Carnutes and Senones sent to make submission and beg for pardon. Cæsar granted it for the time, and then devoted his energies to the destruction of Ambiorix, and the chastisement of the Treveri and the tribes on the Rhine.

But it was only a short respite, not pardon, that they were granted. Returning at the end of the year from his hunt for Ambiorix and taking his revenge upon the Eburones, Cæsar brought his army back to Reims and then convened the Council of Gaul. An inquiry was held into the conspiracy among the Senones and Carnutes. Acco was condemned to suffer death after the cruel old fashion of the Romans. He was stripped, his neck was thrust into a fork, and he was then flogged to death. But the flames of rebellion thus rudely repressed were not destroyed. They broke out again the same winter with redoubled fury when the absence of Cæsar in Italy afforded an opportunity. The murder of Clodius and the reported anarchy at Rome fanned into a flame the slumbering embers of discontent. The death of Acco was discussed by the Gallic chieftains when they held their councils in their secret woodland retreats, perhaps, indeed, at Chartres itself, and the bitterness of the Roman yoke began to seem intolerable. To regain their lost liberty all were eager for a general revolt. It was decided to begin at once in order to cut Cæsar off from his army in Gaul. When the question rose as to who should incur the danger of leading the way, the Carnutes undertook this duty. They first exacted a solemn pledge of support from their countrymen by the Gallic custom of mingling their standards, then, on the appointed day, under the leadership of Gutruatus and Conconnetodumnus, they gave the signal for the great revolt by murdering every Roman citizen they could find in their chief trading town on the Loire, Orléans. With the terrible struggle that ensued between the brilliant energy of Cæsar and the noble patriotism of Vercingetorix we are not here concerned. Suffice it to say that among his first acts of revenge Cæsar sacked and burned Orléans, the town of the Carnutes. Nothing daunted, the Carnutes furnished 12,000 men to the army raised to deliver Vercingetorix, who was holding Alise with desperate valour. On the fall of that town the Carnutes, in obedience to the advice of their leader, Gutruatus, entered into yet another league for their common deliverance from the yoke of their oppressor. They joined the Bituriges and other peoples of Gaul, but when Cæsar himself marched against them with his sixth and seventh legion they fled with their cattle into the woods. Yet, even in the secret retreats of their mighty forests, they were not safe from the hand of the Roman general. They were compelled to submit and to pass under the yoke, and their chief, Gutruatus, was beaten with rods until he died.

Thus the country of the Chartrains was absorbed into the Roman Empire, and it remained under the domination of Rome, reaping the fruits of that strong administration in the form of roads and good order and the minimum of oppression, until the coming, at the end of the fifth century, of Clovis, the Frankish hero.

Meanwhile, when Augustus gave laws to the conquests of Cæsar, he introduced a division of Gaul equally adapted to the progress of the legions, to the course of the rivers and to the principal national distinctions, which had comprehended above a hundred independent states. The Province in which Chartres (Autricum) now found itself embraced the country between the Loire and the Seine, and was styled Celtic Gaul, or, as it soon came to be known, Gallia Lugdunensis, borrowing its name from the celebrated colony of Lugdunum or Lyons. The principal towns of this Province were still Chartres, Dreux, and, above all, Orléans, to which the Emperor Aurelian was later on to give his name when he separated it from the territory of the Carnutes, and raised it to the rank of a city. For the rest, there were a great number of villages and strongholds even in Cæsar's day scattered about in the clearings of the forest. These would increase in size and importance as the great Roman roads running from Dieppe to Dreux, from Rouen to Paris, and from Paris to Autun, were built, and as the country grew more settled. For Druidism, which had long shown itself a disturbing influence and an irreconcilable factor, was at length proscribed by Tiberius and Claudius, and thereafter, Dion Cassius assures us, the Loire could be navigated in as much security as the Po or Rhone. 'The blue waters of the fair-haired Carnutan' grew familiar, not only to the Roman merchant and official, but also to the Roman poet and traveller.[7]

But if the legend of the Druidical Virgin be indeed true, it would appear that the Druids, equally with the Romans, had done something to prepare the soil for the seed of Christianity. As to the first sowers of that seed there is some dispute, and also as to the first sowing, which some date from the first century, others from the third.

Whether Celtic Gaul was evangelised in the days of the Apostles or not, it is at least historically certain that as early as the middle of the second century the country was sufficiently provided with churches to form the principle theatre of the great persecution under Marcus Aurelius. And as Gaul was notoriously evangelised only piecemeal and slowly, and not by a sudden outburst of religious fervour, it is quite possible that the foundation of the Church of Chartres dates back from the first century. If this is so, it accords well with local traditions drawn from various sources, but agreeing in substance. For it is said[8] that S. Peter sent forth S. Savinian, S. Potentian and S. Albin to preach the Gospel to the Gallic nation. In the course of their mission they came to Sens and converted many virtuous heathen, amongst whom were Sérotin and Eodald. To these two, together with Potentian and Altin, Savinian, warned by a mysterious vision, gave this charge:—'Take unto you,' he said, 'the shield of an unconquerable faith; go through the other towns of Gaul and banish all false superstition by preaching everywhere the truth of the Gospel.' Leaving him, therefore, to organise the church at Sens, they set forth to Orléans, and thence, coming down that Roman road which is still known as the *Chemin de César*, they arrived at Chartres. There, perhaps, they found the altar of the Druids and the statue to the Virgin who should bear the Unknown God. Him declared they unto the people. As the word of the missionaries was supported by the miracles they wrought, and the saintly lives they led, a great part of the inhabitants believed on Christ. 'When they saw this, the holy men of God consecrated a church dedicated to the glory of Mary, Mother of God, and *built just within the walls of the town.*'

The northern walls of Chartres, under the Romans, ran along the street *du Cheval Blanc*, where now the houses of the cloister stand. The site of the Church of S. Potentian may therefore be identified, as on other grounds we naturally should identify it, with that of the Chapel of Notre-Dame-de-Sous-Terre in the crypt of the Cathedral. To that impressive underchurch we will pay a visit at the end of this chapter, and endeavour to describe the various stages through which it has passed. But first we will trace the tragic history of these Christian pioneers.

The rapid advance of Christianity soon brought it into conflict with the Roman administration. Domitian decided to check it when it was observed to be spreading among the subject races in opposition to the State religion. It became the duty of governors in the Provinces to treat the refusal to worship the Emperor's image as an act of sacrilege. There was a governor, Quirinus by name, who proceeded to execute his duty with truly Roman thoroughness and impartiality. He summoned the missionaries of what Tacitus called 'that pernicious religion' to his presence and demanded why they had brought hither the ignominy of their absurd doctrine. They answered him boldly, and bade him cease from the worship of idols and embrace the true faith. But Quirinus hardened his heart. He scourged and threw into prison three men 'hated for their abominations, and known to the vulgar as Christians'; notorious, according to the great Roman historian, 'for their hatred of the human race.' Such cases of persecution as this, it should be remembered, were but occasional exceptions to the general tolerance of Roman administration. The Christians were punished, according to the Roman view, for their inflexible obstinacy, their unsocial habits and indiscreet enthusiasm, rather than for the mere holding of their peculiar religious notions.

In the present instance crowds of believers collected about the doors of the prison into which the martyrs had been thrown, and by their continual prayers for the deliverance of their teachers roused Quirinus to savage action. He surrounded them with his soldiers when they were met together to pray and sing hymns to the Lord, and falling upon them suddenly put them to the sword. Amongst those who had been foremost in the faith was a young girl by name Modesta, whom popular tradition asserts to have been the daughter of Quirinus himself. She, it is said, was seized upon this occasion and brought before her father. His fury was increased to madness when he learned that she, his only daughter, had joined the sect and had been baptized. She must abjure, he declared, or she must die.

'Strike,' she exclaimed, 'I am a Christian!'[9] She was brutally tortured, and her body was then thrown along with the bodies of the other martyrs into a deep well, 'which was situated within the Church of the Mother of God.'

'The sober discretion of the present age,' wrote Gibbon, 'will more readily censure than admire, but can more easily admire than imitate the fervour of the first Christians who, according to the lively expression of Sulpicius Severus, desired martyrdom with more eagerness than his own contemporaries solicited a bishopric.'

*S. MODESTA (SOUTH PORCH)*

The blood of martyrs became here, as elsewhere, the seed of the Church. Quirinus was struck down by sudden death in the midst of his persecutions. His persecutions had only increased the number of the faithful. S. Aventin became the first Bishop of Chartres, and, profiting by the calm which followed Quirinus's death, rebuilt above the ancient altar of the Druids the church which Potentian had consecrated and the Roman governor destroyed. This building may well have lasted down to the final persecution of the Christians under Diocletian. For in the meantime the indifference of some princes and the indulgence of others permitted the Christians to enjoy though not perhaps a legal yet an actual and public toleration of their religion.

The courage and constancy of these first Christians were not forgotten. The well down which their corpses were thrown came to be known as the *Lieu-Fort*,[10] and later as the *Puits des Saints Forts*, in memory of them.

## LE PUITS DES SAINTS FORTS.

It is in connection with this well that one of the most beautiful of the legends of Chartres is told.

'A ceremony is still observed in the Cathedral' (wrote Sébastien Rouillard) 'which surprises many people. The reason of it deserves to be known. When the bishop officiating chants the *Pax Vobis* or a priest the *Dominus Vobiscum*, whether at Mass, Vespers or Matins, the choir does not respond in full, but only the nearest priest in a low voice. Some say that this is a perpetual memorial of the first Christian martyrs, in accordance with the saying of the venerable Fulbert in his third epistle, that the divine service which in times of liberty is celebrated with joy and gladness becometh mute during the days of tyranny and oppression. Others say that the custom arose when the crowds of pilgrims and worshippers in the Cathedral were so large and the resulting noise so great that those who were in the choir and at the altar could not easily hear each other so as to sing the responses.'

But there is another explanation. When Godfrey, founder of the Abbey of Josaphat, was Bishop of Chartres (1116), the usual devout and solemn procession to the grottoes and holy places was being made on the eve of All Saints.

Now among the choristers who bore candles in their hands, chanting in this procession, was one beautiful lad, blue-eyed and golden-haired, the only son of his mother, and she was a widow. It was the one joy of her life to listen to the flute-like notes of his glorious treble, and in spirit to join in those praises of the Most High to which her son gave heartfelt, wonderful utterance. And on this occasion she, as ever, was among the crowd of worshippers, hearing only—a mother's ear is so fond and so fine—amidst the whole chorus of those soaring voices the voice of her beloved son. Suddenly, though the chant had not ceased, there was, for her, silence. She listened and listened in vain for the voice of her boy. Mad with anxiety, she pushed her way through the crowd, only to find a group of grieving priests standing round the Well of the Constant Saints. The boy, all unheeding in the ecstasy of his song, had stepped over the dim unguarded edge and fallen into the fathomless depths.

For days distraught the mother haunted the holy grottoes, ever praying and waiting for her son to be given back to her. At last, on the octave of the feast, the solemn procession wound its way once more through the crypt. The mother listened, dazed with grief, to the chant as it came. But for her there was no music in the sweet harmonies that were sung.

Then suddenly there struck upon her astonished ear the silver notes of that well-known voice, how musical! She raised her eyes, half in hope and half in fear, and beheld, walking in his accustomed place and carrying in his hand a golden candlestick, her lost darling. And his face as he sang was as it had been the face of an angel.

They asked the boy what had happened to him at the bottom of the well, and he told them that he had heard the angels rejoicing and singing in response to the prayers that were being offered in the Church of Chartres. And since that day the choir does not make response aloud to the *Pax Vobis*. For so men hope that they may hear the angels singing.

That this holy well of the martyrs was near the spot where is now the altar of Notre-Dame-de-Sous-Terre we are assured by the repeated testimony of old writers. Numerous efforts were made during the nineteenth century to locate it, and made in vain. But in the year 1901 it was at last discovered behind the wall of that altar. Let us take the present opportunity in our history then to visit the crypt,[11] to behold the first beginnings of the Cathedral, the statue of Notre-Dame-de-Sous-Terre and the new-found ancient well of the martyrs.

'The crypt,' says Raoul Boutrais, in his Latin poem in praise of Chartres (1624), 'lies darkling in a hollow of the earth, resting on many an arch, as long and as wide as is the whole church above it. A dim religious light struggles through the deep-set windows. Enter and behold a sacred altar. Your being is filled with a mysterious awe as you descend. Then by the light of a thousand torches the sacred place becomes visible. The smoke of fragrant incense rises from the altar. Priests move to and fro performing their sacred office before the image of the Virgin. Many offerings of gold and silver, in token of granted prayers, hang at the shrines.

'We pass into recesses dug deep within the earth, and are conscious of a strange emotion. Here was the first origin of the church, when the early Christians sang their hymns in these dark places to escape the cruel punishments of the Prefect Quirinus, and yet undaunted by the cross, the sword, the fire of his mad rage. He snatched this heroic band from their Christ, and flung their mangled bodies into the deeps of a well. Still may be seen the well, fenced about that none may fall therein; for, 'tis said, that some have fallen. And it was not only to sing their hymns that the Christians assembled here, but here they passed their lives for fear of persecution. Therefore in their hiding they dug a well that they might have to drink.'

It is evident from this and other passages that the famous well was in existence in the first half of the seventeenth century; but shortly afterwards 'it was covered up by reason of the vapours with which it filled these subterranean places.'[12] It was covered up, and the site of it deliberately falsified when the sanctuary of the Virgin was decorated and the transverse wall between the real site of the well and the altar was built. After the alterations which were then made were completed (1671), the public was informed that the well was now under the step of the new altar, so that those who knelt there, and had a particular devotion to the Martyrs' Well, appeared to be rendering homage to the Virgin. The statements of the historians to the effect that the well was behind the altar were explained away by the very canon who had superintended the filling up of the well, for he made the misleading assertion that the altar itself had been moved back in the course of the alterations. He was believed. When in the nineteenth century efforts were made again and again to find this well, they were always made on the assumption that the altar had been so moved. The cynical precept which warns us to be on our guard against the occasional untrustworthiness of those who never lie was forgotten. It was not till M. René Merlet's pamphlet, *L'Ancienne Chapelle de Notre-Dame-de-Sous-Terre*, appeared in 1900 that investigations, based on historical research and archæological acumen, began to be prosecuted, and were before long crowned with success. Boutrais's words are now once more true, and 'the well may still be seen' behind the altar of the Virgin.

## CRYPT: NOTRE-DAME-DE-SOUS-TERRE.

The oldest portions of the crypt, and therefore of the Cathedral, that remain to us are to be found in the Martyrium or Chapel of S. Lubin. The crypt, it must be understood, was not in origin a crypt or a martyrium or a meeting-house of prayer dug beneath the level of the soil, but a tiny church set on the crest of the hill, and raised above the surface of the earth. It only became a crypt properly so-called when it had been covered up and the surrounding soil raised by the *débris* and deposits of succeeding years; so that when the new church was built it was erected naturally upon the top of the old. The spade of the archæologist has proved that the soil of a mediæval European town was raised by the accumulation of dust and rubble as much as one or two feet per century. And at Chartres excavations have revealed Gallo-Roman sub-structures at a depth of some eighteen feet. When we reach the Martyrium or Chapel of S. Lubin we shall find there a piece of the Gallo-Roman walls of the fourth century. This probably is part of the apsidal wall of the church of that date. As the church, with the vicissitudes of the town which we have yet to recount, was alternately built and burnt, destroyed and rebuilt, the crypt was developed until it is now the largest in France, and next to that of S. Peter's at Rome, and that of Canterbury, the largest in the world. It consists of two lateral galleries which run from the western towers under the aisles of the upper church, and form a horse-shoe curve beneath the choir and sanctuary 366 feet long, and seventeen to eighteen feet broad; of two transepts, seven apsidal chapels, and the *martyrium* which is under the choir of the upper church.

The successive developments of the crypt may be summarised as follows:—

Against the fourth century apsidal wall, of which traces are found in the martyrium, were built in 858 two large columns to support the new choir above. At the same time the circular wall of the apse was pierced with windows. In order to support the apse of the upper church other two large isolated piers were built in 962, whilst the windows in the circular apse were blocked by a second strengthening wall. The same year saw the addition of a double transept at the commencement of the apse. Fulbert, in 1020, developed these transepts by carrying them out westwards almost to their present extent, and by so doing he left the altar dedicated to the Virgin, though unmoved, no longer before a thick wall, but stranded as it were in a corridor—a situation which aided, and still aids, the progress of the pilgrims past the shrine. The great bishop also extended the crypt by piercing the wall which closed the transepts towards the east, and making the ambulatory out of which opened the three large chapels with deep, round-headed windows (S. Joseph, S. John the Baptist, and S. Anne). To support the vaulting of this ambulatory a new wall was built round the martyrium.

In the twelfth century, when the two western towers were constructed, Fulbert's long galleries were extended and connected with them. The windows were raised and enlarged with the exception of those which were blinded by the porches of the upper church. Four smaller chapels, with pointed windows, were inserted between the large apsidal chapels of Fulbert, and these still exhibit traces of early thirteenth-century painting. At the same period, the transepts being now prolonged, it was found necessary to make two new flights of steps by which they might be entered.

The beautiful doorway of the south staircase dates from this time. Lastly, when the porches of the Cathedral were completed, the transepts were connected therewith by means of vaulted passages, of which the one on the north side is near the Chapel of Notre-Dame-de-Sous-Terre, and the other southern one was turned into the Chapel of S. Nicholas in 1681.

Entering the crypt by the south-eastern door, after noticing the windows of its apsidal chapels, you descend a stone staircase, and by the dim candlelight perceive on your left the long south gallery begun by Fulbert in 1020, and extended in the following century right up to the western tower.

You are now in the original south transept of the crypt, and much of the masonry dates obviously from the tenth century. Turning to the left, the first chapel on the left is now dedicated to S. Martin. It was not originally a chapel, but in the twelfth century was used as an entrance to the crypt. Altered in the seventeenth century, as the windows and vaulting show, it was converted into a chapel in the nineteenth. It contains a few fragments of the original choir screen of the Cathedral destroyed by seventeenth-century vandals.

These fragments, which represent some scenes from the Birth of Our Lord, are very beautiful. Above them, fixed to the wall, are some admirable keystones of the vaulting, and two bas-reliefs with signs of the Zodiac, which still retain some of their original thirteenth-century colouring. Opposite the wooden nineteenth-century *grille* is a stone from the Church of S. Martin-le-Viandier, which was destroyed during the Revolution. Upon this stone are represented S. Eustace hunting, and on his knees before Christ, who appears to him between the horns of a stag; S. Martin giving his cloak to a poor man; the Virgin and Child between S. Louis and S. John.

Below is a fine early stoup from the Cathedral and, in the corner, the sarcophagus of S. Calétric (*see* p. 36). The date inscribed upon it has been changed to suit the date of the translation and festival of this saint, who was Bishop of Chartres, and died 557.

The next chapel on the left is that of S. Nicholas (recently restored by M. Durand). We have already spoken of it. Opposite it is the Chapel of S. Clement, where are some mural decorations of the twelfth century. The figures, beginning from the right, are recognisable as those of S. Nicholas, S. James, S. Giles, and of a King kneeling.

The wooden screen which here crosses the crypt was put up in 1687: behind it on the left is a thirteenth-century piscina, above which is a partly-obliterated twelfth-century fresco of the Nativity. Several windows are blocked by the Cathedral porch; and the lowest and narrowest of these is one of Fulbert's original windows, which was not enlarged like the rest in the twelfth century, because it was blocked at that time by a porch erected in the eleventh century. At the end of the gallery is a large monolithic font, intended for complete baptismal immersion. It belongs to the eleventh century. The capitals of the four columns which flank it are curious and noteworthy.

The plinths and abaci of the last bay of this gallery betray the fact that it was added in the twelfth century, when the old south-western tower (Clocher Vieux), with which a flight of steps connects it, was built. The walls of this gallery, like that of the northern one, are decorated with modern mural paintings illustrative of events in the history of Chartres, or of the saints who have been connected with the diocese. They are already in a bad state, and even at their best they must always have displayed more science than art.

Turning now and retracing our steps we pass the staircase by which we descended and make our way round the horse-shoe curve of the apse. On our right we perceive the seven apsidal chapels, of which the first, third, fifth and seventh are the Chapels of S. Mary Magdalene, S. Ives (*see* pp. 91 *ff.*), S. Fulbert (*see* pp. 69 *ff.*), and the Sacristy. They were added in 1194; whilst the second, fourth and sixth are the Chapels of S. Anne, S. John the Baptist, and S. Joseph, and they date from 1020. The window of the Chapel of S. Anne should be noted. S. Anne is represented carrying the Blessed Mary. When we examine the upper church we shall be struck by the importance of the position allotted to S. Anne in glass and statuary—as, for instance, in the great window of the north transept. The explanation is that Louis, Count of Chartres, who died on the fourth Crusade, sent to the Chapter from Constantinople the head of that saint.

Opposite the Sacristy is the entrance to the *Martyrium* or Chapel of S. Lubin (*see* p. 36), which is immediately under the sanctuary. Of this chapel enough has been or will be said.[13] At this point it will suffice to call attention to the architectural features which serve to illustrate its history. First, the fact that you descend into it by a modern entrance, which has replaced the old staircase and doorway; and secondly, the depth of the base of the round column on the right, indicating the original level of the primitive church floor; thirdly, the hiding place for the treasure; next, the fourth-century wall, with its layers of thin horizontal Roman bricks; and lastly, the circular wall and the ninth and tenth-century piers. The Gallo-

Roman wall on the west is probably a portion of the old *enceinte* of the town.

Going westwards on leaving the martyrium, we pass a staircase on our right and the Puits des Saints Forts on the left, behind the wall of the altar of Notre-Dame-de-Sous-Terre. When this wall was built and the well concealed in the seventeenth century, the circular passage by which the chapel could be approached had also to be made, and the masonry was so treated as to suggest the natural rocks of the old Druidical 'grotto.'

The chapel is at the end of the northern gallery (eleventh and twelfth century), which runs from the base of the *Clocher Neuf*. It is lit by two long rows of pendant lamps. Here, then, is that mysterious shrine which Boutrais has so well described. Here is that famous statue which for a thousand years has drawn countless myriads of pilgrims from all parts of the earth.[14] Kings and commons, rich and poor, scholars and Crusaders, sinners and saints unnumbered have knelt at this shrine since the day when Fulbert, having completed his crypt, left, it is said, the 'Statue of the Druids' in the same place as that in which the Gallic priests had held their assemblies *in finibus Carnutum*, on Carnutan territory. That statue was held in honour till the year 1793, when it was burnt by the Revolutionists before the *Porche Royal*. The present Madonna was made on the model of the old, and erected in 1857, after the crypt, which for sixty years had been used as a cooper's warehouse, was restored to its sacred uses. On the north wall may be seen the traces of three twelfth-century windows, which were blocked when the north porch was built; on the south wall traces of twelfth-century frescoes. Other frescoes in the chapel are recent symbolic work by M. Paul Durand. The vaulting was painted in the seventeenth century.

Whether the statue which was destroyed in 1793 was older than the eleventh century is a doubtful point. Some suppose that the previous Druidical statue '*Virgini Pariturae*' was burnt in the fire of 1020, and that Fulbert had a new one carved and set up then. Others, arguing from the colour of the wood, believe that it dated from the days of the Druids. For the face of the Madonna was 'black, but comely,'[15] like that of the Vierge Noire, Notre-Dame-du-Pilier, in the Cathedral proper. But whether this blackness arose from the action of time upon the wood, or whether it was another instance of that tendency to represent Eastern types and colouring and design, which seems to me very noticeable in the glass and statuary of the Cathedral, cannot be definitely decided.

One other curious point remains to be noted. We are told that the eyes of the Child were open, but those of the Mother who held Him on her knees were shut. The Druids, it is said, intended by this device to signify that faith was still in darkness, and that she whom they worshipped was not yet born. But the eyes of the Child, whom she in the fulness of time should supernaturally conceive and bear, were open; for He was without beginning and without end, the Spectator of all time and all existence.

# CHAPTER II

## Saints and Barbarians

THE early Christians of Chartres were scattered and their churches destroyed during the final persecution under Diocletian. When, therefore, the disciples of S. Denis, S. Chéron and S. Martin came preaching the Gospel through the valley of the Loire, they found but few faithful among the descendants of those who had been converted by the first missionaries. The evangelisation of the Province by S. Martin, the great Bishop of Tours, was commemorated in the title of the church, 'S. Martin rendant la vie,' in reference to one of his miracles, and in that of the Monastery S. Martin-au-Val, as also in the window in the clerestory of the nave of the Cathedral (north) and of the choir. Soldier, hermit, bishop and saint, he established the monasteries of Gaul. Two thousand of his disciples followed him to the grave, and his eloquent historian, Sulpicius Severus, challenges the desert of Thebais to produce, in a more favourable climate, a champion of equal virtue. S. Chéron, after completing his work at Chartres, turned his steps towards Paris, but was assassinated on his way at a place since named S. Chéron-du-Chemin. His martyrdom is represented in a bas-relief of the south porch of the Cathedral.

Then Castor, Bishop of Chartres, profiting by the protection of Constantine, built a second basilica, larger than the first, erecting upon the old site a chapel to the 'Virgin who shall bear a son,' and, above it, the main church and the principal altar.

Meanwhile the Roman Empire in Gaul was tottering to its fall. That confederacy known as the Franks, which had been formed of the unconquered tribes that dwelt about the Lower Rhine and the Weser, had overrun Spain and Mauritania, and had been flung back from Gaul by the brilliant efforts of the Emperor Probus. Again reduced by Julian, they remained for some time loyal allies of the Empire. But under Clodion, the first of the long-haired kings of the Merovingian dynasty whose name and actions are mentioned in authentic history, they advanced as far as the Somme, and established a Gallic kingdom between that river and the Rhine. On the death of Clodion, his two sons quarrelled over their inheritance; one of them obtained the protection of Rome, the other allied himself with Attila. For the King of the Huns eagerly embraced an alliance which facilitated the passage of the Rhine and justified the invasion of Gaul.

*Gargoyle on South Arch*

Chartres seems to have escaped as by a miracle the murderous attack of the Huns and Franks. She owed perhaps to the obscurity of her position the immunity which Paris owed to the prayers of S. Geneviève. But Orléans was besieged and defended successfully by Anianus, a bishop of primitive sanctity and consummate prudence, until the arrival of the Roman and Gothic armies compelled Attila to withdraw his innumerable host of marauders, and at length to give battle and suffer defeat in the plains of Châlons. (451 A.D.)

## CHURCH OF S. AIGNAN.

Was this Anianus that S. Aignan who founded the church which now bears his name; the S. Aignan who, with his three sisters, Donda, Monda, Ermenonda, endowed it, and was buried in the ancient crypt of that church?[16] On his tomb there was formerly to be read this couplet:—

'Corpus in his cryptis Aniani præsulis olim
Carnutum recubat, spiritus astra colit.'

(The body of Aignan, once Bishop of the Chartrains, lies in this crypt: his soul is in Heaven.) The crypt (restored sixteenth century) and the windows of this church are well worth seeing. The lower windows have nine of them sixteenth-century[17] glass, and nine of them nineteenth century, chiefly by Lorin of Chartres, whose *atelier* is in the picturesque Rue de la Tannerie. The upper windows are chiefly seventeenth-century heraldic. The church was often burnt down in the Middle Ages, and for the last time in the sixteenth century.

The architecture is therefore in the style of the Renaissance, though the main entrance belongs to the fourteenth century. The small entrance on the left of the façade is pleasing. The church was sacked during the Revolution and all its artistic treasures stolen. The building itself was used as a magazine, a prison and a military hospital till 1822, when it was restored to religious use by private generosity. The painfully unsuccessful polychrome decorations perpetrated by M. Boeswilwald make it impossible to remember the interior with any pleasure. Perched, as it seems, in the air, the exterior, beheld from the boulevards and bridges south-west of the town, forms, with S. Père and the Cathedral, one of the most prominent features of the most unforgettable view of Chartres. But the tower is destitute of grace, and the building, as a whole, devoid of any beauty of form.

If the nave were worthy of the apse and crypt, it would be another matter, and S. Aignan would be worthy of its place between S. Père and Notre-Dame. Approach it from the Rue Saint-Pierre by the steps of Saint-François, and the east end of the church with the enormous buttresses which support it, and the massive buttressed walls of the street which hold up the old parish cemetery, now the garden of the *Presbytère*, give you the impression of a mighty fortress frowning above you. But seen from a distance this effect is lost.

There is a legend in connection with this church worth recounting.

A poor tailor of Chartres, the story runs, made a contract to deliver himself body and soul to the Devil at the end of the year if his daughter should recover her health and make the fine marriage on which she had set her heart. At the date fixed when the tailor must fulfil his part of the bargain Satan appeared. It was evening. The man's wife threw herself on her knees, and by her prayers and entreaties obtained the concession that the infernal treaty should not be enforced so long as the candle burning in the cottage should last. Then the cunning wife rose from her knees, blew out the candle and ran full speed with it to the Church of S. Aignan, where she hid it near the present stoup, in the first pier on the left at which the masons were then working. Wonderful to relate, the pier was immediately completed, and the candle hidden within it safe from the clutches of the Evil One.

Fifty years after the Battle of Châlons, the Franks, under Clovis, established the French monarchy in Gaul. It was not established by the force of arms alone.

The Merovingian King had always allowed his Gallic subjects free exercise of religious worship. Now, at the instance of his wife, Clotilda, niece of the King of Burgundy, he listened to the Bishop of Reims. He and his followers, who were equally ready to follow him to the battlefield or the baptismal font, were received into the Catholic Church at Reims.

This meant that Clovis had on his side the hundred prelates who, under the Roman Empire, had gradually acquired a sovereign power throughout Gaul in matters temporal as well as spiritual. He paid the price in rich gifts to their churches. 'S. Martin,' he remarked on a famous occasion, 'is an expensive friend.' It was to this alliance with the Church that the establishment of the French monarchy in Gaul was largely due. The valour, policy and seasonable conversion of Clovis soon added the Northern Provinces of Gaul to his kingdom, whilst the great prelates were left free to strengthen their own hold over the people with whose instructions they were entrusted. And with the Franks the social system of nobles and serfs, which was the basis of mediæval life, was introduced.

The Dark Ages creep on. The Frankish conquest of Gaul was followed, says Gibbon, by ten centuries of anarchy and ignorance.

So far as Chartres is concerned, the conversion of Clovis is connected with the name of her first authentic bishop, Solemnis,[18] whom he caused to accompany and catechise him on his campaigns. It is even stated, though without sufficient reason, that Clovis founded the Abbey of S. Père (St. Pierre), of which the extremely interesting fourteenth-sixteenth century church is now all that remains. The rest is cavalry barracks.

Of the secular history of Chartres under the succeeding Merovingian Kings there is nothing worth relating. Whatever there was of sweetness and light in this barbarous epoch survived in the cloister, not the court. One turns with relief from the records of the quarrels and crimes of Clother and his sons to the story of some saintly life like that of S. Lubin, shepherd, monk, hermit, Abbé of Brou, and lastly, Bishop of Chartres in succession to S. Ethère. S. Lubin was a typical and charming saint, whose name and fame still live in the hearts of the people.

His charity to the poor, his compassion for the sick and infirm was without limit. Thus, when Malledegonde, sister of the young Calétric, who lay at death's door, asked the holy Bishop of Chartres for some drops of oil blessed by his hands, he did at once that which she had not dared to ask. He came in person to the bedside of her dear invalid, bathed his forehead, and prayed that he might be restored to health. Then the young man opened his eyes, and seizing the aged bishop's hand declared that he was healed. A bas-relief on the south porch of the Cathedral portrays this incident in stone. In glass, a bishop and enthroned, you may see the saint in the second window of the northern clerestory of the nave. From that moment S. Lubin continued to take a paternal interest in the lad, and on his death Calétric succeeded him as Bishop of Chartres. S. Calétric,[19] according to his panegyrist, combined every virtue with every accomplishment, and was, in fact, the personification of that Roman urbanity which the rude manners of the French had almost banished from the Gallic world. His tomb, as we have already seen, is now in the Cathedral crypt, whither it was removed from the Chapel of S. Nicholas, when that building, which was formerly adjacent to the apse of the Cathedral, was destroyed in 1702 to make room for the present bishop's palace.[20] S. Lubin, like most of the bishops of the sixth and seventh centuries, was still less fortunate in the place of his burial. He was interred in the crypt of

## S. MARTIN-AU-VAL,

which probably marks the site of the chief extra-mural cemetery of the Chartres of those days. This asylum of the dead was more than once profaned by the ravages of the Northmen and the excesses committed during the civil and religious wars. The nave and aisles were seriously damaged in the fourteenth century by the bands of English soldiers and marauders who overran the country at that time. The Huguenots, also, under Condé (1568) utterly devastated the church crypt, violating the tombs of the bishops and wantonly burning the building. The tomb of S. Lubin, indeed, was flung out of the church and was long used for domestic purposes, until at last it was cracked by the frost. Even then it was not safe from the utilitarian spirit of the day. It was turned to account when the foundations of the cemetery wall were being constructed.

The Church of S. Martin-au-Val was restored in 1659. It now serves as a chapel for the Hospice S. Brice, where between three and four hundred inmates are provided for.

It is not without reason that I have spoken of this chapel here, for it is the most important illustration of the Merovingian period at Chartres. Leave the Place Michel and go down the Rue S. Brice till you come to the Rue Vangeon, which is the first street to your left. The simple front of the church with its three little turrets is now before you.[21] Go to the chief entrance of the *Hospital* and say that you wish to see the crypt. It lies beneath the raised pavement of the choir, and it is evident that the greater part of it, like the nave, choir and choir aisles, is tenth-century work. You will have noted in this connection the bold abaci of the piers of the nave and the peculiar elongated, round-headed arches of the choir arcade. But here in the crypt, besides the interesting capitals of the detached piers which support the vaulting, are two capitals of extraordinary interest. They are of grey marble in the western hall, on either side of the tablet to Bishop Lescot. Sixth century; Merovingian; crude and barbaric as the age which begot them, there is yet a vigour and directness about these carvings which make them not merely curious or grotesque. Nor are they meaningless.

They represent, in the symbolic fashion of old days, the principle of life and death, of good and evil. They were intended, even then, as a warning to the faithful who approached the sanctuary, as a reminder of the fact that 'the stones shall cry out.' On the one capital, then, we have a scene of peace and love: two doves supporting the crown of peace, two others kissing. The other capital presents us with a scene of terror. An enormous, savage beast is seen emerging from a forest and seizing a man whose arm it has already half devoured. His friend, meanwhile, has gone to summon aid and is now returning, bringing to succour him a man with a lance....

There is one other matter to mention with regard to this church. That S. Aignan, of whom we have already spoken, and who, some think, was Bishop of Chartres in the third century, was found here, it is said, at the moment of his nomination, lost in prayer. The brethren had to drag him hence by force and carry him on their shoulders to be consecrated in the Church of Notre-Dame. Ever since then the Bishops-elect of Chartres pass the night preceding the day of their solemn entry into the town in pious retreat at S. Martin-au-Val.

Under Clotaire II. the French monarchy was re-established and united. The Chartrain territory was joined to Neustria and thus passed under the government of Pépin d'Heristal, Charles Martel and Pépin-le-Bref[22] successively. And Charles, before becoming King and Emperor under the name of Charlemagne, also ruled Neustria. Pépin, his father, who with the aid of the Pope Zachary, had added to the authority of Charles Martel the crown of Clovis, proved by many gifts to the Church that the gratitude of the Carlovingians could be adequate to its obligations. Among his gifts it is recorded that he assigned to Notre-Dame de Chartres part of the forest of Yveline. Ten years before Pépin was established on the Merovingian throne Chartres had suffered from one among many bitter experiences of the violence of the times.

The annals of Metz record that Hunald, son of Eudes, Count of Aquitane, revolting against Pépin and Carloman, threw himself upon Chartres in 745, sacked and burnt it, and 'did not spare the church consecrated to the Mother of God.' This incident was but a fore-taste of the long and ruinous struggle which the Chartrains were destined to maintain against the invasions of those men of the North, whose appearance on the shores of the Baltic had drawn prophetic tears, it was said, from the eyes of the invincible and enlightened Charlemagne.

The church damaged by Hunald was doubtless the one which had been built in the fourth century. The wooden roof and supports were probably consumed by the flames on this occasion, but the thick Roman walls of the ancient basilica—such as you see in the martyrium—would survive many a burning. The church therefore was easily and quickly restored by Bishop Godessald, and was ere long the scene of a memorable event.

Charles, son of Pépin, King of Aquitaine, had been made prisoner in the kingdom of his uncle, Charles-le-Chauve. He was taken before the meeting of the Estates held at Chartres (849), and there he made a declaration aloud from the ambo of the church to the effect that if he turned ecclesiastic it was of his own free will and for the love of God. He was blessed by the bishops and shorn, clad in the garb of a monk and sent to the Monastery of Corbie. Such was one of the ways in which one got rid of a dangerous rival in those days.

It was during the reign of this grandson of his, Charles-le-Fauve, that the storm foreseen by Charlemagne broke over France in a series of thunderbursts, destroying the fruits of his firm administration and wise encouragement of learning.

Warned by the troublous experiences of the times, the Chartrains were not ill-prepared for defence. But their fortifications were of no avail. We will tell the story as it is told by the monk Paul in his Latin *Cartulaire de Saint Père de Chartres*, which was written between 1066 and 1088:—

'Chartres at that time' (858) 'had a large population and was the richest of the cities of Neustria. It was very famous by reason of the magnitude of its walls, the beauty of its buildings and its cultivation of the fine arts.[23] But there burst upon Neustria a Pagan race from across the seas, who came in their huge beaked boats, and baring the sword of their iniquity cruelly laid waste almost the whole country. They destroyed many seats of the holy and gave them over to the devouring flames: towns, when they took them, they razed to the ground, and the Christians they either slew or led into captivity and sold into everlasting bondage. So furious was the rage of the heathen that they rowed up the Seine ravaging the land on every side, and at length coming to the city of Chartres strove to take it, whilst they laid waste the surrounding territory and rendered it uninhabitable. The city thus cut off from support, and reduced by the loss of many citizens and the enfeeblement of others, was surprised by a night attack and taken. All the Christians were slaughtered like sheep. And the city, which had formerly endured unshaken a ten years' siege by Julius Cæsar and had repelled the Roman and Argolic armies, for it was built of huge squared stones and strengthened by lofty towers, and was indeed on that account named The City of Stones, and it rejoiced in an abundance of aqueducts and subterranean ways by which it could be supplied with all provisions, was now permitted by Heaven to be burnt and utterly razed to the ground by a nation that knew not God. But the patience of God, which thus corrects the worldliness of His people in order that they may not perish hereafter, did not permit the cruelty of those barbarians to pass unavenged. For the Franks gathered from all sides and hastened to the spot where the enemy had left their boats upon the River *Diva*. There, meeting them as they returned laden with spoil, they fell upon them with so violent an onslaught that the Northmen went down before them as in autumn the leaves of the forest fall before the blasts of the north wind.'

So the good monk, with an indignant energy that is almost eloquent. The discerning reader will be able to separate in this story the wheat from the chaff. But the fact is certain that Hastings it was who took Chartres upon this occasion. He burnt the town and put to the sword the good Bishop Frotbold, with many of his followers who had sought refuge in Notre-Dame. The church itself, and the Abbeys of S. Père and S. Chéron, he gave to the flames.

### THE VEIL OF THE VIRGIN—THE CATHEDRAL TREASURY.

Three years later Charles-le-Chauve, paying one of his frequent pilgrimages to the shrine which he afterwards described as the first seat of the Virgin in France, beheld the ravages of Hastings. Partly perhaps as a consolation to the inhabitants for their losses, he now made their church the depository of one of the most precious relics of the Virgin known to Christendom—her veil or inner vestment, presented[24] by the Empress Irene to the Emperor Charlemagne at Constantinople. It is and was known as the Sancta Camisia, or, in popular parlance, the Sainte Tunique or Chemisette. Hence the form by which it is represented in the arms of the chapter and in the innumerable emblems which from the thirteenth century onwards have been prepared in metal or ware as tokens for the pious pilgrim. The immediate result of the possession of this sacred veil and the miracles it wrought was an influx of pilgrims to Chartres, who brought wealth enough to enable the Bishop Gislebert to restore the ruined church. He would seem to have still followed the lines of Castor's church, but he extended it eastwards, over and beyond the Gallo-Roman wall, raising the new sanctuary of the choir so that the floor was two or three yards higher than that of the nave, as in the case of the Church of S. Martin-au-Val, and constructing out of the martyrium a crypt where the veil might be kept safe in the time of danger.

It was not long, if we may believe the chroniclers, before the love and reverence with which all the inhabitants regarded this relic was to be justified and the reputation of the veil as the palladium of the town established.

It was in the year 911 that the Northmen, who had now come to regard Neustria as their own, burst for the last time on the land of France.

The people of La Beauce fled to the forests and the churches for refuge; but the forests were soon in flames and the churches were destroyed by the ruthless invaders. The refugees fled with their flocks to seek protection within the walls of Chartres. With them they brought the relics of S. Piat,[25] as some years before they had brought the body of S. Wandegisile to aid them in their defence. For the Normans were coming, those 'barbarians from across the seas,' and at their head was Rollo, first Duke of Normandy, Rollo, ancestor of the Conqueror, plundering and pillaging churches and abbeys in a fit of religious madness, so the monkish chroniclers aver, against the priests who had converted to Christianity the children of Odin. He had made a vain attempt upon Paris, and now had come down the Seine, rowing as far as he could, then, leaving his ships, marched upon Chartres and invested it. But he was obliged to raise the siege. The dry fact of history probably is that the approach of Robert, Duke of France, with the aid of the Duke of Burgundy and the Count of Poitiers, compelled Rollo's men, who were anxious lest their return should be cut off and were disheartened already by their failure to take Paris, to retire when they failed to take Chartres at the first assault. But the traditional account is certainly more picturesque. At the crisis of the siege it was to the Bishop Gasselin, 'a holy man, glorious and just and true,' that all men looked for comfort and courage. So Bénoit, the Anglo-Norman trouvère, tells us in his poetical history of the Dukes of Normandy. And Robert Wace,[26] Jehan le Marchand[27] and the monk Paul[28] agree with him in his description of the wondrous episode which ensued. For a bishop, Gasselin was indeed a bishop, potent in prayer and skilled in that art of destroying the human species which is war. He put his trust in Heaven, but did not disdain human succour. He summoned the Dukes of Burgundy and France to his aid. Then, on the day when he learnt that they were at hand, he left the walls on which he had kept watch and ward in prayer, and, '*tout esploré et larmoyant*,' called the people to the Cathedral. There he first celebrated Mass and offered supplications; next, leaving the altar, he gave absolution to the multitude. Thereafter, having put on his pontifical robes, he, preceded by a cross, led the citizens in armed procession back to the walls. Suddenly, above the gate which is called New, he unfurled as a banner the sacred veil, flung open the portals, and bade the people fight boldly.

'Vers la bataille vait le pas
Tote la ville sune à glas.'

The sortie was well timed, for just at that moment the helmets and bucklers of the advancing Burgundians and Franks were seen glittering in the distance. The besieged fell with resistless enthusiasm upon the astonished enemy. The enemy, dazed by the glory of the precious relics, caught between the sallying citizens and the relieving force, retreated to the Hill of Lèves and there entrenched themselves. So terrible had been the slaughter that the bodies of the slain (says Paul the monk) heaped in the Eure for a while completely choked the stream. And they tell us that the Place des Épars,[29] in which to-day the principal hotels of the town are found, owes its name to the flight of the Normans who were scattered on this occasion (*s'éparpillèrent*). Others, however, more prosaically explain the name as meaning the 'hub' whence the various roads of the province diverge.

It was at this juncture, when Rollo had rallied his men at Lèves, that the Count of Poitiers arrived on the scene, and bitterly he reproached his brothers of Burgundy and France for having given battle before he arrived. In high dudgeon he set off in pursuit of the enemy. But the Northmen outwitted him. Rollo despatched three soldiers into the plain to sound trumpets and thus draw off the enemy to engage an imaginary foe, whilst he and his followers effected their escape.

This signal victory long left its mark on the land. The plain near the gate where the Normans were defeated was known thereafter as the Field of the Repulse or of the Men Repulsed.[30] And the first bas-relief on the south side of the choir screen, which represents the bishop displaying the holy veil to the besiegers, also commemorates this event.

The veil was brought back in triumphant procession to the Cathedral, and shortly afterwards a skilful goldsmith of the town, Teudon by name, constructed a very rich and beautiful casket of gold and cedar wood to contain it. Many miracles were wrought in favour of the devout who sought the aid of the Virgin, like Edward III. of England and Henry IV. of France, by passing under this coffer. Numerous knights who carried the token of the veil were rescued from the greatest dangers, and women, especially queens, who wore taffeta imitations of it, were protected in the pains and perils of their travail. Countless rings and priceless jewels were inlaid in the sides of the casket and hung upon it by the grateful or the expectant, so that it soon became the most valuable treasure of Chartres, in a treasury, that is, of mediæval jewellery such as we have to make a very systematic effort even to imagine.[31] 'The still extant register of the furniture and sacred apparel leaves the soul of the ecclesiologist athirst.' The register to which Pater refers in the sentence I have just quoted was composed in 1682, and an annotated edition of it has been published by M. Merlet (*Catalogues des Reliques et Joyaux de Notre-Dame de Chartres*). The curious reader will peruse with astonishment and scan with regret the long list of precious offerings which the exactions of kings, the exigencies of warfare and the rapacity of the revolutionists have caused in great part to disappear.

The veil, together with the casket in which it had lain for nearly 800 years, was seized during the Revolution. The casket and jewels were sold. The veil, though rent in twain, was recovered, but not in its entirety (3¼ yards by 6 feet). It is kept now in two coffers of cedar wood, covered with silver gilt. Beneath the veil is another known as the Veil of the Empress Irene, which is made of embroidered Byzantine stuff of the eighth century. The visitor to Chartres should on no account omit to see these curious relics, and the extremely rich enamelled triptich of the School of Limoges (thirteenth century, but in part eighteenth century restoration). For the rest, though the Casket of Teudon, which was valued in 1562 at £8980, without counting the diamonds and rubies, enamels and pearls which adorned it, has disappeared; though the head and the slipper of S. Anne are gone and the relics of many another saint; though the golden eagles of S. Eloi, the sapphires of King Robert, and the gems of Henry III. of England; though cameos and crucifixes of emerald or agate, crystal or ivory, have, like the tapestries of Queen Bertha and the golden girdle of Anne of Brittany, with its fifteen rubies, ten sapphires and sixty-four pearls, and the flagon which contained the blood of Thomas-à-Becket, all been seized and sold by sacrilegious hands, yet there remain to be seen the delicate incense-boat, given by Miles d'Illiers, Bishop of Luçon, in 1540, the graceful chalice of Henry III. (1582), and the green marble altar of the English, dedicated by them in 1420, when Chartres was in their hands.

You will also notice a medal, which was struck to commemorate the outbreak of cholera in 1832 and the part played by the *Sainte Chemise* at that time. For not once only, or only in the mediæval days, has the veil of the Virgin played a part in the history of Chartres. It was taken at the height of the plague, in obedience to the clamour of the people, in solemn procession through the streets, and from that moment, it is said, the plague was stayed, and all who were ill, save two, who had mocked at this act of piety, recovered.

Nor should it be forgotten that it was the possession of this veil which, when Fulbert's Cathedral had been burnt down in 1194, stimulated the desire and provided the means to build a still larger and more beautiful cathedral, worthy to contain it, and to be, in the words of the chroniclers, 'the very couch and chamber of Our Lady.'[32]

A few months after his defeat before Chartres, Rollo the Ganger married the daughter of Charles-le-Simple and embraced the Christian faith. Neustria was ceded to the Normans. Their depredations ceased for a while, but, under the young Duke Richard of Normandy, fifteen years later, there was a heathen reaction in Pirates' land. Their fleets once more swarmed up the Seine, and Chartres was the central point of their attack. United in its defence, loud and frequent rang the cry of the House of France, 'Montjoie!'

mingled with that of the Counts of Chartres and Vendôme, 'Chartres et Passavant!'

'Frachois crie Mont-joye et Normans Dez-aie,
Flamans crie Afras et Angevin ralie,
Et li cuens Thiebaut Chartre et Passavant crie.'
WACE—*Roman de Rou.*

But soon these visitations ceased. Gradually heathen Norman pirates became French Christians, their descendants feudal nobles, and Pirates' land the most loyal of the fiefs of France. Christianity was embraced by all, from duke to peasant. By the people it was welcomed with an almost passionate fanaticism. Every road was crowded with pilgrims. Monasteries rose in every forest glade, cathedrals in every town. The Abbeys of S. Père, S. Chéron and S. Martin, and the Churches of S. Lubin and S. Laumer in the neighbouring vineyards, were re-established and restored. The Church of Bishop Wulphard was built, and this restoration of religious centres meant, in a brutal age, the assertion of the rights of humanity, in an age of ignorance the encouragement of learning, of science and art, in an age of devastation the promotion, by means of pilgrimages, of industry and commerce. The growing number of windmills, wine-presses and tanneries on the monastic properties is the index of the civilising influence of the monks. The fragments of their castles remain as the sign of the more picturesque but less admirable occupation of the knights of chivalry.

# CHAPTER III

## Theobald-the-Trickster and Fulbert the Bishop

'Thiebaut li quenz de Chartres fu fel é engignous
Mult out chastels é viles, é mult fu averous;
Chevalier fu mult prous é mult chevalerous
Mez mult part fu cruel é mult envious.'
ROBERT WACE—*Roman de Rou.*

ROLO, on his conversion, gave his domain of Malmaison, near Épernon, to Notre-Dame de Chartres. The deed of gift was long preserved, and ran in these terms:—

'I, Rollo, Duke of Normandy, give to the Brethren of the Church Notre-Dame de Chartres my Castle of Malmaison, which I have won with my sword, and with my sword I will guarantee it to them, as let this knife be witness.'

A knife in the Middle Ages was a symbol of putting in possession. It was a fitting symbol for the *siècle de fer*, that century of moral and material disorder and disaster in which the country was now involved.

For France was now falling into the iron grip of feudalism. It is the age of castles. As the power of the central authority weakens, the power of the great vassals, dukes, counts, bishops and abbots becomes established as absolute in their fiefs. But during the period of disorder, from which the feudal *régime* emerged triumphant, the serf had waged with his master the same struggle that the vassal was waging with his lords and the lord with the King. The result was similar in all cases. Usurpation of servile tenures accompanied that of liberal tenures, and, territorial appropriation having taken place in every rank of society, it was as difficult to dispossess a serf of his manse as a seigneur of his benefice. The serf, therefore, emerged from the condition of almost absolute slavery in which he was at the time of the fall of the Western Empire, and from the condition of servitude that had been his up to the end of the reign of Charles-le-Chauve. From this time *servitude* was transformed into serfage. The serf having withdrawn his person and his field from his master's hands, owes to him no longer his body and goods, but only a portion of his labour and his income. He ceases to be a slave and becomes a tributary.

With the advent of feudalism the map of the country underwent a change. The Roman arrangement, by which Gaul had been divided into eighteen provinces and 127 dioceses, had been little altered by the Francs, and lasted on under the Carlovingians, but it gradually disappeared in the course of the tenth and eleventh centuries. It was preserved only by the Church, the dioceses of which, up to the time of the Revolution, represented very nearly the ancient divisions of Gaul under the Romans. Before the days of Cæsar it was into *pagi* that Gaul had been divided. The pagus or *pays* persisted now; more numerous than the cities, they continued to split up and multiply. But from 800 onwards most of these pays having set up comtés of the same name and same extent began to be known as such—as, for instance, the Comté of Chartres.

When in 987 Hugues Capet, Duke of France, decided to assume the title of King, the political unity of the Chartrains had long been broken by the territorial usurpations of the great officers of the Crown. The government of the country under Charlemagne had been shared by seven counts—Chartres, Dreux, Châteaudun, Blois, Vendôme, Poissy and Mantes. But by Hugh Capet's time these had been reduced to three—Chartres, Blois and Dreux—and in the person of Thibault-le-Vieux or le Tricheur, who was of Capetan stock, the counties of Blois and Chartres were united. They remained in his family till the death of Thibaut VI., 1218. They were then divided between the two collateral branches of the house, but reunited again in 1269.

Philippe-le-Bel acquired the county of Chartres in 1289, and gave it to his brother, Charles de Valois, whose son, Philippe de Valois, united it to the Crown (1346).

It is convenient to explain this matter of the Comté here, for the present period of the history of Chartres is connected with the dread name of Thibault-le-Tricheur, Theobald the Trickster, Count of Chartres, the *chevalier fel et engignous*, whom Robert Wace describes.

This first hereditary Count of Chartres was the Robert the Devil of the *Pays Chartrain*. Through the whole country side, from Tours to Blois, and from Blois to Chartres, the impression of his dreaded personality is indelibly stamped. The legend still runs that Thibault, the old *Chasseur*, nightly crosses the Loire from Montfrau to Bury with a crowd of his reckless men of arms, bent, you may suppose, on some murderous foray. This turbulent spirit threw himself eagerly into the quarrel between Lothaire and Richard, Duke of Normandy, and took an active part in the cruel war that ensued. He invaded the Duke's territory, and, availing himself of every device, and employing every ruse, for Thibault was '*plein d'engin et plein fu de feintie,*' he took Évreux and advanced even to the walls of Rouen. His line of advance was marked by devastation so terrible that, says the

Norman chronicler, there was not the bark of a single dog to be heard throughout the county.[33]

A peace was patched up, and Thibault married Richard's daughter. But the King and the Count shortly afterwards renewed their machinations against the Duke. The latter was hard pressed, but, thanks to his spirit and the valour of his followers, he proved victorious. He ravaged the country of his enemy, and sacked and burnt the town and church of Chartres. It is said that when Thibault, the hardened old *Chasseur*, came to the town—*sa bonne ville de Chartres*—he began to count one by one the heads of those whom the Northmen had slain. Suddenly he stopped in his counting and began to utter the cries and laughter of a madman. For the head of his own son lay there before him, and the shock of the sight unhinged his mind forever.

The Rue des Changes lies opposite the south-west corner of the Cathedral. Pursue this street and you will find yourself in the modern vegetable market—the Place Billard. It is the site on which—coolly appropriating some territory which belonged to the Monastery of S. Père—Thibault built the castle and donjon of the Counts of Chartres. It was outside the then walls of the town, between the Porte Évière and the Porte Cendreuse. Not a vestige of it now remains, if we except a few fragments of the old enclosing wall. For the donjon was destroyed in

**South Transept**

1587, and the castle in the nineteenth century. The great tower known as the King's or Count's Tower (Tour le Roi, Tour le Comte), was used for a prison, and within the spacious halls of the ancient palace most of the general assemblies of Chartres were held. It was here that for five centuries justice was administered, and it was in the chapel of the castle that the bishop, on his entry, was wont to swear that he would not go contrary to the rights of the prince. And it was here that feudal homage was done, *à cause de la grosse tour de Chartres*.

The castle, with its crenelated donjon, its huge façade on the crest of the hill, its massive walls and buttresses; the Cathedral, with its soaring spires, majestic nave and mystic sculptures, were typical in their juxtaposition. The fortress of the Counts, rising behind armed walls and portcullis; the stronghold of the bishops, secure within the buildings of the cloister, to which there was access only through guarded gates—such, for instance, as that facing the castle, of which you may still see a trace on the corner house of the Rue des Changes and the Rue du Lait—Castle and Cathedral so placed were stone symbols, you might fancy, of the temporal and spiritual powers which ruled with divided sway the old town of Chartres.[34]

For, throughout the Middle Ages, side by side with the persistent power of the bishops and their train of clergy and of serfs, persisted also, but waxing and waning with varying fortune, the power of the Counts. And from the vassals and dependants of these two powers was destined to spring the modern *Bourgeoisie*. The Counts of Blois, of Chartres, of Meaux pass before us in the pages of history, forever raising levies, waging wars and exacting tolls on merchandise. Sometimes they are in accord with the clergy; sometimes in opposition; and at one moment make large donations to the Church, at another rob it. To-day they fight for their King abroad and on their Crusades, while Viscounts represent them at home. To-morrow they are home again, fighting among themselves, or trying to throw off their allegiance to their King. Counts of Chartres or their relatives mount the throne of England and the throne of France. But war and brigandage remain their business. They pillage the bishops, and the bishops excommunicate the pillagers. They raise troops, and the bishops call their parish to arms. They war with the sword, and the bishops win with the aid of their trained ability, the cunning of their counsel, and their pens.

For the great bishops—such as Fulbert, Ives and John of Salisbury—were indeed remarkable men, and they held their own successfully, not only, if need be, against the interference of their Archbishop of Sens, but also with the Counts of Chartres and the Kings of France and England.

The eleventh century above all was an era of notable bishops.

There were, of course, good bishops and bad. Aganon, who succeeded Gantelme, was in the former class, and he devoted himself to the rebuilding and establishing of the ruined churches and monasteries; among them that of S. Père de Chartres, which had been utterly demolished by the Normans. His nephew, Ragenfroi, succeeded him, and continued in the paths of his uncle. He was one of the greatest benefactors of S. Père, to which he added many buildings, and whither he brought twelve monks from the Monastery of Fleury-sur-Loire. Their fervour and discipline, which was to give new life to the community at Chartres, had been acquired under the rule of their abbot, Vulphard, destined to be one of the great bishop-builders of Chartres.

It was under Ragenfroi that Hugues le Grand, father of Hugues Capet, gave evidence of his lively devotion to the Notre-Dame de Chartres by the donation of the domain of Ingré, 'with all its lands cultivated or not, vineyards, pasturage and *prairies*, with its forests and serfs of either sex, and the church which is dedicated to Saint Leu.' So runs the charter, and the object is 'that the brethren deriving therefrom the necessaries of life may have the more liberty to perform Divine service and spiritual exercises, and pour out the more abundant prayers for us, our wife and our whole family.'

Hardouin, Bishop of Chartres, succeeded to his brother's position, but not his religion, says the chronicler; for he was filled with pride and swollen with secular ambition. He waged war with the monks of S. Père, and took from them every privilege and possession he could. And the chronicler adds (writing always from the point of view of S. Père) that several later bishops followed his example, and trod in the same path of sacrilege, wasting their own property and coveting that of others, plotting against the monks and harassing them, and even robbing them of much that the charity of the faithful had bestowed upon them, and, whereas they should have protected them, acting in the blindness of their hearts like tyrants and plunderers. Count Eudes succeeded his father Thibault (977), and the following narrative, which the monk Paul gives us in connection with his name, is sufficiently eloquent of the times.

There was a holy priest, by name Sigismund, whose goodness and sanctity were clearer than the light of day to all people, lay and clerical. Chaste and humble, prudent, prayerful, burning with the fire of faith, yet jocund of speech withal, he shone as an example of all Christian virtues. Now Fulcher, Abbot of S. Lubin,[35] had committed to his care certain vineyards, from which, it appears, the Blessed Sigismund knew how to make good wine. And one day when Count Eudes of Chartres was about to dine, and his men were looking about for the best wine to be obtained, they heard that there was wine to be got for nothing in the cellar of the priest. Overjoyed at the news, they hastened there, and boldly entering the cellar filled their skins and carried them off to the hall. The good Sigismund returned from the house of God and found the chief cup-bearer sitting in his cellar, who mocked him, asking, 'Master, tell me, is that wine of yours very good or not?' 'My brother,' returned the holy man, 'you are no novice at wine, and do not need to be told when you have only to taste for yourself.' 'Give me a goblet, then,' said he. 'Nay; the wine will be better from the cup into which it is drawn.'

The unhappy man placed the cup to his lips, but before he could drink he was seized with a fit, and fell to the earth foaming at the mouth. He was taken back to the palace, and when the Count heard of the affair he summoned Sigismund to his presence and ordered the eyes of those who had stolen the wine to be gouged out and the wine to be restored to its owner. Sigismund, however, when he saw him so roused, would not leave his presence till the Count had calmed his wrath, set the prisoners free, and consented to drink the wine *gratis*. Then the holy man turned to pray, and thanks to his intercession the cup-bearer was restored to his former health.

Count Eudes—whose widow, Bertha, afterwards became for a while the wife of King Robert—died in 995. He was succeeded by his son, Thibault II., and with him the struggle between the spiritual and temporal powers took the form of a claim to present to the Monastery of S. Père.

Fulbert, who was one day to be the great Bishop of Chartres, has left us an account of the matter, preserved and completed by the monk Paul, which is as curious as it is instructive.

'The Abbot of S. Père,' writes Fulbert, 'was very ill, but still in full possession of his faculties, when a monk named Magenard—up to that time a dear friend of mine' (more of a courtier than a priest, says Paul!)— 'slipped secretly out of the monastery by night and hastened to Count Thibault, who was all that time lying at Blois, with the view of begging the post of abbot for himself. The Count sent him back to us next day, accompanied by commissioners, who were to secure from the brethren a magnificent reception of him as abbot. But to almost all of us this conduct appeared as horrible as it was unprecedented. We answered, therefore, that we could not consent to their requests, for the appointment was not legal; and an ambitious schemer who had tried to secure the post of abbot before the abbot himself was dead could not be accepted. Magenard rode back in high dudgeon to the Count, and fanned the flames of the young man's wrath against us. Five days later Gislebert, the abbot, died. The members of the monastery met, and the question was put whether anyone supported the claim of Magenard. One by one the brethren answered no. A deputation was therefore sent to the Count (who was acting as bishop at the time) to inform him of Gislebert's death, and to ask for regular permission to choose his successor. But this deputation was forestalled by the treacherous conduct of two monks, who hastened to Blois and falsely informed the Count that Magenard had been chosen abbot by the brethren. The Count was delighted at the news, and publicly presented Magenard with the pastoral staff. The brethren who had remained at home were incensed at this fraudulent business, and promptly drew up and signed the following protest:—

'Know all the Church that we have not chosen Magenard to be our abbot: we do not approve of him, we do not want him, we do not consent; but we disapprove, refuse, and altogether reject him—we, that is, the undersigned monks of Saint Père.'

Fulbert tells us that all the brethren either signed or witnessed their signatures in his presence. On the next day, he continues, the Count Thibault returned to Chartres and requested to be admitted with formal processions into the monastery. The monks replied that they would willingly so receive him provided that he did not bring the false abbot with him. The Count was enraged, but held his hand for one day. On the following day, however, with a noisy crowd of followers, he forced Magenard upon the Monastery of S. Père. At this violence the holy brethren, fearing to be contaminated by the presence of the intruder, bade farewell, with tears in their eyes, to the sanctuary of the Lord, and took refuge in the Cathedral. The Cathedral also lacked a bishop, and within its walls the two flocks of monks, like sheep without a shepherd, mingled their tears with mutual consolation.

The monks found a resting-place in the monastery of Lagni, and Magenard was installed by a foreign bishop, in the absence of the clergy, amidst the indignation of the people, and in spite of the open protest of the Archbishop of Sens and a few of the remaining monks of S. Père.

Not the least dramatic part of this curious story is its end. Magenard remained quietly in possession of the monastery, and 'there was not one bishop in all France whose heart was touched by feelings of piety or love of sacred law to interfere on behalf of the monks who had been expelled.' But presently (1004), on his return from a pilgrimage to Rome, Count Thibault died, and his body was brought back to be laid next his brother Thierry in the Chapel of S. Père. His gravestone, restored in the seventeenth century, at the time of the reconstruction of the abbey, is now to be found in the Hôtel de Ville. Now, on the death of the Count, Raoul, the Dean of Notre-Dame, who had welcomed the monks of S. Père in their flight, was appointed bishop in his stead. The bitter feeling against Magenard, which had long been smouldering, now burst into flame. He was deprived of his pastoral staff and compelled to pass some days in the bishop's house. But when men saw how instant he was in prayer, and how fervent in vigil, how wise in speech and accomplished in letters, the flames of the quarrel died down. His staff was restored to him, together with the conduct of the monastery, and, adds the chronicler, as long as he breathed this vital air so long did he full well and lovingly feed the flock which was confided to his charge.

Bishop Hardouin died eight days after the destruction of the town and church in 962, and the pious and able Vulphard was appointed in his stead. The people of Chartres set themselves with undaunted energy to rebuild their town, and they seized the opportunity of making their houses more substantial, and of enlarging their churches. Look at the tenth-century remains of Notre-Dame and S. Père, and judge how massive was the material they used. Their houses, of course, were still made mostly of wood. Vulphard devoted himself to the business of constructing a new cathedral, which should be more beautiful than any yet conceived.

The martyrium is the kernel of the crypt of Notre-Dame. The latter half of the tenth century was the period of vast crypts, and Vulphard, not content with merely renewing the martyrium of Gislebert, added a broad ambulatory round it, enclosed with a strong circular wall, which was broken by three advanced chapels. This was intended to make the martyrium, as the depository of the treasure and the Veil, safe from all accidents. We shall see presently how well it fulfilled its purpose. The church itself was extended westwards as far as the line marked now by the labyrinth in the pavement of the nave. Two great piers were inserted in the martyrium to support the raised choir.

In order to understand the growth of the Cathedral, which is in itself, to the eye that can see, an almost complete history of Christian architecture, it is necessary to form some idea of the church which Vulphard built. For in size and site it approached the modern building.

If we count the circular portion embracing the martyrium, and connected by stairs with the main building, it must have been over 100 yards long, and in breadth at least thirty, including the Chapel of Notre-Dame-de-Sous-Terre on the one side, and the sacristy on the south. But the nave and the aisles—the floor of which was on a level with that of Notre-Dame-de-Sous-Terre—were together only as broad as the modern nave by itself.

Like the tenth century Church of S. Martin-au-Val, the choir was raised ten or twelve steps above the nave, and was surrounded by an ambulatory. There was a double transept: and it may be that we can trace it in the recesses which now form the Chapels of S. Savinian, S. Potentian and the Saints Forts on the one side, and the Chapel of S. Clement on the other.

As to the details and ornamentation of the church nothing remains, but we can say from our knowledge of the times, and from a comparison with what tenth century work there is in Chartres, what could and what could not have been, if not what was. There may, for instance, have been a belfry, and, seeing that the great square tower of the Abbey Church of S. Père was at that time being built, there probably was. Perhaps two such towers flanked the two extremities of the façade. They would have had no spires, but a four-sided, pyramidal roof. Squat columns or square pillars, one may suppose, carried the series of plain round arches of brick and stone which connected the aisles with the central nave. But the great 'Triumphal Arch,' as it was called, separating choir from nave, was richly adorned with sculpture and painting.

The capitals of the pillars and their bases would be in most instances romanesque, after the fashion of that which serves as a font in the Chapel of Notre-Dame-de-Sous-Terre, whilst others would be decorated like those of S. Martin-au-Val with foliage and forms of real or fantastic animals, the mystic symbols of Mediæval Masonry, the language in which the Masters of the Living Stone were now beginning to speak. The walls may have been enriched with mosaics and paintings in accordance with the precepts of Charlemagne. Above the aisles may have run a triforium or gallery, set apart for the prayers of virgins and widows. If you look at the entrance of Vulphard's crypt you will see that the doorways were simple, and they offer a striking contrast to the porches of the twelfth and thirteenth centuries with their wealth of sculpture, which records, as it were, in brief the history of Christianity, and serves as a preface to the book of the Cathedral. Without going into further detail, we may add, that as the complete art of vaulting was not yet known, though the small roof of the martyrium may have been vaulted, the large roof of the Cathedral can only have been a flat wooden ceiling.

The building of this church was completed before Vulphard's death. But the decoration of it lagged under his successor. The skilled monks engaged for that purpose disappeared. The artists had retired to their cloister to await their last hour in prayer and fasting. For the end of the world was expected. The ancient and popular doctrine of the millennium possessed all minds. Every sign, it seemed, had been given.

Wars, famine and pestilence, and the ravages of the Normans and Saracens had produced a depression of spirit, which, combined with an erroneous interpretation of the Apocalypse, led men to think that the reign of Antichrist and the end of the world must surely be at hand. The beginning of the year 1000, it began to be believed, was the appointed date of this dread climax.

'A long and unceasing series of signs,' writes one in 985, when bequeathing his property to the Abbey of S. Père, 'bears witness to the approaching end of the world, and of the passing of all things therein.'

Private wars and the revolt of the Norman peasantry, who had dared to utter the word 'commune' and had been ferociously crushed by the feudal barons, the breaking up of the Roman Empire, and Charlemagne's after it, the plague of S. Anthony's fire and the scourge of famine, these and a thousand others not less awful were surely signs enough to fill the world with terror and despair. And what should a man do but seek refuge in the house of God and prepare himself

**FULBERT AND HIS CHURCH.**

by frenzied supplication against the great day of the Lord?

But when the year was passed and the world was still unended, a wave of religious feeling swept over Europe and men went with one accord to render thanks at the holy shrines. Pilgrims crowded to the sanctuary of Chartres to make their offerings to the Holy Veil and to acknowledge the protection of the blessed Virgin. They came also to seek relief from the terrible malady known as S. Anthony's Fire or *Mal des Ardents*.

S. Fulbert[36] himself, the successor of Eudes, was afflicted with this painful plague. William of Malmesbury records the miracle by which he was healed.

'He was sick unto death,' he tells us, 'of the sickness called the Sacred Fire or *Mal des Ardents* (erysipelas), which was devouring his tongue with grievous pain. One night, when his agony was most extreme, he beheld a beautiful lady approach with an air of majesty, attended by a numerous suite. She bade him open his mouth, and the sick man obeyed. Thereupon the mysterious lady did unto him as a mother does who suckles her infant child; she pressed upon his burning tongue some drops of her virginal milk, which refreshed his tongue and healed him instantly.

'Even the cheeks of the saint were sprinkled with the precious liquid, and he, having wiped off some drops thereof with costly linen, left them to the Church of Chartres as relics, and as a token of the miracle which had been wrought in his favour.' 'Qui se veoid encores parmi les reliques,' adds Souchet.

But Fulbert's reputation does not rest on these passive acts of sanctity. An event was to happen shortly which brought out all the energy that lay beneath his mild excellence and his scholarly instructions.

'It was on the 7th September 1020,' says Souchet, 'that the burning of the Church of Chartres happened, on the eve of the nativity of Our Lady. It is not known how or by whose agency this disaster occurred; but there was nothing in this holy temple that the fire did not consume.' Rouillard (1608) piously supposes that lightning was sent from heaven to destroy the church, as a punishment for the sins of the pilgrims, some of whom, among the crowds of both sexes who kept vigil there, may by some act of impurity have defiled the sanctity of the place.

However it may have been, the church was once more destroyed, and, as was happening all over Italy and France at this period, it was destroyed only to rise from its ashes more beautiful than ever. So Angers, Poitiers, Beauvais, Cambrai, Rouen were rebuilt almost as soon as burnt, in the enthusiastic rivalry of the Christian builders of the day. 'Humanity,' in the fine phrase of Raoul Glaber, 'rose from its long agony and set itself to build, and to shake off the rags of its old age in order to put on the white robe of the churches.'

The great bishop with whose name the new Cathedral at Chartres was to be indissolubly connected, the Fulbert of Fulbert's Cathedral, had been the favourite pupil of Gerbert of Reims and had practised medicine in the Monastery of S. Père, where that art was long held in high honour. But Fulbert was more than a mere doctor. He was a poet, a mathematician, a theologian, grammarian and skilful musician as well. When, therefore, he became the head of the School of Chartres (from which a few years later John, called the Deaf, was to issue, doctor of Henry I. and chief of the sect of Nominalists, whose pupil was Rosselin, whose pupil Abeilard) scholars flocked from England, Germany, Denmark and all parts of France to listen to the teachings of the French Socrates, and to receive from his eloquent lips the precepts of wisdom and the counsel of friendship. For his knowledge was immense and his learning encyclopædic, ranging from the minutest details of the exact sciences to the most daring speculations of metaphysics. Fulbert, we are told, like a modern Plato, would often withdraw to a garden near the bishop's palace, watered by the clear stream (it *was* clear in those days), and there, surrounded by his chosen pupils, expound with mingled sweetness and force the tenets of philosophy and the doctrines of faith. 'The teacher of philosophers, the marvel of his age, the sun whose rays gave life,' his pupil Adelmann called him. And among the philosophers he taught, and the rare flowers of intellect which in this age of brute force expanded beneath the quickening rays of his mind, Adelmann enumerates Lanfranc, the Archbishop of Canterbury, Walter of Burgundy, Lambert and Engelbert of Paris and Orléans, Hildier, wise as Socrates and learned as Pythagoras, and Sigo, the musician of the delicate ear. Fulbert's letters,[37] which place him among the most interesting historians of this obscure period, reveal him as a theologian firm and decided, as a statesman eager to enforce order and to secure the administration of justice, as a man broad-minded, charming, enthusiastic, humane.

Inspired by a mysterious voice which bade him 'build a sanctuary worthy of his filial love and the divine majesty,' Fulbert now set about procuring funds to build first a veritable crypt, and then above it the new Cathedral, adopting, however, the general plan of the church left by his predecessor in order to make use of the enormous existing foundations.[38] The subterranean aspect of the old church, built about the grottoes and heaped round by the rapid deposit of rubbish which continually raised the soil of mediæval towns, would naturally suggest this scheme. But to carry it out funds beyond the ordinary were needed.

Fortunately Fulbert was no ordinary beggar. Not only did he know how to use the usual means of encouraging gifts, in money and in kind, from the clergy and people of the diocese by holding special assemblies on the site of the proposed church, and by sermons which promised heavenly rewards for those who took part in the building, but he used his connections with the great world and his power of letter-writing to the best advantage.

He wrote first of all to 'his beloved Lord,' the 'good King Robert,' in whom the historian sees more of a monk than of a sovereign.

'All our resources fail us for the rebuilding of our church, and a great necessity is upon us. Come then to our aid, O holy father; strengthen our weakness and succour our distress to the end that God may reward your soul with all blessings.'

And doubtless the 'father of religious architecture' responded generously to this eloquent appeal from his former teacher.

Meanwhile every belfry in the diocese attested by its silence the disaster of the church and the sorrow of its bishop. 'On account of the disaster,' he writes, 'which has befallen my church, I wish to make known my profound grief to all. In consequence I have commanded that all the bells which are wont to ring with joy and gladness shall attest henceforth by their silence my bitter sadness.'

Fulbert wrote next to his most beloved and pious Duke of Aquitaine, and he received handsome annual subscriptions from him whilst the Cathedral was a-building. 'Your marvellous and inexhaustible charity,' writes the bishop, 'is pleased to overwhelm me with many gifts which I do not deserve. I should blush to receive your offerings were I not sure that you will be magnificently rewarded hereafter.'

Eudes II., Count of Chartres and Blois, was, before he met his death in the Battle of Bar-le-Duc, a generous contributor. That was to be expected from so rich a seigneur for the restoration of the principal church of his own county and town, but deeply was Fulbert touched by the receipt of a contribution from Cnut, King of Denmark and England, who, as William of Malmesbury records, 'sent many sums to the churches across the seas, and chiefly enriched that of Chartres, where flourished Fulbert, renowned for his holiness and philosophy.'

In acknowledging the esterlings of the great Danish King, the bishop speaks of him in terms which the verdict of history has confirmed.

'To the very noble King of Denmark, Cnut, Fulbert, by the grace of God, Bishop of Chartres, with his clerks and his monks, promises the recommendation of his prayers.

'When we saw the offering which you deigned to send us we admired at once your astonishing wisdom and religious spirit—your wisdom in that you, a prince divided from us by language and by sea, are zealously concerned not only with the things around you, but also with the things that touch us; at your religious spirit, in that you, of whom we had heard speak as a Pagan King, show yourself a very Christian and generous benefactor of the churches and servants of God. We render lively thanks to the King of Kings, through whose mercy your gifts have descended upon us, and we beseech Him to make your reign happy and prosperous, and to deliver your soul from all sin.'

Such were the means by which the courtly bishop extracted donations from the great, and such the spiritual consolation with which he rewarded the generosity of his royal patrons.

Fulbert's labours, supported by the enthusiastic devotion of the people, were interrupted by the turbulent behaviour of Godfrey, Viscount of Châteaudun. He, since Eudes had acquired the county of Champagne, and took, therefore, little interest in the affairs of Chartres, had, like the other great vassals of Eudes, followed the example of his suzerain. He was endeavouring, by building himself first the Castle of Gallardon, and now of Illiers, in the very centre of the bishop's possessions, to aggrandise himself at the expense of the King and the Church. Fulbert could not prevail upon the monkish Robert to repress Godfrey by force. The spiritual arms which he himself used only roused the Count to take reprisals by plundering the episcopal farms. Eudes himself, who had assumed the title of Count Palatine, was too much occupied with his own ambitious schemes, and his opposition to King Robert and King Robert's successor, to have either the wish or the time to interfere. For, although he had acquiesced in Fulbert's advice, followed by Robert the Good, that Henry, the third son, should be appointed to succeed to the throne, yet, when King Robert died, Eudes espoused the cause of the fourth. He was obliged to yield at last to the force of Henry's arms, and some years later this turbulent Count was killed at Bar-le-Duc when striving to take vengeance on the Emperor Conrad by attacking his vassal, Gothelon.

In spite of his many reverses, Eudes had greatly increased the power and repute of the house of Chartres. So far as Chartres was concerned he had made many rich presents to the Cathedral and to the Monastery of S. Père. He endowed the small church and foundation which was afterwards to become the Monastery of S. Jean-en-Vallée.[39]

But his chief act of interference was when, on the death of Fulbert, the Chapter appealed to him to uphold their election of Albert the Dean to the episcopal seat against the appointment of Theodoric, a creature of Queen Constance. Eudes, seizing the opportunity of opposing the royal will, declared that he would not admit the new bishop into his town until he had been examined by a bench of bishops, for he was said to be a man of little sense and no education. Theodoric's appointment was, however, in the end made good.

The vast possessions of Eudes were divided between his sons, who, following the family tradition, refused to pay homage to the King. They were surprised by the energy of their royal suzerain, overpowered and held captive for six years. Étienne, the younger, died; but Thibault, at the price of the county of Tours, was set free by Geoffrey of Anjou. Thibault was now Count of Chartres, Blois, Brie and Champagne, but as to the delimitations of their territories endless hostilities arose between him and the Angevin prince. And when his hands were not full with the attentions of this neighbour he waged disastrous war for his King against William I., Duke of Normandy (1058).

But in spite of wars and famine and disease, in spite of the violence of Counts and the weakness of Kings, Fulbert's Cathedral was completed ere his death. The fire had left but a few columns and fragments of wall standing where once was the Cathedral of Vulphard. The winter of 1020 was devoted to clearing away the *débris*, and so active was the work, that by September in the following year Fulbert could write 'we have finished our crypts, and' (this is the reason why he cannot accept the invitation of William of Aquitaine to be present at the solemn dedication of the Cathedral of Poitiers) 'we must devote all our energies to covering them before the inclemency of the winter damages them.' But in the following year the work had made such progress that he was able to undertake a journey at King Robert's request to Rome, leaving the building to his canons and architect. Who that architect was may perhaps be indicated by the entry in the *Nécrologie de Notre-Dame*, under date October 22:—*Bérenger.* 'Berengarius hujus matris ecclesiæ, Artifex Bonus.'

The martyrium had suffered less than the rest of the Cathedral, but it was thought necessary to place a large round column on the Gallo-Roman wall, in order to strengthen the vaulted roof. On this column you may descry the word Fulbert, cut not in modern days, nor yet at any great distance of time.

'The circular part of our crypt,' says l'Abbé Bulteau,[40] 'with its vaulting, is to-day just as it was left then.' But the floor was probably much lower if one may judge by the embrasures of the windows.

The convex wall of the martyrium was strengthened on the outside by a double thickness, for it had to support not only the thrust of the new vaulting, but also the weight of the upper church.

As to the rectilinear portions of the crypt, in spite of the alterations of the twelfth century, we may easily recognise the seal of the eleventh century in the piers and the *abaci*. To S. Fulbert we may also attribute the construction of two sacristies for Notre-Dame-de-Sous-Terre, that on the *south* side now being the Chapel of S. Martin, that on the north the *Cave au Bois*, known formerly as the 'Place of the Iron Chest.'

The upper church was built of the same dimensions as those of the former one, but the ground level of the whole was raised considerably, almost to the height of that of the choir.

The length of the church may be indicated by the excavations of 1849 at the centre of the labyrinth known as *La Lieue*, where fragments were discovered which are supposed to have been the *débris* of the western façade. There was a double ambulatory round the choir and chapels corresponding to those of the crypt, and two sacristies may be reckoned to have been built above those of the Sous Terre.

A transept and two side-doors existed in the same place, but of less size than those of to-day.

The decoration of the Cathedral was left in great part to Fulbert's successors.

Henry I., who came to the throne when death had surprised his father, Robert the Good, as he was copying a manuscript in the Church of Melun, owed his succession in some degree, as we have seen, to Fulbert.

He cancelled his debt in part by paying for the wooden roof[41] of the Cathedral—wooden, for the art of extensive vaulting in stone was not yet understood—whilst Henry's doctor, Jean le Sourd, the Chartrain pupil of Fulbert and leader of the sect of Nominalists in the battle of the schools, was responsible for the construction of the south gate and many other details. Teudon, who had made the Sainte Chasse for the Veil, undertook the principal façade. A big bell weighing 5000 livres was also hung in one of Vulphard's towers, which still stood.

Fulbert died in the year 1028, but so rapid had the work been that he did not die before his Cathedral was complete. For William of Malmesbury (*Gest.*, Vol. II. chap. XXV.) records that 'Bishop Fulbert, among other proofs of his efficient labours, very magnificently completed the Church of Our Lady S. Mary, of which he himself had laid the foundations, and which, moreover,' he adds, 'doing everything he could for its honour, he rendered celebrated by many musical modulations. The man who has heard his chaunts, breathing only celestial vows, is best able to conceive the love he manifested in honour of the Virgin.'

Under Fulbert, indeed, the school of Chartres became famous for its music and for its plain-song renderings of the sacred offices. The celebrated François de Cologne and many others are mentioned as having belonged to this school. But Fulbert himself excelled them all in his compositions.[42] For amongst other beautiful canticles he composed, in collaboration, it is said, with King Robert, the famous responses of the Nativity of the Virgin, a feast which he, in grateful remembrance of his wondrous visitant, was the first to celebrate in France. I shall be forgiven for quoting in the untranslatable Latin this noble hymn of love, which is the most beautiful blossom of the poetic crown of Mary.

'Solem justitiæ, regem paritura supremum
Stella Maria maris hodie processit ad ortum;
Cernere divinum lumen gaudete fideles!

Stirps Jesse virgam produxit, virgaque florem,
Et super hunc florem requiescit Spiritus almus,
Virgo dei genitrix virga est, flos filius ejus.

Ad nutum Domini nostrum ditantis honorem,
Sicut spina rosam genuit, Judæa Mariam,
Ut vitium virtus operiret, gratia culpam.'[43]

Fulbert himself left a great part of his wealth to complete the work which he had begun. That work was carried on by his successor, Theodoric. But it must have been interrupted for a while by the terrible famine which came upon France at this period—a famine so terrible that during its course human flesh, it is said, was exposed for sale, and the bodies of the dead were dug up and eaten. The abundant harvest of 1034 put an end to this infliction, and men turned again to finish the decoration of God's house. It would seem, indeed, as if Theodoric turned this task to the purpose of relief-works. For the monk Paul says of him 'that his abounding wealth, poured out in a lavish stream, issuing ever to provide for the hunger and thirst of the needy, completed the famous work of the court of our gracious Lady, the Mother of God, and makes him worthy of saintly renown.'

But it was not till the year 1037 that the solemn dedication of the Cathedral by Theodoric took place in the presence of Henri I. and his whole Court.

Theodoric was buried by the side of Fulbert, and on his tomb in S. Père was written, 'Holy Virgin, he wished to raise to thee a temple, the design of which the author had taken from Heaven itself.'

# CHAPTER IV

## S. Ives and the Crusades

'A pretty burgh and such as Fancy loves
For bygone grandeurs.'—LOWELL.

THE town of Chartres is clearly divided into two sections—the upper (*quartier du luxe*), modern, unimpressive and inelegant, and the lower, picturesque, poor, mediæval. This lower part of the town is watered by an arm of the Eure,

'Dont l'eau distille
Autour de notre ville,
Et d'un murmurant flot
Maint beau verger enclot,'

as a local sixteenth-century poet has it. Like most old towns, Chartres consisted originally of a small city enclosed by strong walls and of suburbs stretching along the main roads which led to it. As these suburbs increased in size and importance, the enceinte was enlarged so as to include them. This took place at Chartres notably in the twelfth century. But up to that time the area enclosed was remarkably small, for after Hastings had sacked the town 'the inhabitants had not the heart,' says the monk Paul, 'to rebuild all their city, but contented themselves with fortifying the little corner of the ancient town which is still' (1060) 'surrounded with walls.'

The line of the enceinte enclosing this 'little corner of the ancient town' cannot be exactly traced. But

*Étape-au-Vin*

it certainly ran from the Place de l'Étape-au-Vin (the picturesque old shop built out on wooden supports), and, passing behind the Church of S. Aignan, the Castle of the Counts (Place Billard), crossed the Petit-Boucherie to join the Tertre S. Eman,[44] where was the Porte Evière (Porta Aquaria). Tertres, it should be remarked, are, in Chartrain dialect, little streets of stone steps which facilitate communication between the upper and lower towns. The rest of the town was defended by ditches and ramparts. A few wooden forts guarded the bridges.

Within the walls, the Cathedral and the castle frowned over the rest of the town and other churches, representing the double power of bishop and count, around which was growing up the crowd of dependants who were destined, in the fulness of time, to become the bourgeoisie of Chartres. And without the walls lay the Monastery of S. Père, waxing yearly in lands and wealth, stirring the jealousy of bishops and tempting the cupidity of counts. About the castle, the Cathedral and the monastery there were gradually being established groups of artisans who, by instinct and necessity, herded together in distinct quarters of the town, and thus gradually formed the redoubtable corporations and guilds of the Middle Ages—unions which, in the learned and unlearned professions alike, still exercise so potent an influence in England and on the Continent. Already there were the quarters of the money-changers, the saddlers, the skinners, the goldsmiths in Chartres. Later, as we shall see, almost every street will fly the banner of some particular Craft.

The liberty of the peasant was also being gradually asserted throughout this period. He was passing from the condition of a farmer under a proprietor to that of a proprietor owing duties to a lord. From these duties and obligations, again, the tendency now was for the peasant, by purchase or refusal, to free himself.

Side by side with this very gradual exaltation of the humble and meek, there begin to occur, as the era of the Crusades approaches, numerous instances of the voluntary abasement of the great. Old seigneurs, in strange paroxysms of religious enthusiasm, giving up their old way of life, left lance and sword to younger hands and themselves put on the armour of God. The example of these soldiers of the Lord, having become *pauvre et peuple* for the kingdom of heaven's sake, living as mere monks in the Monastery of S. Père, went some way towards inspiring pity and consideration for the truly poor and the naturally low-born.

Generally, also, throughout this period there is a tendency to substitute for arbitrary exactions and violence arrangements settled by charter and definite duties and rights. But it is only a tendency. The amelioration of life was only very gradual. Neither life nor property in the eleventh and twelfth century were, as a rule, what we should call secure. Take for an instance the behaviour of the sons of one Échambaud when they had a difference over the possession of some land with the Abbot of S. Père. They refused to submit their case either to the jurisdiction of the Church courts or of Hélisende, the lady of the land. For they preferred to have recourse to the intervention of a powerful friend named John, living at Étampes, who was a total stranger to the matter in dispute. Relying upon his protection, these sons of Échambaud proceeded to plunder the property of the abbey and to burn the houses of the tenants. They were only induced to cease from their ways and to follow the peaceable paths of justice when the monks presented themselves at Étampes and threatened to excommunicate the town.

Crimes were paid for in cash. There was indeed a regular tariff for injuries done in the Middle Ages. The material damage once made good, the moral damage was left out of account. We learn from the *Cartulaire* the price of a monk of S. Père, for it is there recorded that Richard de Réviers, having slain one of these, Giraud by name, bought the pardon (pax) of the monks by making over to them four acres of land and an annual tribute of *four quartants* of corn. A century later (1239) we find the monks releasing from prison a man, who had slain a clerk, on receipt of a promise to pay *thirty sous tournois* yearly, in addition to certain other minor considerations.

Private wars arising from personal quarrels and ambitions, or damages of the sort described, were very frequent. The intervention of the Crown was rare. We have an instance of the exercise of the royal prerogative, however, when Louis le Gros stepped in and destroyed, after three years' war, the fortress of the Seigneurs du Puiset, who had long been a thorn in the side of Chartres, continually committing brigandage on the Church lands and caring nothing for ecclesiastical pains and penalties. The King abolished the oppressive institutions of these lords, and re-established in their ancient liberty the possessions of Notre-Dame and the Monastery of S. Père.

In the thirteenth century the power of the King grew stronger, and asserted itself over the monastic property. The monks of S. Père none the less retained the right of jurisdiction in their own lands. Thus when Geoffroi, Seigneur d'Illiers, had arrested a murderer in an inn on their property and had hung the man (1229), he was afterwards constrained to admit that he had exceeded his rights. All jurisdiction, he acknowledged, appertained to the abbot and monks; he gave them satisfaction, and paid them a fine.

Whilst they upheld their rights against the encroachments of Grands Seigneurs in this fashion, the monks were no less frequently involved in similar disputes with the *Communes*. Such disputes were often carried for settlement to the court of the King. Occasionally we find the courts ordering a point in dispute to be decided by judicial combat. These combats seldom actually took place. The proposal of them seems to have stimulated both parties to come to some arrangement, or to have frightened one of them perhaps into withdrawal. The absurd and cruel practice of trial by single combat had been borrowed from the warlike tribes of Germany, who could not believe that a brave man deserved to suffer or that a coward deserved to live. The old, the feeble and infirm, therefore, in civil and criminal proceedings, were exposed to mortal challenge from the antagonist who was destitute of legal proofs, and thus condemned to renounce their fairest claims and possessions, to sustain the danger of an unequal conflict, or to trust the doubtful aid of a mercenary champion. Two instances of such challenges are recorded by the monk Paul, and are full of human interest.

The Lord Payen de Rémalard brought an action (1090) against the Abbot of S. Père with regard to some land in the possession of the monastery. The two parties appeared in the Bishop's Court. S. Ives was the Bishop of Chartres, and he appeared among the witnesses for the monks. Geoffrey, Count of Perche and many others were present on behalf of Rémalard. The advocates on either side had begun to discuss and expound the case, when suddenly a servant of S. Père, Laurent by name, burst into the middle of the assembly and cried aloud that he had witnessed the gift of the property in question by the Lady Ermengarde to the monks. Rémalard himself, he further asserted, was present at the time and had made no objection then. Rémalard denied the story; the servant affirmed it again and again. Neither would give way. It was a question of word against word, and who was to decide which was the better? At last, at the suggestion of the monks, and with the assent of Rémalard, Laurent boldly named *diem belli et locum*—the day and place of combat. But on the day, and at the place named, Rémalard failed to put in an appearance—*suam presentiam minime exhibuit*, and the land passed peaceably into the undisputed possession of the monastery.

On another occasion, some twenty years later, the men of God proved themselves too sturdy for their opponents. Again it was the question about the donation of some property. Again one of the witnesses for the monastery, Walter of Treleveisin, offered to make good in a duel his testimony that he had been present on the occasion of the gift. This time once more the offer was accepted, and the opposite party, thinking to succeed by means of many subterfuges which they had prepared, at first put on a bold face. But when there was no sign of wavering on the part of the monks, the adversary's heart failed him; we are told his conscience smote him. He acknowledged the wrong he had done, and begged pardon of the abbot, promising, in the presence of the whole Chapter, that in future he would champion the cause of the monastery, both by word and deed, in court and in battle.

Occasionally, when temporal power failed to secure them justice, Divine aid helped the monks to maintain their rights. Wiard, son of Drogon de Conflans, found this to his cost when he had wrongfully exacted a horse from the Monastery of S. Père. Each time that he mounted the beast he was attacked by a sudden malady. So much so that, after making four unsuccessful attempts, he gave in and restored the horse to the monks, as is recorded by the monk Paul in the year 1098.

The same writer relates an incident of the same year, which throws a vivid light upon the social conditions of the days of chivalry. War was the profession of your true chevalier and brigandage his pastime. The excesses of a life spent in these occupations were to be repeated and at the same time expiated by the Crusader. The preliminary expenses of equipment for the Holy War were only to be met by selling some portion of his property to the Church. Many transactions of this sort are recorded in the telltale Chartularies of Notre-Dame and S. Père. The incident to which I refer will serve as an example of this:—

Nivelon, son of Faucher, Lord of Fréteval, confesses that, as often as he was carried away by chivalrous ardour (of a sort sufficiently inconvenient to his neighbours), it was his custom to fall upon the village of Emprainville with a troop of his followers and to 'commandeer' all the provisions to be found there belonging to the men of the Abbey of S. Père. But when, in after years, he determined to go on a pilgrimage to Jerusalem, he agreed, in order to obtain pardon for his trespasses and money for his journey, in consideration, that is, of thirteen silver pounds from the monks, to forego this vexatious habit of his.

And he adds that if any of his descendants dispute the validity of this concession, he hopes he may 'be struck down by the thunderbolt that awaiteth on perjurers, and that he may be condemned with Dathan and Abiram to hell fire, and there to suffer everlasting torture.' There is a fine ecclesiastical ring about the legal documents of those days, it will be noticed. Imprecations on breakers of contracts are indeed common enough in mediæval diplomatics. The monk Paul supplies us with an instance in which the guilty man is consigned 'to the everlasting fires of hell along with Nero, who caused the Apostle S. Peter to perish on the cross, and S. Paul the Apostle to perish by the sword.' In another case the hope is expressed that the transgressor may incur, amongst other inconveniences, the penalty of eternal damnation, the loss of his eyesight, and the infliction of the *mal royal*.

Nor was it a marauding knight only or an aggressive seigneur who was likely to interrupt the even tenor of a man's way in those times. There were not infrequently bishops in his path also—bishops of the feudal, fighting, robbing sort, whose style of blessing was a blow with a sword.

Notable among these persecuting Bishops of Chartres is Robert of Tours, Cardinal and Legate (1065), who excommunicated a whole parcel of monks because they refused to accept the abbot he wished to force upon them. Then, too, there was Arrald, deceitful and fair of speech, against whom the chronicler is mightily wroth. But the bishop must at least have had a sense of humour. For his dictum was that gold and silver and the precious ornaments of the Church had no place in a monastery; they were only provocative of pride and the occasion of wantonness in the monks. Therefore he would take such things away, to save them from temptation. He remarked, too, that it was a wicked thing for monks to eat fish or the fat of beasts; they ought to eat simple herbs only, and he advised them to strive to be xerophagi, or eaters of dry, plain food. And to help them, no doubt, he confiscated their fish ponds, for he had a nice taste in good fish himself, and a liking for foreign dishes, 'always indulging,' adds our monk savagely, 'his own natural tendency to gormandise' (ventri suo castrimargiam semper habens vernaculam)![45] But it is the monks themselves who have left us an imperishable tradition of gormandising; even on fast days they would put a fowl in the pot, and salve their consciences with the argument that as birds and fishes had been created on the same day, they might be of the same species; and, as to drink, they were often under the patronage of S. Martin, in cloisters or at the tavern, quite theologically drunk. As early as 847 the councils of the Church were busy with the scandals of monks in inns. And cleanliness of the body they considered to be a culpable vanity, a pollution of the soul.

But, whether Arrald deserved the censure of the monk Paul or not, that kind of bishop was not uncommon in this century. Geoffrey the First, seven years later, was excommunicated for simony and other vices. His simony he had defended with shameless cynicism.

When the King reproached him with having given to others the benefices which he had asked of him, 'I have not given them at all, sire,' he replied; 'I have sold them very profitably.'

But his treason, his adulteries and his perjuries became at last unbearable. Pope Gregory VII. determined to make an example of him. He was compelled to resign his bishopric, and in his stead was appointed one of the greatest of Chartrain Bishops—S. Ives.

The Feast of S. Ives is kept at Chartres on the 20th of May, when his relics, which are kept in the Treasury of the Cathedral, are shown. His name has been given to the passage in the cloister opposite the great north porch, and it lives in the mouth of the peasants as S. Yvre, protector of sheep; his stone image stands near that of Fulbert on the *clôture* of the choir, but his spirit lives most surely in those square grey towers which he began to build, and which, so massive and yet so spiritual, point with their spires heavenwards, like hands that have been clasped and raised in prayer.

A man of high birth, he had joined one of the severest Augustine orders, who eat neither fish nor meat; a man of great talents, he had improved them by study under the famous Lanfranc, at the Monastery of Le Bec. There he had been the friend and fellow-student of Anselm, who in later years paid him a visit at Chartres, on his way from Canterbury to Rome. The characters of the two men, as revealed by their lives and letters, are much alike in their sweetness and their strength. S. Ives was a man before his time; in every way superior to his century. A scholar, he was also a man of action, a statesman of indomitable will, a theologian of surpassing acumen and enthusiasm. He did not, like Fulbert, found a school of philosophy, but he made of his monks practical philosophers. As a canonist his famous 'Décret' caused him to be consulted by high and low, learned and learners alike, on questions of theology, jurisprudence or conduct. On questions of practical politics his advice was sought by Popes and Kings, whether of France or England; by Counts and Seigneurs, and men of low degree. It was always given with sympathy, science, and a charming humility. His letters are indeed full of sweetness and light, of dignity and logic, of firmness and vigour, tempered by Christian charity and meekness. Take, for an example, his reply to the Bishop of Orléans, who had consulted him on the question whether a free man, married to a woman of whose servile condition he had been ignorant, could divorce her and marry again. 'If the laws of the world are to be consulted,' S. Ives writes, 'the answer must be that, marriage between equals alone being legitimate, the divorce ought to take place. But if we consult the law of God, which makes us all equal, and is careless of social conditions, we shall answer, No.' And elsewhere he says, 'Reject these pretended trials by ordeal of fire and sword. It is tempting God, and I have often seen the innocent punished and the guilty acquitted by this means.'

Such was the pure and fearless spirit of the man who was now called to govern Chartres, and who set himself to introduce order, discipline and a right tone in a diocese which had suffered much from Geoffrey's lawless rule.

It was much against his will that he left his monastery at Beauvais to take up what he called 'the heavy burden of the episcopate' (Letter III.).

And since he was not willing to receive the insignia of his pastoral charge from the throne, the Canons of Chartres dragged him by main force before Philippe, and compelled him (as Anselm in England also was forcibly compelled) to receive the pastoral staff from the King.[46]

Geoffrey, however, the deposed bishop, was not the man to retire without a struggle. He enlisted the support of his uncle, Bishop of Paris, and of the Archbishop of Sens. Gently but firmly S. Ives ignored their protests, resting his claim on the supreme decision of the Pope. The storm wore itself out against his unflinching calmness. But scarcely was he settled peaceably in possession of his bishopric when, like the conscientious man of action that he was, S. Ives felt bound to stir up another storm, destined to make itself felt throughout Christendom.

The union of Philippe the First with Bertrade de Montfort was a flagrant violation of the laws of the Church. Against this adulterous marriage S. Ives arose and protested. In order to understand the part S. Ives took in this matter it is necessary to realise that the sanctity of marriage was a point, the observance of which, in his aim of securing not the appearance only but the reality of virtue, S. Ives had set himself to enforce in all classes. He deals with the subject in his letters with broad judgment and sound sense.

In the case of princes—for the sake of example—he had continually exerted himself to prevent or to annul marriages which transgressed the laws of holy matrimony.

Now, therefore, with immense courage, he determined to stop the adulterous and incestuous union of the quinquagenarian Philippe I. with Bertrade, third wife of Fouques, Count of Anjou. For the King wished to repudiate Queen Bertha and to make a wife of that fascinating and ambitious woman.

To quiet all scruples and objections, he began by endeavouring to obtain the consent of the bishops, and especially that of S. Ives (S. Ives, Letter XIII.), whom he tried to trick into giving his assent. But S. Ives would be no party to such a business. Though he could not dissuade the King, he persisted in opposing and condemning his action. He warned his brother bishops not to be mute dogs that know not how to bark. He wrote to the King that he would rather have a millstone round his neck and be cast into the sea than aid and abet by his presence this unrighteous union with Bertrade.

It was a noble letter; but the purpose of the writer was not achieved. The marriage took place. It remained to punish the honest bishop. Perhaps Philippe might have forgiven him, but Bertrade was not the kind of woman to forgive such opposition.

Hugues II. du Puiset, Viscount of Chartres, was her tool. Acting under instructions from the Court, he pillaged the lands of Notre-Dame. Then, profiting by the presence of the bishop in his country house near Fresnay,[47] he seized him and held him prisoner.

When news was brought to Chartres of the seizure of their bishop, people and clergy alike rose to arms to rescue him. But he wrote forbidding them to use violence for his sake. 'War,' he said, 'is for wolves, not for shepherds. I did not obtain my bishopric by arms, and by arms I do not care to recover it.' In like manner he restrained the nobles who were eager to fight against the King in his defence, and, for fear of stirring up rebellion, he refused for a long time to publish the letters which the Pope had despatched, denouncing the scandalous marriage of Philippe. As a reward, his lands and property were ravaged and sacked, so that, when in obedience to the Pope's command he was at length set free, he found himself reduced to absolute penury. But his firmness gained him his point in the end. Morality was vindicated. Philippe, excommunicated, made his submission to Pope Urban II., and although he withdrew it under Pascal II., he finally, with Bertrade, made the *amende honorable* before the assembled bishops in Paris (1104).

S. Ives had taken his part in that famous Council of Clermont, in which, after the Roman Pontiff had hurled from this tribunal in the heart of France his anathemas against the French King, the Church confirmed the Truce of God by which it was determined that (1095) 'on all days monks, clerks and women, and those with them shall abide in peace; but on three days of the week any injury inflicted by anyone upon another shall not be counted an infringement of the peace; but on the other four days (Thursday-Sunday) anyone who injures another shall be held guilty of breaking the holy peace, and shall be punished accordingly.' Men who lived by violence were to be violent only three days a week—men who lived by the sword were to keep it sheathed more than half the year. The check upon the unbridled power and wanton cruelty of the barons implied by this moderate enactment constituted one of the greatest steps in the direction of alleviating the distress of the poor, the weak and the educated; of encouraging travelling and trade, and promoting civilisation that was taken in the Middle Ages.

S. Ives proceeded with the utmost vigour to persuade the nobles of his diocese to accept the peace which they were tempted to reject as contrary to their privileges, and also to see that it was observed thereafter by them and by others within the limits of his own jurisdiction. And thus, by helping to deliver the weak from the power of the strong, he contributed towards preparing the way for the movement which was soon to give the people a voice in their own affairs and procure for them their municipal franchise in the form of 'Communes.'

Meanwhile this same Council of Clermont had provided an outlet for the energies of the knights of Christendom, which were restricted by the Truce of God. The Crusade had been promulgated.

The enthusiasm of the people had been carefully prepared. The fantastic figure of Peter the Hermit, dressed in a woollen tunic and a cloak of coarse cloth, his arms and feet alike bare, and his eyes flashing with magnetic frenzy, had appeared among them and heated their imaginations. At the sound of his eloquence every heart caught fire, and a nation of soldiers was burning to exhibit at once its piety and its valour by the conquest of the Holy Land. The merit and glory of that undertaking had also been preached by the clergy in every diocese. When, therefore, the Pope ascended a lofty scaffold in the market-place of Clermont his eloquence was addressed to a vast concourse of well-prepared and impatient enthusiasts. The answer to the summons to arms was unanimous. The orator was interrupted by the shout of thousands, 'Diex el volt! Diex el volt!' For so the popular tongue corrupted the cry of the clergy, 'God wills it!' (Deus vult). 'It is indeed the will of God,' replied the Pope, and he gave them as a mark of their sacred and irrevocable engagement the symbol of the red, the bloody cross to be worn on their breast or shoulder.

Thus in a paroxysm of religious fervour began that Crusade which was to end in the rapine of a mediæval raid, and in the disastrous *dénouement* of Nicæa.

The effects of the Crusades were as varied as the motives of the Crusaders. For though all were inspired, one need not doubt, by a genuine religious desire to regain the Holy Sepulchre for Christendom, by the belief of merit, the hope of the reward of plenary indulgence promised by the Pope, and the assurance of divine aid, yet other motives and instincts were present in the breasts of many. Collectively, the Crusading Gaul exhibited a perversion of that instinct of expansion to which French excursions into Britain and Russia, across the Pyrenees, the Alps and the Rhine, to America, India, Madagascar and Algiers, have continually borne witness, and which now survives the population's power to expand. Individually, the desire to rescue the Church, mingled with the hope of military glory and the prospect of unlimited plunder, were sufficient inducements for the barons to cease from petty wars in their own land, and to gratify, as a penance and against the nations of the East, those passions which, when indulged at home, had involved them in the discipline of penance. And in the case of their followers, among many other motives, the love of freedom prompted. For, under the sign of the Cross, the peasant attached to the servitude of the glebe might escape from a haughty lord and transplant himself and his family to a land of liberty, just as the monk might release himself from the discipline of his convent and the criminal elude the punishment of his crime.

Of the effects of the Crusades I shall only mention those which are directly illustrated by the story of Chartres. They rolled back the tide of Mahometan conquest from Constantinople; they brought together East and West, and led to the awakening of the human intellect which was to put an end to the dark ages; they opened up new markets and stimulated trade to a wonderful degree—these great results they had, but they only affected Chartres indirectly. More directly we see the effect of them in the relations between the powers that were. By weakening the resources and influence of the barons they strengthened the authority of the Kings acting in alliance with the citizens. And this alliance broke up the feudal system, gradually abolished serfdom, and substituted the authority of a common law for the unstable will of chiefs, whose arbitrament was private war. Last and not least permanent of the effects of the Crusades was the influence exercised by the East upon art. The Porche Royal of the Cathedral, and the stained glass windows which are the glory of Chartres, would not have been as they are had Peter the Hermit never led his hundred thousand pilgrims to destruction, or if Bohémond, Prince of Antioch, had not taken the Cross in the sanctuary of Notre-Dame.

The foundation of the Abbey Josaphat-Lès-Chartres, which, like so many other religious foundations rich in lands, in relics and in books, was destroyed in 1789, affords another example of the indirect influence of the Crusades upon the institutions of Chartres. This abbey[48] was situated about two kilometres from Chartres, under the Hill of Lèves, on a site which in its topographical relations resembled that Valley of Jehosaphat to which its founder, Bishop Geoffrey, the successor of S. Ives, had vowed to go, but came into the bishopric instead. Even so S. Bernard recalled the town of Tyre to the memory of all Christians in the name of Tyron, which he gave to the monastery which he founded in Le Perche on lands given to him by S. Ives.

It was to the Abbey of Josaphat that, up to the days of the Revolution, the musicians and choristers of Notre-Dame made yearly, in the vintage season, a strange kind of equestrian promenade, known as the *Chevauchée*. This probably represented the survival of some feudal obligation. The chevaucheurs in a dignified Latin speech obtained leave from the Chapter to perform their functions, and then, before leaving the Cathedral, they used to sing the office of the day. But once *en route* the cavalcade became as noisy and riotous a scene of carnival as the Feast of Fools. Riding on horses and donkeys, clad in outrageous garments of all colours, armed with swords, wearing absurd hats, and making a deplorable noise with all kinds of instruments, the cacophonous cavalcade made its way through the laughing, boisterous throng, to *déjeûner* at the Abbey of Josaphat. The Feast of Fools, to which I have referred, like this amazing excursion, was celebrated in the odour of scandal down to the end of the eighteenth century. It was a feast widely popular in France, but much more licentious than religious. It was held at Chartres on the 1st of January. An admirable picture of the Feast of Fools as observed at Notre-Dame-de-Paris five days later is drawn by Victor Hugo in the first chapters of his novel of that name.

Clerks of the choir dressed up in grotesque costumes, elected a *Pape des Fous* and a college of ridiculous cardinals, and then performed an indecent parody of the sacred offices. They danced in an abandoned fashion in the sanctuary, and ran about the city committing a thousand extravagances and bandying jests with the ribald crowd. There was another Feast of Fools in carnival time, which was authorised in 1300 on the condition that it was celebrated *dévotement*. That condition was not observed, and the feast was abolished in the following year. But that of January 1st continued till the 'scandals, insolences, turpitudes and abuses' which attended it led to its being forbidden in 1479 by the Church authorities. But the people preferred their Saturnalia to the danger of ecclesiastical anathemas, and the feast maintained its indecent existence for many years to come.

S. Ives had accompanied Urban preaching the Crusade through France. He returned now to Chartres and preached it there. Numerous were the Crusaders who went from the Chartrain country. It was fitting that, as in Foucher (*historien un peu trop conteur*), Chartres was to boast one of the chief chroniclers of the Crusades, so among her sons there should be many, like Gautier-Sans-Avoir, Raoul de Beaugency, and Gérard de Cherisy, to do knightly deeds worthy to be chronicled. The Battle of Gorgoni was won by the valour of the Count of Chartres and his followers, and Raimbaud Croton, a Chartrain, it was who first scaled the ramparts of Jerusalem. But none among the Chartrain Crusaders exceeded in bravery and brilliant daring Évrard, Viscomte of Chartres and Seigneur du Puiset. It was he who at the passage of the *Orontes* (El far) stood at the head of the bridge and, like another Horatius Cocles, held it against the enemy. It was he again who, when Jerusalem had just fallen into the hands of the Crusaders, won the admiration of the whole army by a bold feat of arms. A party of Christian soldiers were put to flight by the desperate resistance of a troop of the enemy. Their flight was barred by Évrard, whose anger found vent in a scathing volley of reproaches.

'Vile troop of cowards,' he cried, 'is it to fight you have come here, or to figure in a ballet? Are you children playing at soldiers, or little girls footing it in the chorus of a dance?... Away with fear, take courage, and remember you are Francs and born of brave sires. My ensign,' he nobly added, 'shall guide you—follow you me.' Thus speaking, he rushed into the fray, and, inspired by his example, the Crusaders succeeded in overwhelming the infidels.

The part played by Count Étienne was at first less noble. He had married Adèle, daughter of William the Conqueror, and, like his wife, he was distinguished in this age of the sword by a love of art and letters. He wrote poetry, and Hildebert, Bishop of Le Mans, rashly compared him to Vergil. 'Gentiz homme, noble barun,' so Robert Wace describes him.

Summoned from more congenial pursuits, he sailed with Robert, Duke of Normandy, to join the army which was then encamped before Nicæa. In a letter to his wife he described the hospitality with which the Emperor Alexis received him at Constantinople. 'He treated me with so much distinction,' he says, 'that I could only tear myself away from him with tears.' He proceeded to amass booty both before and after the taking of Nicæa, and his letters acquaint his wife with his increasing wealth and his military preferment, but he grows anxious to return to France with his enormous loot. His cowardly retreat from Antioch and the treacherous representations by which he dissuaded the Emperor Alexis from relieving the Crusaders, who were now pressed by the army of Kerbogha, gained him a poor welcome in France when he returned. The subsequent taking of Jerusalem exposed the deserting Crusaders to unlimited contumely, and filled them with remorse. French irony expressed itself in biting *sirvente*, short satirical poems by fighting troubadours like Bertram de Born, the Provençal nobleman, who gave to Richard Coeur-de-Lion his nickname of Yea-and-Nay. Those faint-hearted knights who had stolen back to their baronial halls were denounced with cutting invective.

'Marques, li monges de Clunhie
Veuilh que fasson de vos capadel
O siatz abbas de Cystilh,
Pus le cor avetz tan mendic
Que mais amatz dos buous et un araire
A Montferrat qu'alors estr' emperuieur.'[49]

Stung by such taunts, Count Étienne seized an opportunity which was given him of making a fresh expedition against the Turks. On this occasion he amply redeemed his reputation, and after many deeds of heroism he laid down his life for the cause whose sign he bore. Before setting out he had secured the blessing of the bishop by two interesting concessions.

It was a long-established custom of the town and a right by usage of the Counts of Chartres that, on the death of a bishop, his palace should be sacked. To S. Ives, when his new palace was finished, Count Étienne now granted a charter renouncing this barbarous practice. But none the less Thibault, his son, sacked the bishop's palace upon the death of S. Ives. The other concession made by the Count was with regard to the liberty of the cloister, which, the canons maintained, was outside all secular jurisdiction. The quarrel which sprang from this question of the rights of the cloister was destined to last for three centuries. For the present it was forgotten in the more absorbing interest of the Crusades.

From the time of Fulbert onwards, the canons, on one pretext or another, whether by buying houses, claiming jurisdiction, or openly demanding the right of enclosing their cloister by walls and gates, had begun to encroach—so at least it was regarded by Counts and townsmen—upon the domain of Chartres, and to set up by degrees a town within a town, the cloister which stretched from the Rue de Cheval Blanc on the north to the Rue au Lait on the south, and from the Percheronne on the west to the Rue Montonnière, a continuation of the Rue Muret, on the east. The rights claimed by the Chapter were at last acknowledged and established by parliamentary decree, 1470; but only, as we have said, after centuries of bickering with the Counts. They, feeling themselves assailed both as to their pockets and their powers of jurisdiction by the privileges extended by the Church to those who attached themselves to the cloister, expressed their feelings by frequent armed raids into the precincts, pillaging the shops[50] which had sprung up beneath the shade of Notre-Dame and carrying off unfortunate clerks as prisoners to be ransomed from the great Tower. The Church retaliated with its one all-powerful weapon—excommunication.

The cloister[51] was finally enclosed by thick walls and by nine gates—mostly destroyed in the eighteenth century; but of some of them traces may still be seen—the *Porte Neuve* and the *Porte de l'Étroit-Degré*, giving on the Rue du Cheval Blanc; the *Porte des Changes* (Rue des Changes), and *Porte aux Herbes* (Rue au Lait), *Porte Évière*, entrance of Rue Saint-Eman; *Porte Percheronne* (Rue du Soleil-d'Or), *Porte des Carneaux* (Rue Sainte-Même), *Porte des Lices* (Marché-a-la-Filasse), *Porte de l'Évêque* (Rue Muret).

One of the handsomest of the old houses of the canons that remains is that at the corner of the Rue des Changes, facing the south porch of the Cathedral. Utilitarian France has sadly restored this old thirteenth-century house, and turned it to account as the Post Office, just as she has planted some villainous cavalry barracks on the site of the old monastic buildings of S. Père, and converted into a military bakehouse the interesting old House of Loens.

Attached to the cloister was the Hospital or Hôtel-Dieu of Notre-Dame. It was founded about the tenth century; restored and spoilt in the eighteenth century. The hospital has recently been removed to a more suitable spot, and the old Hôtel-Dieu, with its thirteenth-century chapel, now serves for the École Mutuelle of the town. It stands in the south-west corner of the space which has been cleared in front of the Cathedral, between the Rue Fulbert and the Rue de la Cathédrale.

***Street Entrance to Old Hôtel de Ville***

The departure and death of Etienne left Chartres and its bishop more than ever exposed to the brigandage of the Viscount Hugues, who was always in a state of excommunication, and whose bands of mercenary robbers held the roads, so that S. Ives could not attend the great Council at Sens or at Paris. With his violence, as with the greed and slackness of his own clergy, S. Ives carried on unceasing war, and it was not long before he found himself involved also in a bitter quarrel with the Countess Adèle, widow of Etienne. The Chapter had bound themselves by oath not to admit into their ranks any of those known as *conditionarii*—men, that is, freed from serfdom but still held under servile obligations to the Countess. The Countess exerted herself with extraordinary energy and persistence to advance the claims of certain clients of this description. S. Ives strove to calm her and to support his Chapter. The Countess retorted by violent reprisals and seized the wine of the precentor, Hilduin, in the street des Corroyeurs. S. Ives threatened her with excommunication, and she interdicted the canons from the use of the roads, and of bread and water throughout her domain. It was time to give way, and S. Ives, by a judicious compromise, obtained the Pope's consent that the Lady Adèle's men should be admitted to share in the revenues of the Cathedral.

In support of his suzerain the Viscount Hugues had been devastating the diocese. But a new Crusade saved S. Ives from his enemies. Bohémond of Tarentum, Prince of Antioch, came to Chartres to marry Constance, daughter of the King, and to receive the nuptial benediction from the hands of S. Ives, to whose efforts the marriage was due. The Countess Adèle displayed on this occasion a hospitality worthy in its magnificence of the daughter of William the Conqueror and of the noble House of Thibault the Trickster. The marriage ceremony was performed, and thereafter, before a vast assembly standing on the steps of the altar of the *Vierge-aux-Miracles*, the Prince of Antioch related his wonderful adventures, and bore witness to the miraculous protection afforded to him by God in the former Crusade. Men listened and wondered and waxed enthusiastic. When Bohémond concluded his discourse by inviting his listeners to follow the example of the first Crusaders, a crowd of knights rushed forward and then and there took the sign of the Cross. Foremost among them was the excommunicated brigand, Hugues, Viscomte de Chartres.

S. Ives died at the end of the year 1115. But during his busy lifetime there had been springing up the great monument which is his in Chartres, the Western Towers and the Porche Royal of the Cathedral, with its sculptured kings and queens, than which no sculpture in the world is more beautiful. During his lifetime also it had been necessary to rebuild in great part the Church of Fulbert. The rapidity with which it had been built in troublous times of war and famine may account for this necessity. S. Ives increased the length of the building by some twenty-five yards and, whilst carrying the nave and aisles one bay further west, he prolonged the crypt to the foot of his new towers, adorning it with mural paintings, of which traces yet remain. The towers were built at the end of each aisle, and the lower part of the west front, though actually the same now as that then built, lay back at that time on a line within the eastern sides of the towers. It was afterwards brought forward so as to be where it now is, flush with their western sides.

S. Ives also constructed the two new entrances to the crypt, with staircases and passages, through the Cave du Bois on the north and S. Martin's Chapel on the south. The roof of the apse was also renewed, and an angelot or guardian angel set thereon.[52] But one of the chief works of S. Ives was the construction of the beautiful Jubé,[53] of which we have seen the few remaining fragments in the crypt.[54] Meanwhile the rest of the Cathedral, its chapels and altars, were being adorned by the pious generosity of the people of all classes. The choir was paved with marble and mosaic, and tapestries were hung round it where now runs the sculptured *clôture*. The beautiful glass through which the light still pours its coloured streams were being set up in the lower lights of the western façade, and in the sacristy was accumulating that collection of jewels and relics, of chalices, censers and crucifixes, of liturgies bound in silver, gold and precious stones, and of ecclesiastical ornaments, which was to render the treasury of Chartres one of the richest in the world, till the Vandals of the eighteenth century laid their sacrilegious hands upon it.

In order to obtain funds for the building of his towers and the restoration of his church, S. Ives, like Fulbert before him, begged freely of Kings.

It will be understood that his relations with Philippe were not of the kind to encourage him to ask for aid in that quarter. But he sent two monks to Henry I. of England with a letter, in which, after expressing the pious hope that Henry would continue to walk in the footsteps of his father, and recognise that, as the body ought to be subject to the mind, so ought the civil government to be subject to the ecclesiastical, he tells him that he is the servant of the servants of God, and not their master; their protector, and not their lord; and then adds that the bearers of the letter will explain to His Highness the needs of the Church, which he is conjured to satisfy with the same generosity as his parents showed.

It is scarcely surprising that a letter couched in such terms was not productive of alms from the English King who had taken his spouse from a nunnery; nor was an appeal to Matilda in the following year 'to show that love for the Queen of the Angels which the Queens of the Angles have always so generously displayed' any more successful. But a third more likely letter knocked, to borrow S. Ives's own phrase, at the door of Henry's generous heart with better result. Queen Matilda was charged with the duty of replying to it, and she made many gifts to the Church, among which were several bells, of which S. Ives writes in acknowledgment that 'they are doubly dear to us, both on account of your piety and of their own sweet melody. Every time that they are put in motion to indicate certain hours, our ears are soothed with such delicious music that your memory is renewed within our hearts.' He also reminds her, amid many such graceful sayings, that the roof wants mending; and at her death we find that his words bear fruit, for she made many bequests to the Cathedral, and left money to defray the expenses of a lead roof. But it was not only Kings and

Queens who fell under the charm of S. Ives and the love of his Church, and it was not only the great who received his thanks. Such phrases as the following occur again and again in the Necrology of Notre-Dame:—'On Nov. 24th, died Jean, son of Vital, the clever and faithful carpenter of this Church, who always worked with love and zeal at the work of this Church.' That is but one name among the thousands, who now, with an extraordinary outburst of enthusiasm, came from far and near to build the superb monument of Chartres Cathedral.

# CHAPTER V

## The Cathedral and Its Builders

'By suffrage universal it was built
As practised then, for all the country came
From far as Rouen, to give votes for God,
Each vote a block of stone securely laid
Obedient to the Master's deep-mused plan.'
JAMES RUSSELL LOWELL.

'Like some tall palm the mystic fabric grew.'
REGINALD HEBER.

'Elle est enfin, cette basilique, la plus magnifique expression de l'art que le Moyen Age nous ait léguée.'—J. K. HUYSMANS.

THE grey spire of the Clocher Vieux,[55]—

'molten now in driving mist,
Now lulled with the incommunicable blue,'

was not completed till near the end of the twelfth century, for upon the soffit of the topmost window facing the Clocher Neuf you may read in great Roman letters the name of the master of the works, HARMAN, 1164. N.D.D. Such, at least, is the inference drawn, though it may well be only the weary vigil of a watchman who nightly gazed over the plains of La Beauce on the look out for beacon signals of alarm, or for the first evidence of a fire in the town, that is recorded in these deep-cut letters. The foundations of the old tower at any rate were laid as early as 1091, and both the square towers were finished by 1145. They carry the spires that are the pride of Chartres, and which have given rise to the popular saying that the perfect cathedral, if it could ever be built, would be composed of the spire of Chartres, the nave of Amiens, the choir of Beauvais, the porch of Reims.[56]

Of the two spires, the northern, Clocher Neuf, with its airy staircases and pierced traceries, built by Jean le Texier, called Jean de Beauce, in the sixteenth century, is the more popular, the Clocher Vieux the more beautiful. The former is flamboyant, decked out with delicate ornament, graceful, rich, and feminine; the latter sober, severe, robust, clad, you might fancy, like a man in armour. These giant towers, indeed, and their aerial pinnacles are not twin sisters, but rather, it might seem, sister and elder brother, with their points of resemblance and their points of difference; the one, weatherbeaten and grey, but still preserving, in spite of the wrinkles of old age, a noble, male and mellowed beauty; the other, the young sister, smiling through the lace of a wedding veil, comely as a bride, fair as the spouse of Christ.

The one, fashioned by the Byzantine chisel, sprang into complete being in the heroic ages of faith, in the days of war, and beheld at its feet Thomas, exiled from Canterbury, and Bernard, when preaching the second Crusade, hailed there by bishops and barons as generalissimo of that great enterprise. The other rose, after a long peace, under the hands of the still Christian architects of the Renaissance, when all dangers and difficulties had been surmounted. She arose in her smiling elegance, rose till it seemed that she would touch the stars, and her mantle shone with a thousand lights and sparkled with a thousand

***The Spires of Chartres***

ornaments. Statues and buttresses, gargoyles, arabesques and crochets pile themselves in successive stages, until the eye loses the sense of everything but a sort of architectural lacework.

The Cathedral is truly a Bible in stone. And just as in the sculptured porches the mediæval masons carved in a symbolic type, which the illiterate could read, the story of the Pentateuch and the Gospels; just as in their jewelled windows the monkish glaziers told again the same Bible story for all to see and understand, so it would seem that here in Chartres, the architects also, but by fortune rather than design, have symbolised in stone the Old Testament and the New. In that amazing window of the south transept the prophets of the former dispensation are portrayed carrying on their shoulders the naïve evangelists. Similarly the builders have made the Romanesque crypt to carry the Gothic upper church, and the old tower, eloquent of Byzantine art, massive and superb, confronts the joyous, soaring sister who has sprung up, from like foundations, at his side, the last effort, or rather the last amusement, of that Gothic art which is typical of aspirations that are justified, of a faith that is fulfilled.

The Clocher Vieux combines to the highest degree grandeur with harmonious unity of proportion. From the bottommost stone to the highest there is never a break in the perfect line; and the plain massive base of enormous quarried stones, some of which, they say, measure ten feet by three, passes into the light octagonal spire, covered with its curious coat of mail or fishes' scales, by imperceptible and inevitable gradations. It is a triumph of sheer beauty of proportion unaided by the art of ornament. The transition from the square tower to the tapering *flèche* is, in spite of this simplicity, so exquisitely treated that it cannot be distinguished. It is a perfect masterpiece of masonic skill. Two terrible fires and more than 700 winters have left it with not one stone displaced.[57]

The mere size of the enormous blocks of stone of which the base is built will fill the most casual visitor with astonishment. It has been suggested that they formed part of those city walls described by the monk Paul which once ran close to the Cathedral, and which were at this period being dismantled in order to admit of the enlargement of *enceinte* of the town. But we know, from independent contemporary sources, how the labour required to quarry and fetch these huge masses of material was supplied. It was supplied by popular enthusiasm, inspired by religious fervour. For though the work of building, impeded by plague and famine, and a terrible fire which destroyed the town in 1134, went on slowly at first, in 1144 a great outburst of devotion occurred throughout the land. Whole populations arose and came to Chartres to labour at the work of God's house. A noble rivalry urged every man to toil, and women even took their share in a burden which their faith rendered light, in a task which their devotion made both pleasant and honourable.

'In this same year,' writes Robert du Mont, Abbot of Mont S. Michel, to quote one only among all the twelfth-century chroniclers who mention this fact, 'In this same year at Chartres men began to harness themselves to carts laden with stones and wood, corn and other things, and drag them to the site of the church, the towers of which were then a-building. It was a spectacle the like of which he who hath not seen will never see again, not only here, but scarcely in all France or Normandy or elsewhere. Everywhere sorrow and humility prevailed, on all sides penitence, forgiveness and remorse. On every side you could see men and women dragging heavy loads through the marshy bogs, and scourging themselves with whips. Miracles were being done on every side, and songs and hymns of praise sung to the Lord. You might say that the prophecy was being fulfilled which says, The Spirit of Life was in the wheels of their chariots.'

A curious confirmation of this statement exists in the form of a correspondence which passed at this time between the Bishop of Rouen and the Bishop of Amiens.

'Mighty are the works of the Lord,' exclaims Hugh of Rouen. 'At Chartres men have begun in all humility to drag carts and vehicles of all sorts to aid the building of the Cathedral, and their humility has been rewarded with miracles. The fame of these events has been heard everywhere, and at last roused this Normandy of ours. Our countrymen, therefore, after receiving our blessing, have set out for that place and there fulfilled their vows. They return filled with a resolution to imitate the Chartrains. And a great number of the faithful of our diocese and the dioceses of our province have begun to work at the Cathedral, their mother.' The north-west tower of the Cathedral of Rouen, the Tour S. Romain, was built in this way. The visitor will notice its resemblance to the Clocher Vieux of Chartres, and this letter will explain why in workmanship and spirit it does so resemble it.

These poor Norman workmen departed on a new crusade, as it were, of chisel and trowel to offer their labour for the adornment of Our Lady's Church. They travelled in small bands, forming part of a vast association, and, so the bishop informs his reverend brother, admitted no one to join their company unless he had first been confessed and done penance, and laid aside all anger and malevolence, and been reconciled with his enemies. One of their number was chosen to lead them, and under his directions they drew their waggons in silence and humility, and presented their offerings, not without penance and tears.

There is yet another letter which I shall readily be forgiven for quoting, so graphic is the picture which it gives. It is the text to which the beautiful window in the south aisle of the choir furnishes the perfect illustration. The Abbot Haimon of S. Pierre-sur-Dive wrote to his brethren of Tutbury, in Staffordshire, a small priory dependent on S. Pierre, in the following strain:—

'Who has ever seen or who heard in all the ages of the past that kings, princes and lords, mighty in their generation, swollen with riches and honours, that men and women, I say, of noble birth have bowed their haughty necks to the yoke and harnessed themselves to carts like beasts of burden, and drawn them, laden with wine, corn, oil, stone, wood and other things needful for the maintenance of life or the construction of the church, even to the doors of the asylum of Christ? But what is even more astonishing is that, although sometimes a thousand or more of men and women are attached to one cart—so vast is the mass, so heavy the machine, so weighty the load—yet so deep a silence reigns that not a voice, not a whisper even can be heard. And when there is a halt called on the way there is no sound save that of the confession of sins and the suppliant prayer to God for pardon. There, whilst the priests are preaching peace, all hatred is lulled to sleep and quarrels are banished, debts forgiven, and the union of hearts re-established. But if anyone is so hardened that he cannot bring himself to forgive his enemies or to beg the pious admonitions of the priests, then his offering is withdrawn from the common stock as unclean, and he himself is separated, with much shame and ignominy, from the society of the holy people. Forward they press, unchecked by rivers, unhindered by mountains. You might think that they were the children of Israel crossing Jordan, and for them, as for the children of Israel, miracles are wrought. But when they come to the church, they set their waggons in a circle so as to form, as it were, a spiritual camp, and all the following night the watch is kept by the whole army with hymns and songs of praise. Candles and lamps are lit on each waggon; the sick and the feeble are placed thereon; the relics of the saints are brought to them in the hope that they may find relief. The clergy at the head of a procession, and the people following, pass by and pray with renewed fervour that the sick may be healed.'

Then occurred scenes such as may be beheld to-day before the grotto in the mountain village of Lourdes. For Chartres was the Lourdes of the Middle Ages. The maimed and the halt recovered their powers, leapt from the waggons and flung away their crutches; the blind received their sight, the sick were healed, and all joined, after returning thanks before the altar, in the task of building the house of their Redeemer.

You see their work, you behold the material in which they wrought, as you stand before the western façade[58] and gaze in wonder; for the stones, it seems, have become intelligent, and matter is here spiritualised. But you will almost cease to wonder when you remember the spirit in which they wrought it. Such was the spirit, and such only could be the spirit, which produced the master-art of Gothic, and led the daring architects from step to step in the attainment of their triumphs, as they left behind them the heavy piers and the thick dark arches of the Pagan Romanesque and arrived at last at the perfect expression of the Christian spirit in their soaring arches, their airy buttresses, and their pointing pinnacles flaming upwards to the skies.

Seven miles distant from Chartres lie the quarries of Berchères-l'Évêque, whence, in the spirit and manner that has been described, they brought this 'miraculous' stone—miraculous, for it was in a vision that the existence of the quarry was said to have been revealed. Miraculous one may almost call it still, by reason of its quality of hardness, its gift of wear, and the exquisite tones which it has taken on with years. Of the two towers the old one is the better built; many of the stones of the other were laid in too little mortar and have consequently split. These blocks of stone are marked with various masonic signs, a fact which confirms the supposition that the two towers were built by the Frères Maçons or Logeurs du bon Dieu, as they were called, those famous associations of the Middle Ages, corporations of artist workmen, who were indeed 'masters of the living stone.'

The first time that the traveller beholds the porches of Chartres he is filled with admiration for the exquisite effect of the whole, and afterwards for the exquisite details of which that whole is composed. He may, if he is of an imaginative temperament, fall into some reverie and picture to himself a host of historic fantasies.

But later he will begin to realise that the sculpture which had pleased his eye and inspired his dreams is not a mere ornament of the building. Each part of the Cathedral, like the Cathedral as a whole, is the superb product of the intimate alliance of nameless architects, nameless sculptors, nameless painters of glass, working with the one object of setting forth the glory of God and His Son and the Virgin to the multitude, of illustrating for all unreading eyes the Word of the Lord. The Cathedral is a Bible in stone, and the porches a gospel in relief, a sculptured catechism, a preface and a *résumé* of the book. Each stone, thus understood, is seen to be a page of a great drama. This drama is the history of humanity from the creation of the world to the day of the Last Judgment. Within, the same story is repeated. The jewelled windows are there not only for the sake of the holiness of their beauty, not merely to provide the pilgrim with the dim religious light suitable to his mood, or that the placid sunshine of La Beauce may be transformed into imperious angry fire. The five thousand figures in those legendary lights are the commentary and the repetition of the sculptured text without.

Who conceived, the question arises again and again, this admirable plan, this marvellous whole? Who were the artists of Notre-Dame? We are in great ignorance of the matter, and the question cannot be definitely answered.

The cloister we know was the only refuge of art; the monasteries the sole asylums for those who would study science. And to those peaceable retreats painters, sculptors, artists perforce retired to practise, to invent, to teach the secrets of their trade; secrets, alas! of colour among them, which have been irretrievably lost to this scientific generation. We know, for instance, that in the Monastery of Tiron, which S. Bernard founded on lands given to him for that purpose by S. Ives, more than five hundred artists of one sort or another were to be found. S. Bernard insisted on the observance of that point in the Benedictine rule which recommends that 'if there be artists in the monastery they shall with all humility practise their arts.' These monks, we also know, established a branch at Chartres, 'near the market-place.' Perhaps, therefore, S. Bernard paid his debt to S. Ives and the Chapter of Notre-Dame by furnishing the hands which carved the statues and the storied capitals of the three bays of the western façade.

In the S. Sylvester window, to the right of the entrance to the Chapel of S. Piat, and in the S. Chéron window of the Chapel of the Sacred Heart of Mary, the old glass painters have well represented the masons of Notre-Dame. Here is a beardless dresser of stone, there a sculptor with his rough, pointed cap. The iron hardness of the miraculous stone yields to the untiring application of chisel and mallet, and beneath their ceaseless blows its formless mass by degrees becomes shapely. Above the workers appears the chapel in which the window now is. A mason in a round hat is quietly laying a cornice stone, whilst his help-mate, carrying a piece of sculpture, climbs up a little ladder. In the background four other masons, shaven and clad like the common people, are busy shaping the statues of kings—the very statues which now, representing the ancestors of Christ, stand in the porch without. The statue is as yet only blocked out: the artist is beginning to model it with his chisel. His companion the while, warm with his past exertions, is drinking. The royal statue begins to be distinguishable. The eyes and the mouth are leaping into life: the crown is being adorned with pearls, the sceptre decorated, the robe and mantle draped, the hands modelled. The man who has blocked it out has finished his task and takes his rest; his companion carves, polishes and puts the finishing touches to the work he has begun.

What were their names? No one knows. The names of some of the donors are preserved in the necrologies of the grateful canons, but of all the clever artists of Notre-Dame hardly one has left his name behind him, like the Robbir who carved his signature beneath the combat of David and Goliath on the north porch.

This is in no way surprising, when we remember the spirit in which these works were done. The Cathedrals were built and decorated for the glory of God, not for the glorification of the artists. Men dedicated to the Church their money and their labour for the remission of their sins, and not with the object of acquiring fame. We have seen, and shall see again, how whole populations rose up and came on a pilgrimage from afar to build and to rebuild the house of God, when to the enthusiasm of the Crusades succeeded the holy ardour of religious construction and men took the Cross, not to depart to war in the East, but to labour humbly at the work of God, Our Lady and the saints. Then from the distant cloister came forth the architect, and artists and, at the voice of a bishop calling for aid, the sacred work began. The peasants quarried stone and brought material, the young men dressed it, and the masons raised the lofty piers and fashioned the groined roof beneath the eye of the 'master of the work.' The pilgrims would sojourn, perhaps, for a year in the town, labouring with such ardour that when the light failed they would often continue by the light of torches. Not far from the site of the church, in some adjacent monastery, the glass-painters designed and stained and fitted into the leads their coloured windows, and the sculptors chiselled bas-reliefs and statues. A man's labour was his offering, his art very often his best and only alms. His name was one name only among a thousand, his work might surpass in excellence but it would be the same in spirit with that of a thousand other pilgrims like unto himself. Why should his name therefore be recorded?

So it came about that the 'master of the work' received from the many workers statuary of varying excellence, and gave it all its place in the Cathedral. Among the thousands of sculptures at Chartres or Reims many are of very inferior merit. Many a chef-d'œuvre, on the other hand, on which the pious sculptor has lavished all his skill is hidden in inaccessible nooks, or scarcely visible in the loftiest part of a building, thus showing clearly the motive of devotion which inspired the worker.

It was in this sense, then, that the Cathedral of Chartres was built 'by universal suffrage,' as Lowell put it, just as the entire population from the Coquet to the Tees, headed by the Earl of Northumberland, rose up to build the Cathedral of Durham. The nearest modern analogy to such enthusiasm is to be found in the history of Christianity in Uganda or in the building of the church at Swindon by the united, unpaid efforts of the working men of that town. It was the living faith of the people, not the mere feudal requisition of their labour by the bishops (corvées) which created the mediæval temples, faith strong and simple as that which inspired Sabine of Steinbach or her who laid the last stone of the Dom of Köln.

It would, however, be misleading to suggest that, because many pilgrims worked for the love of God, all the workers were unpaid. We hear of occasions when money failed and

'Ne porent pas païer assez
Li mestre de l'œuvre aus ouvriers.'[59]

Such things as the Jubé, the porches and the rose windows, executed after elaborate consultations and under the supervision of the 'master of work,' were inspected again by a clever master from another country. The chief workers were lodged in houses of the cloister belonging to the Chapter, who granted them doles from time to time and furnished them yearly with gloves and a mantle.

The *naïveté* of the mediæval artists is one of their chief charms, but there is often a spice of wickedness in their work. Read the *fabliaux* and mysteries of the time, from the Bible of Guyot de Provins to the play acted on the Piazza of Troyes in 1475, and you will find passages enough that offend the taste and are worthy of the actors in the Feast of Fools. The satire of the *Trouvères*, whether they are scourging monks, barons or sovereign pontiffs, is often extremely gross. Similarly, while the Count of Chartres was chanting in chivalrous fashion the praises of his lady, the porches of the Cathedral were receiving into their niches here and there the representations of certain ugly vices and their punishment, such as Dante ere long was to translate into the harmonious verses of his *Divina Commedia*. Fallen nuns and erring queens are delivered over to grinning demons, and Satan rubs his hands at the sight of his innumerable victims (south porch). S. Augustin might protest against the apocryphal Scriptures, and Popes denounce the legendary poetry of the early centuries, but painters persisted in depicting with excessive freedom the histories of S. Thomas and S. James, and sculptors still waxed wanton when they carved the sins of the Prodigal Son. S. Bernard, the enigma of his age, was constrained to cry out against the grotesque ornamentation of the churches.

But it is not the mere naughtiness of some satirical mason giving expression to the humour of the people which accounts for all the mediæval grotesques—for the Imp of Lincoln, the Noah of Bourges, the Devils of Notre-Dame-de-Paris, the Ass of Chartres. Vices were portrayed in order to illustrate their punishment. 'Let faithful souls but see the Passion of Our Lord represented,' says an old writer, 'and rarely will they fail to be filled with compunction and to raise their eyes to heaven.' To the impressionable, childlike, illiterate men of the Middle Ages, accordingly, the clergy taught the lessons of dogma and belief through the personages of drama or the medium of art. The sculpted bays of a porch or the storied windows of a nave were a lesson for the ignorant, a sermon for the believer, appealing through the eyes to the heart. The representation of the mysteries and miracle plays showed to him in action and helped him to realise the persons whose figures were already familiar to him as painted on glass, sculptured on capitals, incrusted on the vaulting of the doors. Graphic and dramatic art constituted the books of those who did not know how to read. With the aid of these material objects, as the Abbot Suger, the great artist of

S. Denis, declared,[60] the feeble spirit can mount to the truth and the soul which was plunged in darkness rise to the light which bursts upon its terrestrial eyes. We need not wonder then if the paintings of the Middle Ages have not always the severity of modern ecclesiastical art, for vices were portrayed with a view to condemning them the more thoroughly. The mediæval masons were strangers, it would seem, to the legend of Spinello. Evil for them was always ugly, and the Devil a monster, not Lucifer.

But at Chartres this side of life is not dealt with overmuch. The bases of the pillars of the bays in the south and the western porches give some examples of

*L'Âne qui Vielle*

men and women in the thralls of vice. Apart from these instances, the most famous and striking examples of the masons' satiric warning are the *Âne qui vielle* and the *Truie qui file*. These curious imposts of the closed doorway on the south side of the *clocher Vieux* represent a donkey playing a harp and a sow spinning.[61] They are epigrams in stone, intended to remind us of the maxims, Asinus ad lyram, and Ne sus Minervam doceat; warnings against the pretentious ambitions of the awkward and incompetent, equivalent to the French dictum *Que Gros-Jean n'en remontre pas à son curé*; a proverb of which we have some obvious but homely versions. But of infernal beasts and Vices there is at Chartres, so much is this the Church of Our Lady, a decided scarcity. Of the Virtues there are many: most celebrated is the proud statue of Liberty in the left bay of the north porch, in which some writers have seen a reference to the Communal freedom granted to the people by the Kings, but which is in reality only one of the series of fourteen Heavenly Beatitudes as described by the mediæval theologians, which fill some of the rows of the vaulting of this bay.

On the south angle of the Clocher Vieux there is an angel carrying a sun-dial, of whom one would gladly know more. There is an angel-dial on the corresponding part of the S. Laurence Church at Genoa, and one which much resembles this, and may have been by the same hands, is at the south corner of the cloister at Laon. Our angel stands with bare feet on a bracket, and above his head is a 'Heavenly Jerusalem'—a daïs showing a city with turrets and windows. He is clad in a long tunic covered by a mantle which fits close to his long, thin body. His hands are intended to support a disc on which a sun-dial was traced. His arms are outspread. Clearly the present dial traced on a heavy square stone, with the date 1578, which covers his breast, was an addition of that year, but does not mark the date of the angel. For though the smile which lurks about his fair monastic countenance is scarce angelic, and may suggest rather the disquieting, seraphic types of the Renaissance, yet the whole figure, with its simple and successful treatment of the hair and draperies, is redolent of the Byzantine style, which we shall trace in the family of kings and queens grouped beneath the Porche Royal. To that family he must belong.

**The Angel Dial**

You will move gladly into the porch to study its beautiful twelfth-century sculpture, for whilst you have been looking at this angel you will have learnt that round the south-west corner of the Cathedral, as about the Abbey in Old Palace Yard in Westminster, the wind never ceases to blow, and often blows a hurricane. Before the Hôtel-Dieu, which was quite close to the Clocher Vieux, was destroyed, the gusts of wind were so violent that the passage called *L'Âne qui vielle* had the reputation of being impassable. One Canon Brillon, a hundred years ago, wrote a poem in which he related that 'On a time Wind and Discord were travelling over the plains of La Beauce and suddenly turned in the direction of the Cathedral. Arrived at the foot of the towers, Discord left his companion, asking him to wait near *L'Âne qui vielle* whilst he went into the Chapter-house. Contentious business detained him there so long that the Wind is still waiting, waiting for him outside;

Le Vent dehors l'attend encore!'

As I struggle through Old Palace Yard I often wonder whether it is in the House of Commons or in the Chapter-house of the Abbey that Discord is so busily engaged, for the wind here, as in Chartres and at Kill-Cannon Corner at Lincoln, is always waiting outside, a truly Gothic draught![62]

The western porch is composed of three large bays, of which the middle one was, as always in Christian churches, known as the Porte Royale. This name was given it because in the tympanum Christ was always represented triumphant, the King of Kings. Nor, as you gaze at the wealth of statuary and ornamentation upon which, as upon the architecture, the artists have lavished all their resources and all their skill in their endeavour to illustrate the Story of the Triumph of Our Lord, will you grudge this entrance its other names of Porta Speciosa and Porta Triumphalis. The sculptured figures are of every size. Once the whole porch was a blaze of colour. Of this colour and gold you may still see a few traces left.

Begun about 1110, under S. Ives, this typical example of early Gothic work was not completed till nearly 1150, and among those who wrought the images which people it were, some think, the artists who had worked at the Porch of S. Sermin at Toulouse, and knew that of S. Trophimus at Arles.

They would thus connect it with the art of the South, and, through that, with Roman art. It appears to me rather to be directly under the influence and inspiration of Byzantine art. There is to one's eye something Eastern in this work as surely as there is something Eastern also to one's ear in the rhythms of a Gregorian chant. However that may be, nowhere, at any rate, has the story of Christ's Triumph been told so fully and with such a wealth of detail in stone as at Chartres. We are shown here not only His triumph but the events which led up to it. The whole Gospel is revealed to the gaze of the Christian who is about to enter the house of the Lord. The story is taken from the apocryphal as well as the canonical Gospels. It begins with the scenes represented by the thirty-eight miniature groups of the capitals, the figures of which, in spite of their small size and occasional lack of proportion, are full of life and interest. The first series starts northwards from the central doorway, and here the chisel literally reproduces the legend of S. Joachim and S. Anne and the Birth of the Virgin: then follows the story of Joseph and Mary and the Nativity of Our Lord, up to the episode of the Massacre of the Innocents. This brings us to the Clocher Neuf. We must now return to the right hand portion of the central doorway, and take up the story again, moving in the direction of the Clocher Vieux. The events recorded, up to the last appearance of Jesus to His disciples on the Mount of Olives, it is hardly necessary to enumerate.

Thus in this rich stone compendium of the Christian story even the capitals of the pillars, which we are accustomed to see adorned only with foliage, flowers, fantastic figures and mere patterns, have been pressed into the service of the teller of the tale, and recount *in petto* scenes from the life of Christ upon earth. We have been shown Him expected, prophesied, prefigured and again realising the prophecies and fulfilling all the acts of His divine mission. If we look now above, in the tympanums of the three doorways, we shall find the triumph, joys and glory of the life to come portrayed, and the crowning of religion in the person of its Chief. First of all, in the tympanum of the left bay, we have His Last Coming.

The artists of the Middle Ages never omit the scene of the Last Judgment from the western façade of their churches; but, curiously enough, the Last Judgment before us is always interpreted as an Ascension or a Descent into Hell, and writers have been exercised to explain the omission of what after all has not been omitted.

Not only is a Last Judgment required here, but any other explanation of the sculpture fails to suit the attitude of the figures represented. The tympanum is divided into three sections. In the upper portion Christ is standing upright on a ground of fire or cloud. His right hand is raised, His left lowered. Two angels accompany Him, whose pose is not symmetrical, as would be that of censing angels, for Christ is saying to the angel on the right, 'Come, ye blessed of My Father,' and to the angel on the left, 'Depart from Me, ye who work iniquity.' In the central section are four angels emerging from the clouds. Their open mouths, and the gestures of their arms, one beckoning, the other pointing above, indicate that they are heavenly messengers, who have come 'to gather together the elect from the four winds.' And below them, gazing heavenward in holy calm and happiness, sit the Apostles, chosen to judge the twelve tribes of Israel. They are clad in long robes and mantles with borders of pearls after the Byzantine fashion. There is room for only ten of them on the lintel (which is nearly 9 feet broad), and several of them are mutilated. We may regret but we cannot wonder that many of the seven hundred statues have suffered more or less from the hand of Time or of men. There is more reason to be amazed that for over seven hundred years they have so successfully escaped the perils of war and of sacrilege that have threatened them.

In the vaulting of this doorway are the signs of the months and the signs of the Zodiac which roughly correspond with them. But since there was room for only ten of the latter, the remaining two were inserted in the vaulting of the right bay, where they are really out of place. Here they suggest the meaning that Christ is of all time, 'the same yesterday, and to-day and for ever.'

The Cathedral can boast five such almanacs, which it may be found interesting to compare—three in the porches, one in a window of the south aisle of the choir, and one (sixteenth century) on the clock of the choir screen.

Mediæval masons followed the example of Pagan antiquity, and like the architects of Persia, Egypt, Greece, Italy, India and Mexico, loved to trace upon their holy buildings the allegories of Time, whether in the form of the personification of the twelve months, of the four seasons, or the twelve signs of the Zodiac. The months are symbolised with extraordinary cleverness of detail, in a manner at once naïve and effective, by the recreations and employments to which they lend themselves.

The zodiacal signs are given in the verses of Ausonius:—

'Sunt Aries, Taurus, Gemini, Cancer, Leo, Virgo,
Libraque, Scorpius, Arcitenens, Caper, Amphora, Pisces.'

And as to the months, they, in the quatrain attributed to the venerable Bede, describe themselves as follows:—

'Poto—ligna cremo—de vite superflua demo;
Do gramen gratum—mihi flos servit—mihi pratum:
Fenum declino—messes meto—vina propino;
Semen humi jacto—pasco sues,—immolo porcos.'[63]

The studious visitor may compare the treatment of them in the windows and porch at Chartres with that which they receive at Venice, Reims, Verona, Sens, Amiens, Bruges and the English churches.

In the tympanum of the right-hand doorway the Virgin (1150) sits, crowned and throned, a sceptre in her hand, sharing the triumph of her Son. The Holy Child is in the act of blessing the world, and on either side are two archangels, censing. Beneath are the chief scenes of the life of Mary—the Annunciation, Visitation, Nativity, appearance of the Angels to the Shepherds and the Presentation of Christ in the Temple; and above, in the vaulting which forms the frame of this picture, are, in one row, six archangels carrying incense in honour of Mary, and, in the other, the seven Liberal Arts, each of them symbolised by two statuettes, the one representing the inventor or paragon, the other the allegory of the art. Here, then, as at Laon, Sens, Auxerre and many other places, we have the carved expression of the opinion of Albertus Magnus, that in Music (Pythagoras), Dialectic (Aristotle), Rhetoric (Cicero), Geometry (Euclid), Arithmetic (Nichomachus), Astronomy (Ptolemy), and Grammar (Priscian), in all the knowledge of the Middle Ages, in fact, the Virgin Mary was well skilled.

The tympanums of the right and the left bays have both suffered much from years: they are blurred and defaced with age, and it is perhaps partly for this reason that, in spite of many fine points, they seem inferior, crude even, by the side of the tympanum of the central bay.

This is one of the most beautiful masterpieces of mediæval statuary. In the centre is the risen Christ, enthroned, triumphant, yet full of mercy and tenderness. An aureole is about His head, His feet are set upon the footstool of the earth. With an infinite pity, it would seem, He beholds and blesses the thousands who for seven hundred years pass, and have passed, beneath Him into the Cathedral. With one hand He blesses, with the other He holds the book sealed with the seven seals. He is there, clad in an antique mantle, which falls in a cascade of folds about His naked feet, a bearded Christ, with long, straight hair, and an expression of sweet gravity, and the artist has succeeded somehow in convincing us that this is the Christ expected and foretold, fulfilling the past as He will fulfil the future, and reigning for ever in time upon earth, and hereafter for ever beyond time in heaven. Above Him two angels hold a large crown, destined for the eternal King of the Ages.

He is surrounded by the four-winged symbols of the

**TYMPANUM OF THE ROYAL PORCH.**

evangelists. On the lintel, as if on the first step of the throne, are grouped beneath an arcade, and in pairs, as they were sent forth to preach the Gospel, the twelve Apostles. And, to complete the scene from the Apocalypse, in the rows of the vaulting above, are the twelve angels and the heavenly choir of four-and twenty elders, having every one of them a different and curious mediæval instrument of music. They are clothed in white raiment, and on their heads are crowns of gold.[64]

They form, as it were, a living halo round the King of Ages, in a picture of incomparable grandeur and simplicity, the conception of which reveals not only the genius of art, but also, and, above all, the genius of faith.

But we have not yet completed the tale of the western porch. It yet remains to mention those strange colossal figures, which are by far the most beautiful and remarkable among all these

'Dedicated shapes of saints and kings,
Stern faces bleared with immemorial watch.'

These curious figures, these seven kings and seven prophets and five queens, these nineteen survivors of the twenty-four once here, with their thin, elongated bodies, their small heads, their Eastern drapery, their anatomical faults, and their haunting faces, may strike you at first as unattractive, bizarre. But nothing is more certain than that, if you study them, you will find in them an unutterable beauty and an ineffable charm. For this is the most spiritual and fascinating sculpture in the world, wrought with an infinite delicacy and an inimitable cleverness of detail, by the hands of artists who were consummate in their craft, and had learned, if not the perfection of form of the old Greeks, yet the secret, as it has been said, of spiritualising matter.

**PILASTER OF THE ROYAL PORCH.**

The figures stand upright, with an air of inviolable repose, beneath canopies like that of the Angel-sundial, heavenly Jerusalems, miniature Zions. Their hands are glued to their sides, their drapery falls, in most cases, in straight parallel folds; a halo is, or has been, behind the head of each. They are clad in the long, rich robes of the East. Over some of these a kind of dalmatic reaches to the knees. The girdles and the broidered robes, the arrangement of the sleeves and veils, and the jewellery of the crowns they wear, all demand the closest study. The hard stone has been handled with such precision and such feeling that you might almost fancy it, here, a delicate brocade, and there, a necklace of veritable jewels. You could almost untie the knots of those girdles, unplait almost the long braided tresses of those mystic queens. And the heads of these silent watchers, who have waited here and watched, with ever the same living smile about their thin, ironical Gallic lips, are portraits startling in their lifelike reality.

The bare feet rest upon pedestals which are not the least exquisite portions of these sculptured monoliths. For they are richly ornamented with carved chequerwork, so delicately chiselled as to seem the work of a goldsmith rather than a mason; mosaic patterns, which, like the borders of the stained-glass windows, betray the influence of the East through the medium of the Crusades. An exception, however, must be made in the case of the three first statues of the left bay, next to the Clocher Neuf. These have no halo, and the pedestals on which they rest their feet are groups of enigmatic beings. The first, a king who has been given by some modern restorer a thirteenth-century Virgin's head, treads underfoot a man, now scarce recognisable, enfolded by two serpents; the second, a king also, rests upon a woman, who holds with one hand the tail of a dragon, on which she is trampling, and with the other she fingers a tress of her long, plaited hair; the third, a queen of grosser type, but very richly clad, has beneath her feet a curious group, composed of a large ape, two dragons, a toad, a dog and a basilisk with a monkey's face.

It has been supposed that this group represents the benefactors of the Cathedral, William the Conqueror, Henry the First and Queen Matilda. But this explanation, like that of the last-named group as representing the Deadly Sins, is mere conjecture. Nor can we do more than name as kings, prophets and queens the remaining sixteen statues which line the porch. The fourth and fifth, counting from the Clocher Neuf, are prophets, Isaiah and Daniel perhaps, according to the suggestions of M. l'Abbé Bulteau: the eighth, ninth and tenth, Ezekiel, James-the-Less and Thaddæus; the eleventh, thirteenth and fourteenth, kings with missals and sceptres in their hands, may be Edward the Confessor, Charlemagne and Cnut; the fifteenth, S. Paul; the sixteenth, a haloed, virgin king, beardless, and full of the holy charm and freshness of youth, S. Henry (1024); the seventeenth, S. Peter;

the eighteenth, S. Constantine; the last, a queen, much defaced, like several of the others, Pulcheria, beloved of the Byzantines.

**PILASTER OF THE ROYAL PORCH.**

There yet remains the sixth, seventh and twelfth of the statues, the absorbing, seductive, inexpressible queens of the central bay. Her sexless shape, the book in her hands, her expectant gaze, rapt as it were in a vision of the ages, proclaim the first to be a nun rather than a queen, albeit she is clad in royal raiment;—S. Radegonde, Queen of France (582), Bulteau suggests.

The second is younger, and her beauty of a more earthly type. She wears a halo, and is clad like the other, save that she has no mantle, and her head is not shrouded in a veil. Her long hair falls in two plaits over her shoulders, and the tight-drawn body of her garment reveals the curves of her figure. Her expression is that of a rebellious, artful and vindictive nature, and, if she is rightly supposed to be Queen Clotilde, she is, as M. Huysmans[65] remarks, Clotilde before her repentance, the Queen before the saint.

The last, the angelic mysterious queen with the sweet, ingenuous smile, and the great deep eyes, is, according to local tradition, Bertha *aux grands pieds*, mother of Charlemagne. Her right hand once lay open upon her breast, and there it has left its impression. In the left hand she carried a sceptre, terminating in an ornament that still remains. She is clad in sumptuous raiment, most delicate in texture, and fringed with lace. Her figure is elongated, so that she seems to be like some rare lily swaying forward on its stalk. And thus, beneath her eyebrows slightly raised, she smiles down upon the visitor in the childlike grace of her chaste simplicity, *saintement gamine*.

Of the other statues that complete the company of Christ—martyrs, prophets and patron saints of donors in the jambs of the doorways, or between the other figures—I shall only call attention to the merchant on the right pier of the *Porte Royale*, who is being robbed by the earliest cut-purse in mediæval sculpture, and to the name Rogerus, cut above the broken head of an adjacent butcher. Was this the architect Roger who built the *Tour-Grise* at Dreux, and who was then chosen by S. Ives to build this western porch?

M. Bulteau suggests the question. But it cannot be answered.

Over the three doorways two pilasters with simple mouldings run up on either side of the central window as far as the rose, terminating in symbolic carvings—the northern one in the head of an ox, representative of sacrifice, symbolising here, it is said, the abolition of Judaism, with its sacrifices and cult; the southern one in that of a lion holding a man's head, which is the Lion of the tribe of Judah, and here symbolises Christ triumphant in the hearts of men.

The two towers, the old spire, and the western porch described, together with the west front up to the rose-window, including, therefore, the three enormous windows (34 feet by 13 feet, and 28 feet by 9 feet), and their unrivalled treasure of twelfth-century glass, which, through repeated dangers, has been preserved to us, are all that remain of the Church of Fulbert, rebuilt by S. Ives.

For in 1194, when Regnault de Mouçon was bishop, and when they were about to begin the spire of the Clocher Neuf, the Cathedral was destroyed by fire. *Mirabili et miserabili incendio devastata*, says a manuscript of the year 1210, now in the Vatican, and Jehan le Marchand in his *Book of Miracles* writes of this year:—

'A Chartres prist en la cité
Un feu qui ne fu pas a geus,
Car trop fu grant et domageus ...
Moult fu grant douleur dou veoir
Telle iglise ardoir et cheoir.'

It is worth while to quote this and other accounts because the patriotic desire to see in the present building the Cathedral of Fulbert has led to some unpardonable garbling of evidence, with a view to concealing the fact of this fire.

Guillaume-le-Breton, who died in 1226, records in his Latin poem, 'The Philippide,' written in honour of King Philippe-Auguste, that the church was burnt at this time. 'It was so ordered,' he infers, 'in order that the present church might be built and shine in its unequalled splendour.[66] For the former one was not yet worthy to be called the "mestre maison de Marie." Completely rebuilt of hewn stone, and covered throughout its whole length by a roof as it had been by the shell of a tortoise, it now need have nothing to fear from fire till the day of judgment. And from that fire springeth the salvation of the many by whose efforts the Cathedral was rebuilt.'

The account of another contemporary, William of Newbridge, the chronicler of the wars of Philippe-Auguste and of our Richard, whose lion-heart lies in the tomb at the Cathedral of *Rouen*, gives another explanation of the burning, and incidentally throws a vivid light upon the state of the country at that time.

'The troops of King Philippe,' he says, 'had retired precipitately from Évreux on the approach of King Richard. Now the King of the French, to wipe out the dishonour of this shameful retreat, threw himself with implacable fury on Évreux, which he had already sacked a short time before. He did not even spare the Church of S. Taurin, so famous in that country. He gave orders, indeed, that it should be given to the flames, and, as no one in his army would, for fear of God, execute so sacrilegious a command, the King himself, it is said, with some abandoned men called Ribauds, entered the sacred edifice and set fire to it. It is said, further, that he transferred to Chartres the spoils of the Church of S. Taurin; but these spoils were as fire to that famous city. It fell, in consequence, a prey to the flames, and was almost completely destroyed.'

All the inhabitants of the town, we learn from the author of the *Book of Miracles*, clergy and laymen alike, lost all their houses and their wealth in this disastrous conflagration. Yet their distress at their own losses was as nothing compared with their grief at the destruction of the church. But when the *Sainte Châsse*, containing the precious relic which they called

'la gemme
Et la gloire de leur cité'

could no more be seen, their sorrow passed all bounds. Bitter tears filled their eyes, and they cried aloud that the glory of Chartres and of the whole country side was departed. They despaired of their town, and were ready to quit forever the homes which they no longer had the heart to rebuild.

But the legate of the Pope, Mélior, Cardinal of Pisa, who happened to be at Chartres, summoned the bishop and Chapter, and called upon them to take courage and to begin rebuilding their Cathedral. He exhorted them to fast and pray that their sins, which had brought upon them this calamity, might be forgiven, and to set an example to the laity by emptying their purses,

'Por loer ovriers et maçons
Qui sache bien et tout ovrer.'

His eloquence met with such success that the bishop and his clergy devoted the greater part of their incomes for three years to the work of rebuilding and paying those 'skilled labourers and masons.'

Next he called together all the people, and exhorted them also to devote themselves to the task. And when he had finished speaking there emerged from the depths of the crypt some devoted clerks, bringing with them the holy casket and its priceless contents, 'the true mirror and the precious treasure,' which all thought had been destroyed. The people fell on their knees in a transport of delight, weeping tears of gratitude and joy. For a miracle had been wrought. As Jonah was kept from harm three days in the belly of the whale, as Noah was preserved from the flood and Daniel from the lion's jaws, so these devout servants of the Lord had been saved alive in the deep recesses of the martyrium, 'in the grotto near the altar which the men of old had prudently constructed,' whither they had retired with the Veil, and had lived unharmed and unafraid, whilst the walls and roofs of the Cathedral fell about their ears, and the molten bells and glass surged in a fiery flood around them.

Their appearance gave point to the eloquence of the cardinal. All classes, in gratitude, devoted themselves to rebuilding the Cathedral. And, in order that resources might not be lacking, in order that pilgrims might come from far and near, bringing money and labour to supplement the contributions of the Chapter and people, a series of miracles was wrought.[67]

It appears, says the chronicler Jehan de Marchand, with whose poetical legends, let me advertise the reader, I shall fill the remainder of this chapter, that the first miracle which roused the enthusiasm of the people was the healing of a little child of Le Perche, young Guillot. His tongue had been cruelly cut out by a knight whom he had surprised in an intrigue. Poor and mutilated, the orphan lad fled to Chartres to beg his bread. Kneeling there, on Shrove Tuesday, before the altar of Our Lady, he burst suddenly into loud praise of God, albeit he was tongueless. All the people when they heard him were filled with amazement. They crowded to the scene of his healing to render thanks and make their offerings before the altar, whilst the boy, that he might not be stifled by the crowd, was placed upon a scaffolding near the Châsse of S. Lubin. And the Virgin, 'qui voloit la chose parfeire,' obtained for him that on the day of Pentecost he should receive a new tongue. 'This child,' says the author, 'object of a double miracle, is still living in our midst.'

At the news of these marvels multitudes began to come together from every part, bringing waggons and carts laden with corn, wine, iron and all things useful or necessary for the building of the church. Jewels also and precious things they brought. The devotional enthusiasm of 1145 was repeated. The marvellous spectacles presented to-day by the Grotto of Lourdes were seen then at Chartres.

'Undique dona ferunt burgenses atque coloni,
Pontifices, clerus cum militibus dare pronis!'

So great was the crowd of pilgrims that they were obliged to pass the night in their carts about the Cathedral, for they could not all find shelter within the Cathedral, and the clerks coming to perform their offices therein could not for the press make their way into the cloister.[68]

These pilgrims were but one wave on the ocean of Catholic devotion: pilgrims, whether kings like Charles, coming to replace an image disfigured by profane Huguenots, or courtiers bringing with them the very presence and perfume of the Paris of their day, or pious wanderers from the remotest provinces of France and from strange lands beyond the seas, scholars from the universities and weather-beaten travellers from the New Continent, with outlandish offerings to Our Lady, they wash forever against the hospitable shores of Chartres, and break peacefully upon the gray cliffs of the Cathedral. A trace of their offerings, stranded on the shores of time, is to be found in the coins dug up in the Butte des Charbonniers in 1846, now in the Musée; coins which range in date from the earliest days of the Roman occupation down to the latter part of the sixteenth century, and which bear the superscription of innumerable kings and dukes and princes of various climes.

Of the wave of pilgrims which now occupies our attention you may see a record in the first window in the clerestory of the choir on the north side. There, beneath a Virgin enthroned and the blazon of the bishop,

Regnault de Mouçon, are two groups which show what manner of men were they who came to swell the tide of workers for Our Lady of Chartres, and through whose aid, says the chronicler, the piers, the vaults and the altars of the Cathedral rose as if by magic.

The Chapter was not content to sit idly and wait for miracles. They had recourse to human means. To obtain contributions towards the expense of this *mestre maison de la Reine des Cieux*, they sent priests afar to collect in all the countries and cathedrals of Europe. Now a young Englishman who had been studying in the schools of Paris and was returning home passed by Soissons by chance and entered the church. A Chartrain preacher was describing in eloquent and touching terms the disasters that had befallen Notre-Dame of Chartres. The audience was so moved by his eloquence that they all emptied their purses in response to his appeal. But the young Englishman had nothing to give except a golden necklace, which he intended for the girl he loved in London. Moved by the words of the preacher, after a long struggle, he made the offering of this necklace and, leaving Soissons, set out for the sea, passing the night in the barn of a friendly innkeeper, for, as we have seen, he was penniless. Overwhelmed with fatigue, he fell asleep upon the straw. But in the dead of night the barn was filled with a celestial light, and, waking, he beheld three women of rare beauty, one of whom revealed herself to him as the Lady of Chartres. Then she restored to him his necklace, and he vowed to consecrate himself to her service. He returned to his own country,

'A Londres dont il fu nais,'

and after taking leave of his parents, withdrew to a desert island, where he lived the chaste life of a hermit and enjoyed the ineffable bliss of communion with his fair visitant.

Richard Cœur-de-Lion, King of England, when he heard of this miracle, conceived a great veneration for the Church of Chartres, and, although he was at that time at war with Philippe-Auguste, he welcomed, encouraged and endowed with alms the emissaries of the Chapter, gave them safe conduct through his lands, and himself did obeisance before the sacred coffer and its relics. It was he who told the tale of this miraculous vision to his sister, Countess of Blois, and he loved to speak of it to the faithful on every occasion.

Thus the solemn voice of the Church, through the agency of these emissaries, made itself heard throughout the land, promising 'indulgences' to those who responded generously to her appeals, and threatening with anathemas those who dared to pillage the convoys of the pilgrims. The inhabitants of Château-Landon, as our poet relates, stirred, man and woman alike, by the discourse of their pastor, resolved to load a waggon with wheat and take it to aid the workers at Chartres. They yoked themselves to the waggon and began to pull with all their strength, but the road was so heavy that they made but slow progress. Ere they reached Chartres they ran short of provisions. The villagers gave them bread out of their small store, and behold, the loaves of bread were multiplied unto them, and they found, when they had eaten, that the villagers had as many loaves as they had had at first.

The inhabitants of Bonneval, of Puiset, of Pithiviers and of Corbeville, filled with a like spirit and parting on a like errand, experienced similar miracles, thanks to 'la dame, qui est salu de cors et d'ame.'

The Bretons, also, who were established at Chartres in the street called La Bretonnerie, met together and decided to go out together to Berchères-l'Évêque and bring back as their tribute a waggon-load of stone, a task in which none but a Breton born should take a hand. They set out, therefore, one evening, every man of them who could help with collar or trace, but ere they could regain the town with their burden the sun went down behind a thick bank of clouds; there was no moon nor any light, but in marvellous wise an obscure and dreadful night was upon them. The unhappy pilgrims soon lost their path, and wandered astray over the vast plains of La Beauce. Blind terror seized their hearts, but God sent three brands of flaming fire before them to lighten their way. Rejoicing and amazed, they regained the road to Chartres, whose *iglise et la tour* (church and the tower) were rendered visible by these heavenly torches. Then they deposited their offering and spread abroad the news of the miracle which they had beheld.

Of another sort was the marvellous deliverance of a rich merchant of Aquitaine, who, whilst he was bringing on his horse a barrel of oil for the lamps of Notre-Dame, was made prisoner by the English soldiers of Cœur-de-Lion. To him, in answer to his prayer, the Virgin appeared, and she enabled him to pass out of the prison into which he had been thrown, without the knowledge of his gaolers.

The fame of these and other wonders of the sort, narrated by the pilgrims and repeated by the inhabitants of the town, soon filled the countryside and spread to the more distant provinces. The renown of the Church of Chartres filled the land and reached beyond the seas. In La Beauce every hamlet was eager to contribute something to its glory. Those who had no possessions to offer gave their services loading and drawing vehicles: the roads were crowded with these humble servants of the Lord. The blind, the dumb, the lame and the halt awaited in each village the passing of the pilgrims and besought to be allowed to join their company.

Rich and poor, all came to Chartres with their offerings, so that, in the words of the chronicler, money came to support the workmen, rather from the hand of Providence than human purses.[69]

The deduction of the historian from the legends of our Trouvère is one which we shall find illustrated by the Cathedral windows. It is, that this Cathedral is a popular and national monument, built by the free labour of the people gathered together freely from all parts of France, joining and rejoicing in the new democratic movement of the Communes, and recording, therefore, in stone and glass their new aspirations, their new dignity.

# CHAPTER VI

## Mediæval Glass and Mediæval Guilds

'I gaze round on the windows, pride of France!
Each the bright gift of some mechanic guild,
Who loved their city and thought gold well spent
To make her beautiful with piety.'
JAMES RUSSEL LOWELL.

'Fine coloured windows of several works.'
FRANCIS BACON.

THERE are in the Cathedral one hundred and seventy-five stained-glass lights, 'storied windows richly dight,' and of these almost all date from the thirteenth century. Remembering the glass of the following century in S. Père and the later windows of S. Aignan, we shall not care to dispute the claim of Chartres to be the *locus classicus* of mediæval glass.

The three western windows of limpid blue belong, as we have said, to the twelfth century. And we know that by the year 1220 all the great legendary lights of the nave and all the windows of the choir, with the exception of those given by S. Piedmont of Castile and Jeanne de Dammartin, had been placed in the bays. Almost all the original glazing remains. There is, of course, fine thirteenth-century glass in England, at Canterbury for instance, and at Lincoln, whilst Salisbury and York are scarcely to be surpassed for the pale beauty of their silvery grisailles. But we have nothing in this country to compare in quantity, and therefore in effect, with the gorgeous glass which illustrates the great French churches. It is at Reims, Le Mans and Bourges, and most of all at Chartres, that are to be found the largest and most complete and therefore the most gorgeous galleries of the deep, rich mosaic glass of that date. At Chartres, throughout the whole vast expanse of jewelled lights, there is scarcely one that is not early, and there are very few that are not of the thirteenth century.

Consider the list of them now as they have come down to us across the ages, in spite of fires and sieges, artists and vandals, cleansing and restoring, in spite of the winds that sweep across La Beauce and the desire of the people to read: in spite even of the eighteenth-century architects and their eagerness to throw daylight upon their abominable deeds. This is the reckoning:—One hundred and twenty-four great windows, three great roses, thirty-five lesser roses, and twelve small ones! And in these are painted 3889 figures, including thirty-two contemporary historical personages, a crowd of saints and prophets in thirty-eight separate legends, and groups of tradesmen in the costumes of their guilds. This is the national portrait gallery of mediæval France! It is one of the most precious documents of mediæval archæology. It is one of the most rich and poetical applications of symbolic art.

Amazing, unspeakable are the glories of this unrivalled treasure of stained glass. 'I gaze round on the windows, pride of France!' Language is futile in the presence of their rich, deep, gem-like colouring, and the memory of them, faint though it must be, compared with the intense impression conveyed by the immense reality, makes the tongue to falter, the pen to fail.

'I gaze round on the windows, pride of France!'

The building is Aladdin's cave, and the glass a myriad jewels set in lead lines and in tracery of stone! But metaphors are unavailing, epithets are quite powerless to convey the beauty of the light which pours through them. It is as marvellous, and it changes as unceasingly as the ever-changing hues of a sunset on the western shores of Scotland, or on the iridescent waters of the Venetian lagoons. And it is even more brilliant than these. When the noonday sun is darting his angry rays across the aisles, or soft rain-laden beams streak the spaces with stripes of bloom; when the shades of evening have begun to fall, or when the dawn is gathering strength, and is now lighting the dim distances of the vast nave, you may sit and gaze round on those windows. You watch the wine-red, the blood-red, the yellow and the brown of the Rose of France and the lancet lights beneath, till the memory of all other beauty upon earth fades in the intoxication of that stupendous colouring. You turn at last, and, since no memory, however vivid, can retain to the full the impression of the beauty of that glass, you are startled into another ecstasy. For you have forgotten that there can be other windows as beautiful. You cannot believe that there are other colours as exquisite, until you see once more those blues and greens, ultramarines and peacock blues and azures, and those fiery reds which shine in upon the astonished sight from the windows of the south transept and the aisles. And still there remain the lights of the choir and the apse, and still the old glories, ever new, of the azure of the western lancets, the sapphires and rubies of the western rose.

The reds, like those at Reims, are everywhere wonderful; the saffron also and the citron yellows, the brown and the emerald green; but most superbly beautiful of all are the blues, the lucid transparent azure of the twelfth-century lancets, and the deep sapphire, the blue of Poitiers, which fills the lower windows of the nave. The secret of its manufacture is lost, but you can understand, when you behold it, how easily that story was believed which said that in order to secure this depth of blue the monkish glaziers used to grind sapphires to powder and mix them with their glass. There is only one thing that can be compared with the stained glass of the North, and that is the mosaics of the South, of Ravenna, Palermo, San Sofia.

You 'gaze round on those windows, the pride of France,' and as you feast your eyes upon the sparkling azure and the blood-red rays that stream from the rose, you understand also how easily the lad who saw it for the first time was led to say, when suddenly above him the organ burst forth into music, that it seemed to him as if the window spoke!

The Cathedral offers to the student of glass a perfect model, not indeed of detail, for upon the path which leads to the perfection of detail the thirteenth-century glazier had still many steps to take, but of effects in decorative colouring. In the rose you have a confused effect of colour, in which there is not any too definite form to spoil the charm of the broken bits of colour upon the senses. The meaning is there, too, as we shall see, many meanings, simple and elaborate, direct and mystical. But it is in the lancet windows of the nave that the row of otherwise (let it be confessed) ungainly figures supplies us at once, by means of the drapery, cloaks and borders, with that mixture of colour and shade that makes colour beautiful, and with those broad masses of stain combined with absolute simplicity and severity of design which should be the ideal of the glazier. And they are not crowded with too much story.

The lesson of the army of saints and martyrs which they represent is printed in large type, so that it may be easily read and understood from the distant level of the nave. Each light exhibits one enormous figure of a saint, with features strongly marked, clad in bright robes of blazing colour, set off by a border that is more sober in tone and opaque. The fire dies out of these broad patches of limpid blue and emerald green, of flaming red and saffron yellow, as they approach the deep, cool borders of brown and black, violet and grey, mingled with lower tones of red and green. You see, then, the object and the successful result of these bold designs of huge saints. The mediæval glaziers had considered the position which their glass was to occupy in the Cathedral. They did not merely design it with a view to its being effective in the studio. There is another point to be noted. Working, as they did, with small fragments of the precious glass as it came out of the melting-pot, and binding each fragment in lines of lead till the whole formed a pattern or drawing in a leaden framework, they were able to watch and test their work in its progress. Thus, watching and testing, they were able also to arrange for the proper mingling of the rays diffused on all sides by each piece of the mosaic. They did not aim so much at painting a good preliminary design upon paper as at producing a fine effect of colour in glass. When in succeeding centuries painters invaded the realms of glass they would appear to have ignored the obvious requirements of the new medium in which they were to work. Experimentally and intuitively the mediæval glazier, on the other hand, must have studied the whole question of radiation as it affected his task. And the result is, that for the most superb effects of stained glass we have to go, not to the pictures burnt on the large sheets of glass by famous painters, but to the designs of the thirteenth-century anonymous monkish craftsmen. In the matter of stained glass the latter had this advantage also in their favour. They had to work with a material which, being less scientifically compounded, was artistically immensely superior. In the manufacture of the old pot-metal something was left to Nature, much, that is to say, to accident. The colour, in other words, was not so evenly and exactly spread as by more modern processes. Being more unevenly distributed, it would frequently tone off at the edges, and the rays diffused from it would mingle in a softer harmony with those of the neighbouring coloured fragments. And greater variety was obtained, because a chemically imperfect process never gives two batches of glass from the pot quite alike. In early work, again, the fact that large pieces of glass could not be made was also on the side of the craftsmen. Perfect colour is the product of varied colours; the multiplicity of small pieces of glass set in deep black lines of lead yielded a result of rich, deep colouring, which is in the nature of things not to be obtained from one large sheet, however fine.

But though the palette of the early glazier was so rich in quality with those splendid reds and ineffable blues, the secret of which has long been lost, and other primary colours, it was poor in extent. To this poverty must be ascribed the curious colouring of many details. Beards are often painted blue, and faces usually brown. Some shade of a rich purplish brown was in fact the ordinary flesh tint of the early glazier. In the window of the north transept, where S. Anne is portrayed, we have a very striking example of this. The brown face of S. Anne is there so large (it must be at least 2 feet in length), that the craftsman has been able to glaze it in several pieces. The eyes are of white, and so strongly leaded that they seem to stare out of the picture.

The sunburnt effect of their brown visages only accentuates the Oriental aspect of many of these glass figures. As at Bourges, so here, the influence of the East is plainly visible, not only in the hieratic type of the personages and their sumptuous apparel, but also and still more undoubtedly in the mosaic borders by which they and the medallions beneath are framed. The tones are rich and soft as those of a Persian rug;

the patterns and devices are clearly related to those in Byzantine ivories and enamels. Nor will the simile I have used seem inept when it is remembered that at this very time imitations of the Persian rugs brought home by the Crusaders were being deliberately manufactured in Paris.

The enjoyment of colour is one of the finest of pleasures, but it was not merely to give pleasure that this glass was stained, and these figures drawn in lead. There is a reasoned aim, a definite symbolic purpose in all mediæval art, and not least in the art of stained glass.

We have seen how the huge figures of the guardian saints in the nave are made to stand out from their borders and tell, in spite of the height at which they are placed, their story, plain for every eye to see. If you now look at the windows of the lower row, of the aisles that is, you will notice that the breadth and importance of the borders which form the framework of the circular and quatrefoil medallions are striking. They are not, however, intended to make the medallions stand out—if they were, they would fail in their object—but to give the effect of an immense blaze of subdued, indeterminate colour.

That effect is reasoned: the light in the nave is subdued for a mystic purpose. It is not the chance result of light playing upon a fortuitous collection of coloured fragments of glass. It is a result knowingly and scientifically produced by the artist. The dim religious light which fills the threshold of the temple grows less dim as it approaches the centre of the Cross; it borrows still more transparent colours from the painter's palette as it circles round the choir, and in the sanctuary gives place to the most lively and brilliant tones, which pour in from above. 'What poetry is there,' exclaims M. Ferdinand de Lasteyrie,[70] 'in this immense gamut of tones, so cleverly arrayed. It is an admirable symbol of the light of Christianity escaping in great floods from the summit of the Cross, but throwing a lesser brillance upon those who stand afar off.'

To produce this striking effect the artist has availed himself of very simple means. In the aisles the windows are cold in tone, and the medallions,[71] as we have said, set in very broad borders. And these borders themselves, filled with a variety of patterns and ornaments, are composed of an infinite number of pieces of glass, mosaic work, the leaden frames of which contribute to the desired gloom. It is a clever application of the 'legendary' style, and the very choice of subjects here is in keeping with the place they occupy. The same tones prevail in the lofty windows of the nave, but there the figures are larger; huge saints and tall apostles look down from their posts upon the Cross of Christ and guard His church, S. Piat at their head; and the broad bands of colour give more access to the light. Advancing to the centre of the Cross, you perceive that the aisles are still plunged in a gloom, which is rendered yet more obscure by the unlit spaces of the great transept doors. But the roses set on high throw rainbow lights aslant the transepts, which mingle at the entrance of the choir with the mysterious tints of the nave, and the gallery of lights beneath these roses seem intended to effect the needed transition between their transparent loveliness and the opaque mass of stone beneath. In the apse, again, with its unique double aisles and the series of chapels, which form, as it were, the crown of thorns about the head of Christ upon the Cross, symbolised by the Church, there reigns a luminous obscurity. Here we have once more storied windows with medallion subjects and broad borders of topaz, emerald and ruby, rich and deep, and warmer in tone than were those of the nave. And in the centre of this sacred aureole of chapels rises the sanctuary in a blaze of light, like Jesus in the midst of His Apostles, and floods of warmly-coloured light pour down into the choir through the huge figures which fill the windows. 'It seems,' says M. Lasteyrie, 'that the artist has borrowed a ray of light divine to animate his work, a ray which is brilliant at first but dies away at the entrance of the sanctuary, as if to indicate the spot in which the Christian enters into communion with his God.'

The mediæval artist, however, was not content with a reasoned effect of colour, however beautiful. His windows must be 'storied' as well as 'richly dight.' They must repeat in glass the lessons read to the people by the statuary without. In those three superb twelfth-century azure windows of the west the Tree of Jesse, the Childhood of the Saviour, and the principal scenes of the Passion are represented. The rose above them, with its rubies and sapphires in a deep setting of stone, tells again the story of the Last Judgment. From the wounds of Jesus, who is seated on a throne of clouds, flows the blood which saves or condemns mankind. Angels, cherubim and apostles surround him. An aureole in quatrefoil is about His head. Above shine the instruments of the Passion, and four angels are blowing the last trump. The earth opens and the sea gives up its dead. Emerging from their tombs, the dead look towards the Supreme Judge. S. Michael (as on the south porch) is weighing souls in the balance. Some are being led to Abraham's bosom, whilst others, dragged by demons, fall into the vivid flames of hell.

A panel under the centre circle was destroyed by a cannon ball in the siege of 1591. It has been replaced by some fragments from another window. The rose of the north transept is called the *Rose of France*, because it was given to the Cathedral by S. Louis and Blanche of Castile. The Fleurs-de-lys of France and the Castles of Castile recall this fact when you see them repeated in their blue and gold in the medallions and the spandrels of the window. The rose itself is not so large as that of Notre-Dame-de-

Paris, nor so delicately graceful as that of Amiens, but, as in the case of the western rose, the boldness of the masonry and the clear depths of the colouring lend to it a charm and beauty all its own. It represents the *Glorification of Mary*, the subject of the noble porch without.

In the centre, Mary seated on a throne, holds in her arms the Saviour of the world, and receives the homage of the angels, the Kings of Judah and the prophets, who are painted in these circles of twelve medallions. The panels of the second circle are rectangular.

Beneath the rose are five tall pointed windows of unforgettable splendour and extraordinary interest. King David with his harp of gold, Solomon the monarch with the blue fleur-de-lys and Jeroboam worshipping his calves of gold below, both stand forth from a background of purple, prefiguring the Kingship of the Son; Aaron, the high priest, with the rod that budded and the book of the law, wearing a curious red hat, and beneath him Pharaoh engulfed in the Red Sea; Melchisedek, with chalice and censer, and beneath him Nebuchadnezzar in front of the statue of gold, silver, iron and clay, represent beforehand the Priesthood of Christ. And all these rich Oriental figures support the enormous brown-faced portrait of S. Anne, who sits in the central light and carries the infant Mary.

The great white eyes of these figures seem to stare across at the rose of the south transept opposite, which represents the fulfilment of all that they had foreshadowed—the *Glorification of Christ*. The story is repeated by the statuary of the south porch without. This window was founded by Pierre Mauclerc, Count of Dreux and Duke of Bretagne, who figures therefore with his wife and family and arms in the lower portions of the windows below the rose.

The arms of Dreux and Bretagne also appear with fine effect in the twelve quatrefoils of the rose, which correspond to the rectangular panels of the windows opposite. In the centre of the rose Christ enthroned blesses the world and holds in His left hand a large chalice. The surrounding medallions contain eight angels censing the four beasts and twenty-four elders before the throne, referred to in the Book of Revelations.

As in the north transept, five large pointed windows beneath complete the subject. The central figure is that of Christ presented to the faithful in the Virgin's arms, whilst on either side are the four evangelists carried on the shoulders of the four great prophets; S. Matthew seated on Isaiah, S. Luke on Jeremiah, S. John (beardless, as always in mediæval portraiture, to typify his virginity) on Ezekiel, and S. Mark on David. The strange position of these naïve evangelists is intended to symbolise the fact that the new dispensation rests upon the old, even as the Christian Gothic of the upper church is built upon the Pagan Romanesque of the old basilica, the crypt beneath.

To the east, in the apse, seven great windows repeat the motive of the Glorification of Mary, and the artists, who, throughout this Cathedral of Notre-Dame, are never weary of portraying its patroness in every guise and every form, at every age, and almost as of every clime, represent her as receiving homage from the personages of the Old Testament, and even of S. Peter.

Not the least famous, not the least fascinating of these innumerable Madonnas, though candles are no longer burnt to her as they were of yore, is the window—the second in the south aisle of the choir after leaving the transept—which is known as the Notre-Dame de la belle Verrière. She is clad in bright vestments of azure, and, like the Virgin who appeared to the peasant girl at Lourdes, she has about her head an aureole of blue. Deep tones of red and brown form the background of the window from which the figure of the Madonna stands out, so that you might almost believe that she is about to step through into the dark aisles of the Cathedral that is hers.

This window belongs to the thirteenth century, but it is probably modelled on an earlier one of which there is mention. Like the three twelfth-century windows of the west, and especially the southernmost of these three, it is strikingly Byzantine in character. The Miracle at the Marriage of Cana and the Temptations of Christ fill the lower part of the light.

In the case of the remaining windows the evidence of design is less obvious than in that of the groups with which we have dealt. Much was evidently left to the caprice of the donors, who usually chose to represent the lives, the struggles or the martyrdoms of their patron saints. Thus the episodes of the life of a local priest, S. Laumer, are recorded in a series of medallions, just as one of his miracles is related in stone in the south porch. The storied window suggests at once practically all that we know of him. Some time in the seventh century, it is said, he kept his father's sheep near Chartres, but afterwards, having learned his letters, he was ordained priest and entered a monastery. But he longed for a life of prayer and solitude, and fled to the forest where he hoped none would follow him. It was vain; disciples, hearing of his sanctity and the miracles he wrought, flocked to him. Again he fled and settled in the woods near Dreux. But his cell of green leaves and wattles soon became the centre of a colony of monks, so that he was fain to recognise the call of God and to build a monastery there. Of the miracles recorded as wrought by him there is one characteristic of his gentle individuality. During the night some robbers stole a cow belonging to the monks. The brethren were in despair. The robbers, however, lost their way in the tangled forest. They wandered all night and all next day, unable to discover the road. At last, as evening settled in, they saw the darkness of the forest lighten, and, still driving the cow, they came out upon the clearing of the monastery. S. Laumer himself stood before them. They fell at his feet, asking his pardon and imploring him to direct them aright. He raised them and said, 'I thank you, kind friends, for finding and bringing back to me my strayed cow. You must be very tired and hungry. Follow me.' They followed him into his hut and he set before them such food and drink as he had, and they ate and drank and were refreshed. Then he set them on their right road, and they departed—but without the cow.

Or take, as another example, the third window of the north aisle where the lesson of the life of another saint, not local, is taught in another series of medallions, because S. Eustace was the patron saint of the founder. In the bottom panel, Placidius, a centurion of the guard in Trajan's day, appears hunting a stag. A miracle is wrought which brings about the conversion of the Pagan hunter. For a cross of light shines between the horns of the fugitive. Overwhelmed by the sight of this prodigy, Placidius dismounts from his horse, kneels down and is baptized. The change wrought within is described in the upper panels. Great calamities befall him; his wife is taken from him; his children are devoured by wild beasts. But Eustace, filled with a perfect trust in God, bears all with Christian resignation. He retires to a distant land, and there his virtue waxes daily until at last he is deemed worthy to suffer martyrdom for his faith. Together with his wife he is roasted alive in the belly of a brazen bull.

Thus in all simplicity the glaziers paint the legends which the people have learned. They tell the story of a man's life from his birth, and do not even hesitate to represent his faults, because these windows were intended to serve as an illustrated catechism for the poor and ignorant, and the saintliness that has no touches of things human proves for ordinary people discouraging. In the lower panels of the windows, therefore, the early years of the saints are shown so that we may be comforted and inspired by the knowledge that they too shared in the weaknesses and the miseries of our nature. And above, when they have risen superior to their trials, we see them in a halo of sanctity, performing miracles by their faith. Frail man has shaken off this vile earth and goes on from strength to strength, according to the simple expression of a chronicler, until he arrives in the house of the Eternal Father, whose glorious person dominates the whole window. As in the case of the sculptured porches so here, when we study and admire the conception and execution of these storied windows, the question arises, Who was it who arranged, who was it who coloured this glorious glass?

And again the answer must be that we know not. The artists of the twelfth century have not been careful in this matter: the object of their fecund imagination and their exquisite workmanship has been this only—the majestic expression of the burning faith within them.

One name only, that of Clement, the Chartrain glazier (*Clemens, vitrearius Carnotensis*), found on a window in the Cathedral of Rouen, has come down to us. And Clement, it is supposed, designed the window which recounts the legend of S. Martin. That name alone survives out of all the artists whose work has for over seven hundred years been the admiration of all Europe!

The donors of the windows, on the other hand, shine there amid a blaze of heraldic glory. You may still behold Louis de Poissy on his white charger and at the head of his men, clad in full armour, setting forth on the Crusade. Ferdinand III. of Castile also, S. Ferdinand, you may see, wrapped in mail for the defence of the faith, and Blanche of Castile, who so often brought her young son to Chartres and inspired him with his so tender devotion to Notre-Dame. Pierre Mauclerc is here, that turbulent spirit who expiated his offences against order by his immense generosity to the Cathedral; Thibault VI., Count of Chartres, the very valiant Crusader; Amaury de Montfort, Constable of France; Pierre de Courtenay; Bouchard de Marly, of the noble house of Montmorency—these and a whole gallery of other counts and barons and knights of chivalry live on in the church which they endowed with their gold and for which they fought with their swords.

But we have seen that this Cathedral was built not by the generosity of the great alone. It was in every sense a popular, a national monument, raised to the glory of God by the contributions and labour of all classes. And if the humble donors have scarcely dared, like the great lords, to represent themselves individually, they have fortunately not shrunk from perpetuating, under the guise of the guilds through which they subscribed, the record of their no less interesting personalities. They all figure in the windows founded by their several trades; masons and skinners, drapers and goldsmiths, bakers and armourers, butchers and tanners, cobblers and water-carriers even, are all portrayed at work with the simple realism of the Middle Ages.

A whole book, and a very interesting one, might be written as a commentary on the thirty or forty trade corporations here depicted. It would exhibit the commercial history of a mediæval shrine, the mart of pilgrims and the *bazar* of the devout.

All the trading corporations of the Middle Ages were close and exclusive bodies. Admission to them was only possible by the long and narrow path of apprenticeship. Economically, their general aim was to limit competition by limiting the number of masters, by limiting the number of embryo masters in the shape of apprentices whom each master in a guild might receive. Their general result was to maintain a high standard in the quality of the work produced, and by discouraging the modern ideal of quantity to provide a certain and sufficient employment amongst all those who were fortunate enough to be within the sacred circle of their union.

An apprentice was an unmarried lad of from fifteen to twenty years of age, bound to his master for a certain number of years by the payment of a fixed fee and an oath. As elsewhere, so in France,[72] the master was responsible not only for teaching the apprentice his trade, so that he might in due course be approved a master-workman himself, but also for his moral training. By the rules of the craft he was required to cherish the boy 'beneath his roof, at his board and at his hearth.'

If he did his duty, in fact, the master treated the apprentice as his own sons and thrashed him as heartily. The apprentice frequently returned the compliment by making him his father-in-law. Shortly before the expiration of his apprenticeship the young craftsman was examined by a board of *jurés*, and was called upon to give a practical exhibition of his skill. If he succeeded in satisfying them that he could fashion a proper doublet or bake a good loaf of bread, he was allowed to call himself a workman, to practise his trade, and to take his share in the management and the benefits of his guild. Those benefits often included comprehensive schemes of charity and mutual aid. The widows and indigent members of a corporation were provided for by funds to which all had contributed their quota. The standard of efficiency was maintained not only by the vigilance of the jurés, who examined each finished article before it was offered for sale, not only by the fear of a fine which might be inflicted for defective work, but also by the pride and sense of honour fostered in each individual craftsman. It was lowered on the other hand by the excessive conservatism of the guilds, who forbade any underselling or departure from customary models, insisted on a minute and absurd division of labour, condemned all inventions, and nipped all developments in the bud.

Such, briefly, was the constitution of the famous mediæval guilds, such were their faults and excellences. The record of these Cathedral windows helps us to realise their importance in the history of Chartres, and also enables us to imagine the state and the character of the old town's trade. In spite of the exactions and taxes levied by bishop and count, chapter, monastery and viscount, the merchants of Chartres flourished mightily in the thirteenth century, and the fairs of the town held during the four feasts of Our Lady rivalled in importance even those of Brie and Champagne. Chartres was one of the seventeen towns in France where the trades were separate and distinct, and each trade had its statutes regulated and enforced by jurés in the manner I have sketched. She owed her commercial activity to the gatherings of pilgrims at the shrine of Notre-Dame, and when these gatherings ceased her trade drooped and dwindled away till once more, as in the Merovingian days, it was confined to traffic in wool and corn.

Take first, for instance, the window which gives us the story of S. Eustace, the third in the north aisle of the nave, and the third in the north clerestory of the nave, with its medallions of apostles and S. Thomas of Canterbury, that favourite saint of the Middle Ages. They were given by the furriers and drapers, the *Bourgeois*, as they were called, of the River, members of the renowned corporation known as the *Métier de la Rivière*. This *métier* included the professions of the woollen-drapers, combers and cleaners, felt-makers and dyers.

Six jurés were elected annually by the masters of the guild, whose duty it was to examine, and pass or reject every piece of cloth or wool-work made at Chartres or anywhere within a radius of three leagues. Latterly every piece approved was stamped with a leaden trademark. The trade flourished and brought great reputation to the town from the twelfth to the sixteenth century. But the wars with England, and plague and famine greatly affected its prosperity. These and other causes led to its gradual decay and final disappearance.

The tanners and cobblers who gave the third and fourth windows in the south aisle of the nave formed one corporation, and the curriers were for a long time included under the heading of tanners. The latter were attracted to Chartres by the excellence and quantity of the skins to be obtained there, and by the peculiar quality of the water of the Eure, which, together with the bark supplied by the trees of the neighbouring forests, was specially adapted for curing them. The tanners flourished exceedingly, and were accustomed to celebrate with great magnificence at the riverside Church of S. André the feast of their patron, S. Louis. The difficulty of procuring skins and other accessories had considerably injured them by the time of the Revolution, and their industry, like that of the shoemakers, has to-day no more than a quite local importance. But the river is still to some extent the scene of their labours. For though agriculture is now the chief industry of the department, and though the great fairs of May and September are great no longer in comparison with their splendid past, the commerce of Chartres is not altogether dead. There is a considerable traffic not only in corn and wool but also in sheep and horses, and a walk along the river banks between the Pont Neuf and the Porte Guillaume will

show you that the chief *ateliers* of the district are the wash-houses of the tanners and the wool-workers. Along the base of the mouldering wall which skirts the diverted arm of the Eure lie the backs of old houses with their adjoining tanyards. Many of them, too, are garnished with little wooden galleries, lavatories of the town's soiled linen. 'These galleries are filled with washerwomen, who crane over and dip their many-coloured rags into the yellow stream. The old patched and interrupted wall, the ditch with its weedy edges, the spots of colour, the white-capped laundresses in their little wooden cages—one lingers to look at it all.'[73]

Wine was another commodity for which Chartres was once famous. The author of the *Book of Miracles* tells us of a troubadour who left his companion to pursue his pilgrimage alone whilst he himself paid a prolonged visit to a *cabaret*.

'Car la parole et le renon
Des bons vins avoit entendu
Qui a Chartres erent vendu
Clers seins nes et delicieux.'

The monks, it seems, had not planted their vines in vain. But, alas! the modern vintage of La Beauce cannot claim any of the epithets assigned to it above. The *grands clos de très bon vin* of which Souchet speaks (1640), which cardinals had found excellent in 1506, and which were sold with pride and profit at the *Étape-au-vin* or the various taverns, is but a thin and dreary liquor to-day. Either the soil has been exhausted and the grape lost its virtue, or the taste of the former connoisseurs was faulty. No doubt their standard of taste in wine was lower than ours. A cup of sack, I doubt, would not prove so pleasant to the modern palate as it is to the modern ear. But even so the vintage of La Beauce must have suffered a sore deterioration. The flourishing condition of the old tavern-keepers and vintners is indicated by their generous donation of the magnificent window which records the chief events of the life of S. Lubin (second in the north aisle of the nave).

It remains to close this chapter with a bald list of the subjects of the windows, taken in order, starting from the western front and moving round the Cathedral from the Clocher Neuf along the north or left-hand side.

1. Rose Window. Last Judgment. Described above.

2, 3, 4. Below it the three twelfth-century windows, of which the one on the south side contains twelve circular panels representing the later events from the life of Christ (Transfiguration to Supper with Disciples at Emmaus). The arrangement of the windows should be compared with that of the Notre-Dame de la Belle Verrière, which, though made of thirteenth-century glass, was copied in design from an earlier one of which mention is made. The centre window of the three (32 feet 10 inches) contains the Virgin and Child in the head, and in twelve panels the chief events of the Gospel story from the Annunciation to the Entry into Jerusalem. The northern one is a Jesse window, on which the genealogical tree of our Saviour is shown. Among the branches are the first four Kings, then the Virgin, and Christ surrounded by the seven gifts of the Holy Ghost. On either side of the tree are seven prophets.

*North Aisle of the Nave.*

5. Story of Noah. Given by the Carpenters, Wheelwrights and Coopers.

6. Story of S. Lubin (*see* p. 36). Given by the Tavern-keepers and Vintners.

7. Story of S. Eustace (*see* p. 163). Given by the Furriers and Drapers.

8. Story of Joseph. Given by the Moneychangers and Minters.

9. Story of S. Nicholas. Given by the Grocers and Druggists.

10. *La Nouvelle Alliance*. Given by the Farriers and Blacksmiths. (Seven panels were removed in 1816).

*Clerestory of the Nave* (North).

11. Lancets (*a*) Temptations of Christ.

(*b*) Jonah, Daniel, Habbakkuk.

Rose    (*c*) Bishop (S. Etherius?) with two suppliants at his feet.

12. Lancets (*a*) S. Laurence, as a deacon, with the Evangelists, and below,

on his gridiron.

(*b*) S. Stephen, and, below, his Martyrdom. Also a group of Weavers.

Rose   (*c*) S. Lubin, in pontifical robes on a throne. Two Innkeepers offer him wine.

13. Lancets (*a*) Six medallions in which appear two pairs of Apostles, and, below, Furriers and Drapers.

(*b*) S. Nicholas, and below, Curriers and Leather-dressers.

Rose   (*c*) S. Thomas of Canterbury and two Knights invoking him.

14. Lancets (*a*) Six Apostles seated in quatrefoiled panels.

(*b*) An Apostle, and below, the Moneychangers.

Rose   (*c*) The Virgin Mary holding in her lap the seven gifts of the Holy Ghost: Wisdom is represented by Christ, the other gifts by white doves with a simple nimbus, bound to the aureole of Christ by red rays.

15. Lancets (*a*) S. Giles in the act of blessing, and below, celebrating Mass before the King.

(*b*) S. George of Cappadocia in thirteenth-century armour, and below, nude on a wheel of swords.

Rose   (*c*) S. George on horseback slaying a dragon.

16. Lancets (*a*) Christ, and below, Abraham about to sacrifice Isaac.

(*b*) The sacrifice of Isaac repeated, and above, a bust of Christ with the letters Alpha and Omega, 'the beginning and the end.'

Rose   (*c*) Scenes of tilling.

17. Lancets (*a*) A Martyr and S. Martin of Tours.

(*b*) S. Martin cutting his cloak and beholding Christ in a vision.

Rose   (*c*) The donors, with an inscription, 'The men of Tours have given these three windows.'

*North Transept* (below the Clerestory).

18. A free version of the story of the Prodigal Son.

19. The story of S. Laurence was portrayed in this window, but the central portion of it was removed in 1791, when the Chapel of the Transfiguration was made.

20. Removed 1791.

*North Transept, Clerestory* (West Side).

21. Lancets (*a*) The Death, Assumption and Crowning of the Virgin.

(*b*) Angels announcing the Birth of Christ to the Shepherds, and below, the Presentation in the Temple. Below again, and in the

Rose    (*c*) Philip of France, Count of Boulogne, uncle of S. Louis, on his knees before an altar, and on horseback.

22. Lancets (*a*) The Annunciation and the Visitation. Below, Mahaut, Countess of Boulogne.

(*b*) S. Joachim and S. Anne visited by Angels. Their meeting at the Golden Gate of the Temple. Below, Countess Jeanne, the donor.

Rose    (*c*) The Virgin Mary.

23. Thirteenth-century grisailles, with border of the Lilies of France, and the Castles of Castile.

24. The Rose of France, and beneath,

25, 26, 27, 28, 29. The five pointed windows described above (p. 159).

*North Transept, Clerestory* (East Side).

30. Lancets (*a*) S. Thomas and S. Barnabas.

(*b*) S. Thomas and S. Jude, and below, the Canon who gave the window.

(*c*) Christ seated between the sun and the moon, and holding a globe blazoned with the arms of Castile.

31. The Lancets of this window contain four more Apostles, like the last,

and

The Rose, a portrait of the same munificent Canon.

32. Lancets (*a*) S. Eustace and the Stag, his Baptism, before the Idols. Below, an Armed Knight on horseback.

(*b*) The Annunciation, Birth of Christ, and the Adoration of the Magi. Below, the wife of the aforesaid knight.

Rose (*c*) Christ seated.

33. The seven large windows (46 feet high) of the choir apse repeat the story of the north rose—the Glorification of the Virgin. In the first (north) is

34. Aaron, and an Incense-bearing Angel, with the donor (Gaufridus) and his family. Below,

35. Ezekiel, David, and a Seraph. Below, the Butchers.

36. Events from the Life of S. Peter. Below, the Moneychangers.

37. The Annunciation, Visitation, Motherhood of the Virgin. Below, the Bakers bringing bread.

38. Moses, Isaiah and Incense-bearing Angel. Below, the Bakers.

39. Daniel, Jeremiah, a Seraph. Below, the Drapers.

40. Scenes from the Life of S. John the Baptist. Below, the Moneychangers.

*The Clerestory of the Choir* (North).

41. Lancets (*a*) The Virgin enthroned, and the escutcheon of Regnault de Mouçon, the bishop.

(*b*) Two groups of Pilgrims, and, below, the donor, kneeling, Robert de Bérou, sub-deacon and chancellor of the Cathedral. The plain glass border was inserted 1757.

Rose (*c*) Christ seated between two three-branched candlesticks.

42. This window was founded by S. Ferdinand, King of Castile, who appears on horseback in the rose. The other two lights were removed in 1788 at the request of Bridan, in order to set off his marble Assumption below.

43. The same fate attended the next but one, founded by S. Louis, whose figure was allowed to remain in the rose.

44. Lancets (*a*) S. Martin working miracles.

        (*b*) S. Martin giving away his cloak, and beholding Christ in a vision. Below, and in the

    Rose    (*c*) Jean de Châtillon, the founder, on horseback, and kneeling.

*Clerestory of the Choir* (South).

45. The lancets were destroyed in 1773. The founder, Amaury, Count of Montfort, remains in the rose. He appears again in the rose of the next window.

46. Lancets (*a*) S. Vincent, with millstone about his neck, on the land and on the sea. Below, the donor, Petrus Bai....

        (*b*) S. Paul. Below, the Curriers.

47. Destroyed 1788.

48. Lancets (*a*) S. John, S. James the Great, the Adoration of the Magi. Below, the arms of Montmorency.

        (*b*) The Birth of Jesus, the Flight into Egypt, and below, the donors, Colin and his wife, before a chess-board.

    Rose    (*c*) Robert de Beaumont on horseback.

*South Transept* (now being restored).

  49. Destroyed 1791.

  50. Destroyed 1792. A border alone remains.

  51. S. Apollinaris of Ravenna and Hierarchy of Angels (1328).

*South Transept, Clerestory* (East Side).

52. Lancets (*a*) S. Christopher, S. Nicaise and the donor, Geoffroi Chardonnel, Canon of Chartres.

        (*b*) S. Denis presenting the oriflamme to Henry Clément.

    Rose    (*c*) S. John the Baptist.

53. Lancets (*a*) S. Protais and S. Gervais.

(b) S. Cosmas and S. Damien. The same donor as above, kneeling.

Rose   (c) The Virgin Mary.

54. Lancets (a) (b) Two Prophets, and donor, Jean de Bretagne.

Rose   (c) The Virgin Mary.

55. The rose of the south transept and the

56, 57, 58, 59, 60. Five large pointed windows, as described above (p. 160).

*South Transept, Clerestory* (West Side).

61. Lancets (a) (b) Malachi and Micah, and below, the arms of Mauclerc.

Rose   (c) Pierre Mauclerc, the donor, on horseback, and in full armour.

62. Lancets (a) Destroyed 1786. Border remains.

(b) S. Paul, the first hermit, and S. Antony. Below, a Deacon serving at an altar.

Rose   (c) S. Ambrosius, the Archbishop (?).

63. Lancets (a) (b) S. Paul and S. Peter.

Rose   (c) The donor, a Canon of Chartres.

*South Aisle of the Nave* (starting from South Transept).

64. This window formerly recorded the miracles of the Virgin, wrought in the thirteenth century. But only one out of sixteen medallions remains complete.

*Vendôme Chapel.*

(Founded 1413 by Louis de Bourbon. Two chests contain remains of S. Piat and S. Taurin.)

65. Below, six Angels bearing the arms of Bourbon-Vendôme, and a piece of another window representing the Death of the Virgin. Above, on left, Jacques de Bourbon kneeling; S. Louis of France, S. Louis of Toulouse, Louis and Jacques de Bourbon; on right, S. James, in similar company. Above, again, the Virgin and Child, next to a lady, crowned by two angels; S. John blessing a chalice, S. John the Baptist, with the Lamb.

In the head of the window, the Crucifixion, and, on the right, the Holy Women; on the left, the Jewish Priests and the Centurion. Above, Christ judging the world, between Mary and John praying, and the angels summoning the dead, who rise from their tombs.

66. The Death, Funeral, Assumption and Coronation of the Virgin. Below, the donors, Cobblers.

67. The Story of the Good Samaritan. Below, the Cobblers, *Sutores*.

68. The Life of S. Mary Magdalene. Below, the Water-carriers.

69. The Life of S. John the Evangelist. Below, the Armourers.

*The Nave, South Side, Clerestory.*

70. Lancets (*a*) S. Symphorian and his Martyrdom.

       (*b*) Mostly hidden by the organ.

Rose   (*c*) S. Hilary.

71. Lancets (*a*) (*b*) Destroyed 1648.

Rose   (*c*) S. Gregory the Great.

72. Lancets (*a*) S. Bartholomew and Moses.

       (*b*) S. Caletric and the donors, the Turners.

       (*c*) S. Augustin.

This window also is partly hidden by the organ.

73. Lancets (*a*) S. Philip and Jeremiah.

       (*b*) S. James the Less and the donor, Gaufridus.

Rose   (*c*) S. Jerome.

74. Lancets (*a*) S. Faith, and below, her Martyrdom.

       (*b*) The Virgin, and below, the scene of Christ saying, Noli me tangere (Touch me not).

Rose   (*c*) S. Solemnis, Bishop of Chartres.

75. Lancets (*a*) S. Peter, and below, the donors, the Pastry Cooks.

(*b*) S. James.

Rose   (*c*) Christ with the signs Alpha and Omega.

76. Lancets (*a*) S. Laumer, and below, his death-bed scene.

(*b*) Meeting between S. Mary of Egypt with Zozimus, and below, her burial.

Rose   (*c*) S. Laumer.

*The Chapels of the Ambulatory and Apse.*

77. Subject unknown. Given by Geoffroi Chardonnel.

78. Life of S. Nicholas. Given by Etienne Chardonnel.

Rose, Jesus and the four beasts.

79, 80, 81, 82. Four interesting grisailles with coloured borders.

*Sacristy.*

83. Grisaille, fourteenth century.

*Chapel of S. Joseph.*

84. Story of S. Thomas.

85. S. Julian. Given by the Carpenters, Wheelwrights and Coopers.

86. Grisaille, picked out with colour.

*Chapel of the Sacred Heart of Mary.*

87. Story of S. Savinian, S. Potentian, S. Modesta (*see* p. 18). Given by the Weavers.

88. Story of S. Chéron. Given by the Sculptors, Masons and Stone-dressers.

89. Story of S. Stephen. Given by the Shoemakers.

90. Story of S. Quentin. Given by Nicolas Lescine, Canon of the Cathedral.

91. Story of S. Theodore and S. Vincent of Saragossa. Given by the Weavers.

*Windows between the Chapels.*

92. The legend of S. Charlemagne and S. Roland, told in great detail and with remarkable clearness, after the versions of Turpin and Vincent de Beauvais.

93. S. James, the Apostle. Given by the Drapers and Furriers.

*Chapel of the Communion.*

94. Grisaille, ornamented with arms of House of Castile.

95. Lives of S. Simon and S. Jude. Donor, Henri Noblet.

96, 97, 98. Scenes from the life of Christ, given by the Bakers. Nine of the panels were removed in 1791, and like those of the two next windows, which depict the incidents of the lives of S. Peter and S. Paul, they have been very skilfully restored.

*Entrance to Chapel of S. Piat (see p. 44).*

99. Grisaille, fourteenth century. S. Piat in ecclesiastical robes.

*Chapel of the Sacred Heart of Jesus.*

100. Grisaille. S. Nicholas restoring three children to life (fifteenth century).

101. Life of S. Rémy. The donor below kneeling.

102. S. Nicholas.

103. Story of S. Marguerite and S. Catherine of Alexandria. Donors, Marguerite de Lèves, and her husband, Guérin de Friaise, with her brother Hugues de Meslay.

104. Life of S. Thomas of Canterbury. Given about thirty years after his murder by the Tanners and Curriers. John of Salisbury, Bishop of Chartres, had been the secretary of Thomas à Becket, and an eye-witness of his murder.

*Chapel of All Saints.*

105. The story of S. Martin (by Clement, the glass painter of Chartres, whose name is recorded in a similar thirteenth-century window in Rouen Cathedral?). Given by the Shoemakers.

106, 107. White eighteenth-century glass.

108. Fourteenth-century grisailles. The Annunciation. Two coats of arms.

Rose, Christ blessing.

109. Signs of the Zodiac and Months of the year. The life of the Virgin. Rose, Christ crucified. Given by Thibaut VI., Count of Chartres, for Thomas, Count of Perche, killed in the Battle of Lincoln, 1217.

110. Notre-dame de la Belle Verrière (*see* p. 161). Above, the Virgin (whose mouth has been skilfully restored), enthroned and crowned, with Christ between her knees, surrounded by angels bearing candlesticks and censers. Below, the Marriage at Cana, and the Temptation of our Saviour in the Wilderness, on the Temple and the Mountain.

111. Scenes from the lives of S. Antony and S. Paul, the first hermit. Given by the Basketmakers.

     Rose, Virgin and Child.

# CHAPTER VII

## *The Cathedral*

'Monument unique, et qu'il faudrait comparer aux gigantesques constructions de l'Egypte, aux monstrueuses pagodes de l'Inde pour lui trouver des analogues.'—DIDRON.

'Notre-Dame de Chartres! It is a world to explore, as if one explored the entire Middle Ages.'—PATER.

THE Cathedral of Chartres is gifted to a peculiar degree with the quality of impressiveness. This quality it owes to the living unity, the animated harmony of its members, and also to the sensation of space, not emptiness, to the impression of massiveness which is yet not heavy, suggested by the whole, whether viewed from near or afar, and equally by the parts, such as the west front or the nave.

'Dependent,' says Pater, 'on its structural completeness, or its wealth of well-preserved ornament, or its unity in variety, perhaps on some undefinable operation of genius, beyond, but concurrently with, all these, the Church of Chartres has still the gift of a unique power of impressing. In comparison, the other famous Churches of France, at Amiens for instance, at Reims or Beauvais, may seem but formal, and to a large extent reproducible, effects of mere architectural rule on a gigantic scale.'

The main body of the Cathedral was completed by 1210, for it is written in the Latin version (1210) of the *Poem of Miracles* that one day there came a shining light which dimmed the candles that were lit, and a noise as of thunder that drowned the voices of the many faithful praying in the church, and that a belief sprang up that the Virgin herself had appeared to honour with her presence the Cathedral built to her praise.[74]

The north and south porches, which were not part of the original plan, as is evident from the manner in which they have been applied to the walls and the buttresses cut away to admit them, would appear to have been begun in this same year 1210.

But the dedication of the Cathedral was long deferred. It did not take place till 1260, when S. Louis himself, the devoted benefactor of the Cathedral, whose personality has filled the north transept, the Rose of France and the north porch, attended with all his family, and with multitudes of people from every side, princes and dukes and peasants, and the bishop, surrounded by his seventy canons, joined in the solemn dedication of the temple.

By the fire of 1194 the whole of the upper church had been destroyed. The narthex, with the western porch and its three twelfth-century windows, alone remained. Beyond the church stood the two towers still, but their bells and woodwork were all gone, and the masonry was so charred that traces of the fire may be seen to this day.

Briefly, the steps that were now taken to give us the Cathedral which we have may be summarised as follows. Four apsidal chapels were added in the crypt, completing thus the favourite Gothic number of seven; all the soil of the crypt (except the martyrium) was levelled up to that of Notre-Dame-de-Sous-Terre; aisles were constructed over the corridors of the crypt; a vast transept was added; an enormous choir, with double aisles and apsidal chapels, was erected over new vaulting of the crypt; the narthex was displaced and made room for two new bays in the nave; whilst the west porch was moved skilfully westwards, with the same object, and set in a line flush with the two towers. Traces of this latter process will be found in the fact that the three doorways, having existed before the present nave and aisles, do not now correspond with them, and traces of what was once exterior masonry of the towers may also be seen *inside* the present church, between the Chapel of the Seven Sorrows and that of the Calvary.

At the same time, above the triplet window, in a severe quadrangular framework, was inserted the splendid Rose window, which is a masterpiece of masonry, a superb creation, recalling at once to mind the magnificent circular window of Lincoln, which, however, was a good score years later, and also—for the thick radii of the circle still suggest the spokes of a wheel quite as much as the petals of a rose—the rather earlier Wheel of Barfreston (Kent, 1180). It is 46 feet in diameter, and has been set, designedly, not in the exact centre of its flat stone frame, in order to counterbalance the inequality noticeable in the breadth of the two towers. There, with its double row of sculptured spokes, which radiate from its centre, it looks, to borrow Mr. Henry James's fine phrase, on its lofty field of stone, as expansive and symbolic as if it were the wheel of Time itself.

Above this window stretch a noble cornice and a simple balustrade which serve for communication between the two towers, and above this again are the sixteen niched figures which have earned for this gallery the title of the Gallery of Kings. Higher still is the gable which terminates the front, containing in a niche a colossal statue of the Virgin and Child, and on the apex a statue of Christ in the act of blessing. (Both these statues were re-made in 1855).

The kings stand upright in their niches; their pose is little varied; their costumes uniform. M. Viollet-le-Duc suggested that they represent the Kings of Judah, but there is no reason to doubt the tradition that, like the royal statues at Wells and Notre-Dame de Paris and the stained-glass figures at Strasbourg, they really represent the kings of the country who were benefactors of the church.

The first seven, then, are the figures of Merovingian Kings, the eighth Pepin-le-Bref, as you may tell by his small stature and the fact that he is standing upon a lion, in allusion to his courageous feat when, after challenging the French nobles who despised him for his smallness, he slew a raging lion single-handed, and then demanded, 'Do you think me worthy to rule you now?' The ninth statue was broken by a cannon-ball in the siege of 1591. It was Charlemagne or Charles-le-Fauve. The others are, according to M. Bulteau, Philippe I., Louis le Gros, Louis le Jeune, Philippe Auguste, Louis le Lion, Louis IX., and Philippe le Hardi, in whose reign the gallery was finished (1280).

As at Rouen and at Bayeux, it was originally intended that six new towers, two at each corner of the north and south front, making eight in all, should be grouped round the soaring spire of a central tower which was to rest on the four huge piers at the point of intersection of the transepts of the nave and choir. But they remain incomplete, even as, in accordance it might be fancied with some inscrutable degree, almost every Cathedral in the world is unfinished.

Thus at Chartres the Cathedral type, after which, with tentative, uncertain hand, the twelfth-century architects of Poitiers and Soissons, Laon and Paris had been striving, was struck out at last. It was to serve as a model for Central Europe throughout the thirteenth and fourteenth centuries, just as the sculpture of the western porch was to be copied at Corbeil and Paris, Sentis, Laon and Sens.

The name of the genius who achieved this glorious success we do not know, though the names of the builders of Reims, of Rouen and of Amiens have come down to us. All we do know is, as has been said above, that there was an active school of architects and sculptors, drawn chiefly from the monks of the Monasteries of Tiron and S. Père, established at this time in La Beauce, who worked with humble zeal, anonymous.

But, whatever his name, he succeeded at last, after the efforts and by aid of the efforts of his so many predecessors, in striking out the cathedral type, in shaping the mould in which, with various alterations, modifications, improvements and excesses, all the cathedrals of France were henceforth to be cast. In striking out the type he was himself confined by local conditions, and limited by his lack of experience. By bringing the western façade flush with the western extremities of the towers he was enabled to increase the length of that nave, which he made to leap heavenwards with almost the same joyous spring as that of Amiens, and the length and breadth, and height and strength of that nave, with its massive piers, its splendid vaulting, and its jewelled windows casting their purple and crimson rays across its dark roomy spaces, and the dim distances of the mysterious aisles, render Chartres 'awful' in a manner seldom or never elsewhere achieved by Gothic architect. But the proportion of the nave to the choir, or, again, to the vast transepts, is not perfect, for the builder was limited by the existing towers. As a pioneer, too, he was limited by inexperience. There is, indeed, no effect of heaviness in this nave, for the massiveness of the work, which is almost equal to that which we call Norman, is relieved by the stupendous height. And the solemnity, the overwhelming impressiveness of Chartres are due, it might almost seem, to that accident of ignorance. For if he had dared, if he had known that it was possible and safe, can you doubt that the architect would have added to the soaring spires of Chartres the soaring nave of Amiens? But what we should have gained in sheer beauty we should have lost in character. For Amiens is light and joyous; Chartres is mysterious and sad. Amiens rises as naturally as the sparks fly upward, as ethereal as the flute-like notes of a treble voice, as careless as a child's light laughter. But Chartres it would seem has more sympathy with the sadder, deeper sides of human life; it is older, stronger, more masculine, and more wise; combining the stern philosophy of the Pagan Stoic with the comforting tidings of the Christian martyrs and saints; combining, that is, as never before or since so harmoniously, the Romanesque and the Gothic styles, the rounded and the pointed arch, taking the best of each, and uniting them in a transition that is yet a triumph, in an attempt that is an eternal monument of success.

The transition of style is to be observed on almost every side. Not, indeed, so much in the plain round pillars with capitals in imitation of the Roman composite, and with square abaci, as the eye accustomed only to English work might assume, for these in France were retained much later than in England, even throughout the period of Flamboyant. But in almost every direction you can see the tentative mason at work, leaving the old heavy style with its horizontal lines behind him, and making new experiments, discarding or developing fresh ideas which tended to the achievement of lightness and spring, but as yet hardly daring to believe to the full in the capacity of stone. Here, for instance, in the nave, the blind triforium has not broken yet into one continuous window, as it was soon to do in the Church of S. Père, of S. Ouen at Rouen, and at Amiens; nor have the heavy masses of stone been resolved into a network of delicate tracery, leaving not a span uncovered by its gossamer thread. The desire for lightness, again, which was in time to lead to the adoption of bar tracery is, in the case of the windows, evident, but not fully attained. Combined, however, with the rare opportunities offered to the architect by the excellent quality of the stone of Berchères, it has led him to invent a very simple and handsome type of window, which consists of two lancet lights under one arch, with a foliated circle in the head, the plate tracery of which is peculiarly heavy, and is cut through the solid stone. Between these circular openings, which fill a whole bay between the flying buttresses, and the heads of the lower lights, there is, as at Soissons, Bourges, Reims and so forth, a considerable interval of masonry. The foliated circles themselves are surrounded by a number of small trefoil or quatrefoil openings, not formed of bars, but likewise pierced through the solid stone.

**FLYING BUTTRESSES OF THE NAVE.**

The buttresses of the nave, again, are amazingly heavy and massive, as if the workmen were still afraid to trust them to support the thrust of the vaulting of the roof at so great a height. This is borne by flying buttresses of enormous solidity, composed of an upper and a lower section, which are strengthened in turn by an arcade. The arcading is remarkable for its rugged grace, its masculine beauty. Its round-headed arches, which are supported by short, thick shafts, that remind one of the spokes of the wheel window, are composed of two large blocks of hewn stone.

Compare these flying buttresses with the later and lighter but less pleasing ones of the choir, or with the almost impudent development of the use of them in the Abbey Church of S. Père, and, without any doubt, you perceive in what direction lay the ambition of the transitional architect.

These buttresses of the nave will be best seen from the galleries of the roof, with their graceful balustrading, along which you pass, when, under the guidance of a verger from the Maison-des-Clercs, you make your ascent of the *clochers*, starting from a door near the north entrance and the sacristy. Passing, then, along these galleries, you come to the Clocher Neuf, with its Flamboyant spire, the work of Jehan de Beauce (1507-1513); built after the spire of timber and lead, which replaced the one destroyed in 1194, had been destroyed itself in 1506. It was raised 4 feet by Claude Augé in 1690, so that the present height of the Clocher Neuf is 378 feet, that of the Clocher Vieux being 350. Augé, in the following year, added the enormous bronze vase on the top; the cross above that was placed in position in 1854. There is a vane in the form of a sun (Jesus, the Sun of Justice, the Light of the World) upon this cross, corresponding to the moon on the old spire (Mary, 'clothed with the sun, with the moon under her feet.'—Rev. xii.)

The third storey of the Clocher Neuf into which the gallery brings us is the beginning of the Flamboyant work of Jehan de Beauce. An elegant balustrade connects the parts of the different date. On the south wall of the *Chambre des Sonneurs*, as the third storey is called, is graven in Gothic, but now scarce legible characters, an inscription in six quatrains, in which the clocher tells us the history of the disaster of 1506, and the event of its rebuilding by Jehan de Beauce, the skilful mason, just as the bronze vase above relates in Latin prose the further history of the spire down to 1690, and the name of the bronze-founder, Ignace Gabois.

'Je fus jadis de plomb et boys construit,
Grant, hault et beau, de somptueux ouvraige,
Jusques ad ce que tonnerre et oraige
M'a consumé, dégâté et détruit.

Le jour sainte Anne vers six heures de nuyt
En l'année mil cinq cens et six.
Je fu brulé démoly et recuyt
Et avec moy de grosses cloches six.

Après Messieurs en plain Chappitre assis
Ont ordonné de pierre me reffaire
A grant voultes et pilliers bien massifs
Par Jehan de Beausse, maçon qui le sut faire.

L'An dessu dist après pour l'euvre faire
Assouar firent le vint quatrième jour
Du moys de mars pour le premier affaire
Première pierre et aultres sans ce jour.

Et en avril huitiesme jour exprès
René d'Illiers évesque de regnon
Pardist la vie au lieu duquel après
Feust Erard mis par postulacion.

En ce temps là que avoys nicessité
Avoit des gens qui pour moy lors vieilloient
Du bon du cœur feust yver ou esté,
Dieu le pardont et à ceulx qui s'y emploient.
1508.'

The fourth storey, lit by four large bays, contains two great bells cast in 1840, Marie (C., 13,228 lbs.) and Joseph, the tenor, who sounds the Angelus throughout the year.

The fifth storey, pierced on each of its eight sides by a large bay, contains four large bells of 1845, Anne (D., 2040 kilos.), Elizabeth (E., 1510 kilos.), Fulbert (F., 1510 kilos.), Piat (G., 870 kilos.). The first-named bell is always known as Anne of Bretagne. For she, when visiting the Cathedral in 1510, was so delighted with the voice of one of the lads singing in the choir that she begged him of the canons, and when they granted her request she thanked them in these words: 'Messieurs, you have given me a little voice, and I in return wish to give you a big one.' This she did, giving them the bell which has ever since been called by her name. It was known also by the name of the *Cloche des biens*, for at one season of the year it was rung for an hour every evening to secure an abundant harvest. 'At the first stroke of the bell,' wrote Sablon, in 1697, 'all the people make the sign of the cross and recite an Ave Maria for the products of the soil.'

The fifth storey marks the beginning of the spire, and is itself octagonal. The transition is ingeniously concealed by the richly-ornamented pinnacles at the four corners, which tie the balustrade to the tower and support, each of them, three colossal statues (John the Baptist and the eleven Apostles). Light flying buttresses, adorned with graceful mouldings and admirable grotesques, connect the pinnacles with the tower. Over one of the lights is a Christ in the act of benediction.

The sixth storey, surrounded by a gallery in Flamboyant style, panels of rich tracery and gargoyles, and pinnacles at the corners of the octagon, contains the room of the watchmen, whose duty it was every half-hour during the night to walk round this gallery and give the alarm when they saw a fire in the town. A Latin inscription records that by the peculiar grace of God this pyramid was preserved from the effects of a fire (1674) due to the watchman's carelessness. This good man, Gendrin by name, finding that the hours of the night watch hung heavy on his hands, used to amuse himself by reading. One night the candle fell and set light to his straw mattress, and thence the flames spread rapidly to the timber of the room. The wooden belfry was saved from destruction by the great bravery of a workman named Claude Gauthier. A quotation from Psalms cxxvii., outside the western door, draws the moral, 'Except the Lord keep the city, the watchman waketh but in vain.' It is signed F. Foucault. But the significance of the name has died away.

At last, after having mounted 377 steps, we reach the seventh storey, where hangs the 'Tocsin' bell, 'in accordance with which,' says an old writer, 'all the people of Chartres order and conduct themselves.'[75] It weighs 5000 kilos., and was cast on the 23rd September, 1520, by Pierre Sayvet, as the inscription tells us, 'Petrus Sayvet me fecit.' Another and longer inscription, in beautiful Gothic characters, runs round the bell in two lines. The bell, speaking in Latin verses, tells us that it has been raised 'to the lofty summit of this mighty building to announce the eclipses of the sun and the moon.' And it fixes its date as 1520, with a reference to the great event of that year, the meeting of Henry VIII. and François I., near Calais, on the field of the Cloth of Gold, 'when the Frenchmen met the English and lay down together in everlasting goodwill.'

'Facta ad signandos solis luneque labores
Evehor ad tante culmina celsa domus
Annus erat Christi millesimus adde priori
Quingentos numero bis quoque junge decem
Illo quippe anno quo francus convenit anglum
Perpetuaque simul discubuere fide.'

The arms of the Chapter, the chemisette of Notre-Dame, and the escutcheon of a dauphin will be noticed at the end of the last line.

You reach the old tower from the new by way of the Gallery of Kings or by crossing, within, the vaulting of the nave, beneath the copper roof which has taken the place of the old wooden roof destroyed in the fire of 1836. The old roof was an immense and elaborate construction of timber known to the people as The Forest, because, one old chronicler explains, had the trees of which it was composed still been growing they would constitute a large forest by themselves; because, says another, the sight of it recalled to the people the sacred groves of the ancient Druids, who once performed their rites upon this spot. The magnificent woodwork of the belfry of the old tower was consumed in the same fire, and the huge bells that were once its boast—Mary and Gabriel—were melted down in 1793 to supply the men of reason with bullets.

The great bell of the old tower (Marie) had been re-made in 1723 and carried the inscription—

'Marie-Anne je m'appèle
Et trente mille je pèse,
Celui qui bien me pèsera
34,000 trouvera.'

At the foot of the Clocher Neuf is the extremely elegant little Renaissance clock tower, which was built by Jehan de Beauce in 1520, when he had completely abandoned the Gothic style and adopted the classic manner lately introduced by the Italian artists who had followed Louis XII. and François I. into France. Partisans of pure Gothic may call it mythological, mannered, mundane, but the more catholic lover of the beautiful will not dismiss it so contemptuously. From this pavillon de l'horloge there used to run alongside the nave up to the transept some fourteenth-century buildings, which were demolished in 1860. They served as a lodging for the Sœurs-cryptes, who, when the epidemic known as the Mal des Ardents was scourging France in the eleventh and twelfth centuries, had charge of the Hôpital des Saints-Lieux-Forts, organised in the north gallery of the crypt to receive the crowds of sufferers who flocked to the shrine of Notre-Dame-de-Sous-Terre. The patients were received and nursed in this hospital for nine days and then dismissed, healed or not.[76] From the fourteenth century onwards the plague gradually decreased in intensity, cases became less and less rare, and the staff of Sisters was finally reduced to one, known as La Dame des Grottes.

We will leave for the present the exterior of the Cathedral and return later to the consideration of the north and south porches. For it is time to enter, by the western portal which we know, the sanctuary of Notre-Dame. Here, amid the dim shadows of old dreams, the mystic may indulge his fancy, and here, if anywhere, wandering through this veritable gallery of Madonnas, in escaping from the feverish passions of the world, a man may cool his hands awhile in the gray twilight of Gothic things. More souls, they say, have been healed at Chartres than bodies at Lourdes. In solitude and silence it is best; but wonderful also and impressive is the Cathedral when filled with long trains of pilgrims, whose shuffling feet and murmured prayers echo through the vast nave and resound from the innumerable chapels. These sounds, these sights carry us back in a flash of memory to those mediæval days when Sébastien Rouillard was astonished at the crowds of all nations who congregated here 'and slept all night in the church or in the grottoes for lack of lodgings.' On the very threshold the sloping floor of the west end of the nave, so made that it might the more easily be cleansed, suggests that scene.

Surely the vast nave with its gloomy spaces is filled with the ghosts of forgotten worshippers, and it thrills with the unheard echoes of unanswered prayers. It is melancholy with the records of perverted faith and false enthusiasm, and it is magnificent with the chanted hopes of the faithful and the undying promises of the Risen Lord. The blood of martyrs and the blood of infidels cries aloud from those stones which once resounded with the fiery exhortations of a crusading monk or of a fanatic preaching the extermination of the Jews and the persecution of the Huguenots.

Here knights have kept their vigil and watched by their armour on the eve of a Crusade, and here many a young squire after his night watch by the altar, clothed in vestments of white linen that symbolised his moral purity, has been struck on the shoulder with the consecrated sword and made 'a knight in the name of the Father, the Son and the Holy Ghost.' Hither, again, courtier pilgrims have brought with them the perfume of Paris, and Norman peasants the odour of the fields. Here many a penitent Magdalen has poured out her soul in contrite supplication. Here, too, the hand of the sacrilegious destroyer has wrought its vile work, and yet failed to leave more than a few blots and stains upon the mighty fabric reared by mediæval faith.

You may close your eyes and imagine that you are present at a Mass of old days—a Mass of the dead—a silent Mass, at which no sound escapes from the lips of the praying, and no tinkle comes from the bell that is vainly shaken. Kings do penance before the sacred altar, knights in chain armour kneel and take the sign of the cross; noble lords, clad in velvet and brocade, with plumes in their hats and swords at their sides, carry in their hands tall canes, with golden knobs, and bow to great dames with powdered hair, who hide behind their fans lovely faces powdered, painted, patched. And in the aisles a crowd of youthful artisans, in brown jerkins, dimity breeches, and hose of blue, stand beside young women with rosy cheeks and downcast eyes. Elsewhere peasant women, in their old skirts and laced bodices, sit tranquil, whilst upright, behind them, their young lovers shift their legs and twist their hats in their fingers, gazing open-eyed.

They seem to follow with their silent lips the noiseless priests as they perform that ritual order of Notre-Dame de Chartres, which rejoiced the Gothic soul of Gaston de Latour; a year-long dramatic action, in which everyone had and knew his part—the drama or mystery of redemption, to the necessities of which the great church had shaped itself. For all those various 'offices' which, in pontifical, missal and breviary, devout imagination had elaborated from age to age with such a range of spiritual colour and light and shade, with so much poetic tact in quotation, such a depth of insight into the Christian soul, had been joined harmoniously together, one office ending only where another began, in the perpetual worship of this mother of churches. And Notre-Dame had also its own picturesque peculiarities of 'use,' and was proud of its maternal privilege therein.[77]

You notice the rich tones of the masonry, made richer by the jewelled lights of those rare windows; you notice in the centre of the nave the mysterious maze traced upon the pavement, the scene in old times of much devotional exercise,—la Lieue, it is vulgarly termed, for the miniature pilgrimages, along the line of white stones, with prayers at stated intervals, as once at Reims, Amiens, Arras, and Bayeux, earned many indulgences, and took the place of a journey to Jerusalem. This, with the exception of that at S. Quentin, is the only remaining instance of a labyrinth in the French churches. Above you, around you, tower the piers and vaulting of the nave—

'Heavy as nightmare, airy light as fern,
Imagination's very self in stone.
Solemn the lift of high-embowered roof;
Solemn the deepening vault.'

Something of the power of impressing which this Cathedral possesses is due, one begins to reflect, to the fortunate scarcity of side-chapels, and the complete absence of the tombs, which fill up the spaces, and therefore detract from the effect of so many churches. The reason for this happy freedom from monuments is given by the old writer, Rouillard. 'This church has the special prerogative of being reputed the chamber or couch of the Virgin. As a sign thereof the soil of this church has always hitherto been preserved pure and undefiled, without ever having been dug or opened for any sepulture.' But there was one exception. One military leader was interred there with all honours in 1568, within the precinct of the high altar itself. Much against their will, the canons had yielded to the pressure of the King and the Court, and consented at last to inter in the Choir the body of the Baron of Bourdeilles, the colonel of the Gascons, who had fallen in the defence of the breach against the Huguenots (*see* p. 277). To the sound of tabourins and fifes the funeral *cortège* wound its way through the town of mourning citizens, and the remains of the valiant D'Ardelay were regretfully lowered into a vault to the left of the high altar, which was not to prove their last resting-place. Rouillard, who saw the tomb of the gallant colonel in 1608, adds that many believed then that the body would not long remain where it was. And, indeed, fifty years afterwards, the reverend canons, resenting, on the part of their immaculate Patroness, this intrusion, reported that the corpse itself, ill at ease, had protested, lifting up its hands above the surface of the pavement, as if to beg interment elsewhere. This it easily obtained in the cemetery of S. Jerome.

The nave exceeds in width any in France or Germany. Its width, as also its length, which is short in comparison with the other parts of the Cathedral, was determined, as we have seen, by the position of the two towers. In height it falls short of the naves of Bourges and Amiens, and of Beauvais, which out-rivalled even its sisters, and fell in the moment of its mad success. But it is an unprofitable business, this comparison of cathedrals. One is not less beautiful because another is of larger dimensions, nor less perfect because another is more uniform. This nave has its own qualities, which I have feebly endeavoured to suggest, qualities different from, but not less valuable than the pure beauty of that of Amiens.

Architecturally speaking, Parker put the matter in a nutshell when he wrote that the nave of Chartres was 'nearly as massive as Norman work, although the effect of heaviness is removed by the enormous height.'[78] Detached piers and engaged pilasters support the vaulting, which is as daring as it is strong.

'The main ribs of the vault spring from, or are rather continuations of the tall clustered pilasters, which are themselves continuations of the main piers; and from the points where each of the main ribs rise two other cross-ribs also spring. These at their points of intersection are adorned with crown-shaped bosses, for the most part enriched with carvings of foliage, coloured in part, which have been marred with colour-wash. Lines, in imitation of ashlar-work, have been painted upon the vault' (Massé).[79]

The piers in the nave and transept are alternately cylindrical and octagonal in section, and have supplementary cylindrical or octagonal columns; but in the ambulatory of the choir there are several piers circular in section, with octagonal bases and square plinths, but without any supplementary columns. Such plain round piers, which in England are called Norman, are rare in France. Examples of them are, however, to be found at Laon, Soissons and Paris. The capitals are rich and varied, and consist chiefly of foliage; those of the piers in the Chapel of the Seven Sorrows (Clocher Neuf), and, again, those of the Norman pillars, in the deambulatory of the choir opposite the shrine of Notre-Dame du Pilier, are remarkably fine. But the most noteworthy of the piers are the four 'Toureaus,' as they are called: the enormous piers at the intersection of nave and transept, which were intended to support the central tower and spire, and which rise sheer to the roof, in an unbroken line, to the height of 120 feet. Their faces are covered with a quantity of slender columns.

The arcading of the triforium varies in width and character in the nave, the choir, and the transepts and the apse. The arches of the smaller bays into which each main bay is divided are pointed. The soffit is flat, with a round moulding at the inner and the outer edge. The capitals are richly carved with foliage; the bases are plain and severe.

The clerestory is composed of pairs of tall lancet windows, with a rose window above them, which fill the whole available space in each bay. Of the glass we have spoken in the previous chapter.

The *Flamboyant* period is represented in the Cathedral by the spire of Jehan de Beauce and the *Chapelle Vendôme*, next to the south transept. It was founded in 1413 by Louis de Bourbon, and dedicated to the Annunciation. It has recently been restored. The style is incongruous with this massive transitional nave, but serves perhaps to accentuate the beauty of its masculine grandeur and reserve. The remains of S. Piat and S. Taurin are preserved here; the one is invoked for fair weather, the other for rain by the farmers of La Beauce.

The influence of the *Renaissance* is to be traced in the clock tower at the foot of the *Clocher Neuf*, in the later portions of the *Clôture du Chœur* and, in its most fatal form, in the alterations that were made in the eighteenth century within the choir.[80] The Chapter, about 1750, was composed of men with much taste, all of it bad. A terrible mania for ugliness had seized mankind. Men like Bossuet, Fénelon, Montesquieu and Racine, enamoured of the classical style, declared the Gothic barbarous. At that inopportune crisis of taste the Chapter began to 'decorate' the choir. The result is simply nauseating.

The jubé, the beautiful screen which had come down from the century of S. Louis, required repair. The excuse was welcomed, and it was destroyed. A few fragments only remain in the Chapel of S. Martin in the crypt. The pillar upon which the Vierge Noire (Notre-Dame du Pilier) was then set is said to have been part of the *débris* of this screen. The present grille replaced in 1866 the pretentious iron-work of the eighteenth century.

This achievement of the Chapter seems to have whetted rather than satisfied their shameless appetite for the hideous. 'Sans doute,' wrote Victor Hugo, 'C'est encore aujourd'hui un majestueux et sublime édifice que Notre-Dame de Chartres. Mais si belle qu'elle se soit conservée en vieillissant, il est difficile de ne pas soupirer, de ne pas s'indigner devant les dégradations, les mutilations sans nombre que simultanément le temps et les hommes ont fait subir au vénérable monument.'

Italians were sent for from Milan to wash the grand old stone of Berchères a sickly yellow; the noble simplicity of the piers, capitals and soffits of the arches disappeared beneath a mess of stucco, gilding and sham marble. The choir was treated like an eighteenth century drawing-room. The old tapestry hangings, five of which are happily preserved in the

Museum, were removed, and in their place eight mediocre bas-reliefs in glaring white marble were substituted by Bridan, two of which have been removed to the Bishop's Palace. The old paving of the choir, on which S. Louis and a thousand other illustrious pilgrims had knelt, was also removed, and an utterly unsuitable pavement of black and white marble laid down in its stead. In order to throw light upon the atrocious transformation that had been wrought, several of the priceless thirteenth-century windows were taken out and plain glass substituted. To such an extent was this done, indeed, that in 1786 we find a canon of the Cathedral gravely complaining that there was too much light, and asking for a curtain to be drawn across the window! But the Revolution surprised these canons seated in their new stalls ere the curtains had yet been made to hide the results of their pious Paganism. They were sent to the scaffold, and their church was converted into a Temple of Reason amid scenes of abominable profanity and vile orgy.

The group of the Assumption was preserved by the presence of mind of an architect, by name Morin, who placed a red cap of liberty on the Virgin's head and a lance in her hand. It might have been more reasonable to destroy it. For anything more detestably out of place than this soulless mass of Carrara marble in the old Gothic sanctuary it is impossible to discover without going to Westminster Abbey. It is the work of Antoine Bridan, the King's sculptor, and the Chapter were so pleased with it that they settled a pension on him and his wife, and cheerfully destroyed more windows in order to throw more light upon the monument.

Vandals, alas, are of all time and of all countries. Even the beautiful Clôture, the great horse-shoe wall

***Ambulatory, Chartres Cathedral.
Facing Page 203;***

which, chiselled like a silver bowl, encloses the choir, has been and continues to be horribly defaced and defiled by the ignorant vandalism of impious idiots and pious pilgrims, whose zeal has eaten them up and moves them to write or scratch their names upon the walls of this exquisite though unequal work.

More beautiful than the fourteenth-century screen of Notre-Dame de Paris, but inferior in unity and nobility of feeling to the *Pourtoir* of Amiens, this Clôture, although executed at various periods, is one in design. The plan of forty groups, representing the principal scenes in the life of the Virgin and the Gospel story was drawn up by the Chancellor of the Chapter, Mainterne, at the beginning of the sixteenth century. The work was begun in 1514 under Jehan de Beauce. It was continued in 1611 by Boudin. It was finished by various sculptors at the beginning of the eighteenth century, and the style naturally varies from late Gothic to Renaissance. The earliest work is the best.

It comprises the first twelve groups in the south ambulatory. These were wrought by or under the supervision of Jehan Soulas, a Parisian sculptor, engaged for that purpose by the Chapter (1518). For Jehan de Beauce, being an architect and not a sculptor, was responsible only for the framework, and not for the groups of figures. But that framework is a masterpiece of delicate grace and prolific imagination. A wealth of ornament, of foliage and arabesques, of mythical personages and fantastic beasts, covers the base and the innumerable columns about it. The stone openwork above and the canopies are exquisite in their lightness and finish. Before he died in 1529 Jehan de Beauce had passed completely under the influence of the Renaissance. The elegant and ingenious clock tower, which breaks the series of niches on the south side of the clôture, with its decorative Titus and Vespasian, and so forth, gives evidence of this. The elaborate clockwork with which it was originally provided, and which showed the days, hours, months, time of sunrise and sunset, and signs of the Zodiac, was destroyed in 1793. The initial F, with a crown, which appears on the vertical band, refers to the then reigning François I.

Apart from the infinite variety of other ornamental details in which the framework is so rich, there are thirty-five medallions on the base. The first on the south side refers to the Siege of Chartres by Rollo in 911; the next fifteen to the lives of David, Daniel, Moses, Samson, Abraham and Jonas; the next twelve to mythological subjects—Labours of Hercules— and the last seven are heads of Roman emperors.

The pillars of the screen carry statuettes of founders and bishops, of whom we have already mentioned S. Fulbert and S. Ives at the eastern extremity. The small doors in their beautiful frames give access to rooms of which four were once chapels, and two others served for the night-watchers.

The first group in the south ambulatory represents the angel appearing to S. Joachim, who is watching his flocks with two shepherds and a dog, and announcing the birth of the Virgin. This and the three following groups are certainly the work of Jehan Soulas (1520).

The second group shows S. Anne receiving a similar message from an invisible angel, to whom she listens with the most intent absorption. The servant, whose attention has also been arrested, is portrayed with equally vivid realism. The sculptor was evidently a master of exact observation. There is something Flemish in his closeness to life. The third group, where the aged couple meet and embrace before the Golden Gate, shows a minute and vivid understanding of the gestures of old age, and the attitude of the servant is admirably suggestive of her naïve, sympathetic delight. There is something Flemish, again, in the homely details with which (4) the Birth of the Virgin is portrayed. S. Anne lies on a curtained couch in the background, attended by a servant, whilst another prepares to wash the Infant.

The next eight groups owe much to Jehan Soulas, but they cannot be ascribed with certainty to his chisel. They show (5) the Virgin Mary ascending the steps of the Temple with S. Joachim and S. Anne, (6) the Marriage of the Virgin, (7) the Annunciation, (8) the Visitation.

The ninth group, next to the Renaissance clock, is of extraordinary excellence. It is conceived in a spirit of the most bold and vivid realism, absolutely justified in the result. Mary is sewing and reading a book; Joseph asleep (and not his eyes only but his whole body proclaims profound slumber), learns in a dream the immaculate conception of the Virgin. Then follow three excellent groups—the Adoration of the Shepherds and Angels, the Circumcision and the Adoration of the Magi. In the latter the figure of the Virgin is particularly noteworthy. On the threshold of the Renaissance the sculptor has suddenly left the uninspired style of his day and gone back to the mystic ideal charm of the thirteenth century.

The next two scenes, the Presentation in the Temple (13), and the Massacre of the Innocents (14), with the Flight into Egypt in the background, were finished by François Marchand, of Orléans, in 1542, and, in spite of mutilation and restoration, they reveal the beginnings of the influence which the Italian Renaissance was to exercise upon French art. The Baptism of Christ in the Jordan (15), which follows, is by Nicholas Guybert, who lacked the draughtsmanship and anatomical study of Marchand, but was inspired with a devotional feeling quite foreign to the seventeenth-century work of Thomas Boudin, (16, 17, 18) the Temptation, the Canaanitish woman, the Transfiguration (1612). The Woman taken in Adultery (19) is the work of Jean de Dieu (1681), and (20) the Man born Blind, that of Pierre Legros (1683).

The centre of the *Tour du Chœur*, as it is called, was formerly filled by an altar, above which were relics of several saints in rich caskets (SS. Piat, Lubin, Calétric, Tugdualus, etc.); but those have disappeared, and a fifteenth-century group, representing S. Martin sharing his cloak with a poor man, has taken its place.

Tuby the younger executed the next two groups in 1703. They represent (21, 22) the Entry into Jerusalem, whilst the next six are as late as 1714, and are by Simon Arazières. They depict (23) the Agony in the Garden, (24) the Betrayal, (25) the Trial before Pontius Pilate, (26) the Scourging of Jesus, (27) the Crown of Thorns, (28) the Crucifixion, (29) the Virgin gazing at the dead Christ.

Thomas Boudin, again, is responsible for the next four groups (1611)—(30) the Resurrection, (31) the Holy Women bringing vases of perfume to the Tomb, (32) Christ and the Disciples of Emmaus, (33) Christ dispelling the doubts of S. Thomas.

The remaining eight groups are of the same date, and almost of the same excellence as those by Jehan Soulas at the beginning of the clôture opposite, and contrast favourably with the cold and Pagan feeling of the foregoing. They are probably the work of a pupil of that sculptor, and were made under the supervision, in part, perhaps, with the aid of Jehan Texier, called De Beauce. An inscription of the plinth beneath explains the subject of each scene.

(34.) *Comment Jésus-Christ ressuscité apparoist à la Vierge Marie.* Christ appearing to the Virgin and S. John.

(35.) *Comme Nostre-Seigneur monte ès-cieux.* The Virgin and the Apostles grouped round the stone which bears the imprint of the Saviour's feet, look upwards to the sky, where the robe and feet of the ascending Lord can be seen.

(36.) *Comme le S.-Esprit descent sur les apôtres.* The tongues of fire descending on the day of Pentecost on the Virgin and the eight Apostles round her.

(37.) *Comme Nostre-Dame adore la Croix.* The Adoration of the Cross by the Virgin, accompanied by S. John, Mary Magdalen, Mary Salome.

(38.) *C'est le trépassement de Nostre-Dame.* The Death of the Virgin, who lies upon a couch, holding a taper, whilst all the Apostles attend—S. John weeping, S. James the Less taking off his spectacles, and so forth.

(39.) *Le Portement de Nostre-Dame.* The Virgin is borne on the shoulders of eight Apostles to the Tomb in the Valley of Jehoshaphat.

(40.) *Le Sépulcre de Nostre-Dame.* Four angels raise the body of the Virgin from the Tomb, whilst Christ descending between two angels blesses the body, which has half risen from the grave.

(41.) *Le couronnement Nostre-Dame.* The crowning of the Virgin by the three Persons of the Trinity is a charming group, worthy to be compared with the best of the first twelve in the south ambulatory.

In the dim aisle, opposite the groups of the Clôture which we have just described, is the shrine which draws from every side the greater number of the visitors to Chartres. Notre-Dame de la belle Verrière is, save for the devotion of a few aged peasants, a deserted Madonna, and even the cult of Notre-Dame-de-Sous-Terre or of the Voile de Marie is at the present time less popular than that of *Notre-Dame du Pilier*, the *Vierge Noire*, black also and comely. The chapel in which this statue is placed is next to the sacristy, which was built, like the three gables of the façades, with their turrets, galleries, balustrades and statues, about the year 1310, under the direction of Jean des Carrières, 'mason and master of the work of Notre-Dame.' The Chapel of Notre-Dame du Pilier is not, properly speaking, a chapel, but part of the ambulatory of the choir in which the statue of the *Vierge Noire du Pilier* or the *Vierge aux Miracle*s is set. A priest from the *Œuvre des clercs* is always in attendance; innumerable lamps and candles burn before the shrine, and countless pilgrims kiss the pillar devoutly and obtain the forty days' indulgence granted for that act of faith. 'The column,' said Rouillard (1608), 'is worn hollow by the kisses of the faithful.' The statue dates from the latter part of the fifteenth century, and was originally placed at the foot of the cross above the choir screen. When that screen was destroyed in 1763 it was moved near a pier in the choir, and afterwards, in 1791, banished to the crypt and its place taken by the statue of Notre-Dame-de-Sous-Terre. It was established in its present position in 1806, and set upon a column which is a fragment of the old jubé. Notre-Dame du Pilier was solemnly crowned, in the name of Pius IX., on May 31, 1855, after a month-long festival, and amid a scene of extraordinary splendour and jubilation. Ever since then, on the anniversary of that feast, the statue is borne in triumphant procession round the church.

I do not think that there is any other detail in the Cathedral over which it is necessary to linger. For the crypt and the Chapel of S. Piat have already been described at length. Let us, then, seek the open air and examine the copper-stained statuary of the northern porch, choosing, if possible, the late afternoon for our visit, when the cold stone is warmed by the rose-pink tint of the setting sun. The effect of this gallery of seven hundred thirteenth century statues of all sizes is splendid enough as it is, but it must have been greatly enhanced originally, when, in accordance with the early regulation of the church, every piece of carving was coloured or gilded. The same perfect harmony of structure which distinguishes the western and southern porches is visible in the northern, and the latter is even richer in detail. It was given by the Royal Family, like the rose window above, and, like the south porch, it was added after the plan of the Cathedral was more or less completed. Traces of this fact are evident. Buttresses had to be cut away to make room for it, and it was soon found necessary to insert iron ties to hold it to the main building.

There is nothing outside France which can be compared with the splendour of these porches. And among French churches those of S. Urbain at Troyes, S. Maclou at Rouen, S. Germain at Paris, and the Cathedral of Bourges and of Alby rival, but cannot claim to surpass, in harmonious effect and delicate grace of detail, the open porches of Chartres. The fact that these porches are opened and advanced, verandah-like, beyond the line of the building, relieving thereby the severity of it, is significant. It indicates the change from the primitive architecture of the church. For the early buildings, the style of which was based on that of the Roman basilicas, had closed porches beneath which persons of importance were buried, catechumens were instructed and baptized, and exorcisms of the devil performed. But in the thirteenth century it became the practice, as here with regard to the western façade, to build the entrance flush with the towers, and when later, in the reign of S. Louis, the fashion of lateral porches was revived, they were no longer used for sacred purposes as before, but merely as shelters for the faithful coming into or going out of the church. It was not therefore any longer necessary to build them entirely covered in.

The architect will study with pleasure the arrangement of the arcading and the exquisite plinths of the piers which support it. To the artist the study of the sculpture with which the bays and the piers of the porch are filled will prove of profound interest. Comparing this statuary with that of the western front, he will notice a distinct difference in feeling, a marked advance in style. The overwhelming influence of the East has disappeared. Classical and Byzantine art have given place to the original genius of France. Throwing away the debased classical traditions, the neo-Christian artist has given expression to the new Christian ideal of character in a type of Germanic origin, with wavy hair and prominent forehead, which he has observed from the men and women of his own time and country. He has given expression, that is, to the ideal of humility and graciousness which has been traced by the teaching of chivalry, with all its appreciation of physical perfection and its teaching of noble manners. 'We have then,' it has been well observed, 'in this new art, evidences of a sudden increase in the feeling for pure sensuous charm, and at the same time for spiritual grace.' A perfect union between sense and spirit has arisen, imparting to each a rare intensity. In the grace and movement of the drapery (for the old straight folds have been discarded), and in the simple grandeur of pose as well as in the qualities of truth and self-restraint, these sculptors are nearer to the masterpieces of Greek sculpture than perhaps any before or since. Yet they lack, do they not? something of the intimate mystic charm of the kings and queens of the Porche Royal. In the name of Philosophy and the Republic it was proposed (1793) to destroy them. And this, save for the firm opposition of the deputy, Sargent-Marceau, would have been done.

Some damage, however, they did succeed in doing. The left bay, for instance, is sadly mutilated, and the large statue of Philippe-Auguste, who had provided for the yearly expenses in connection with the work of the porch, has disappeared from the column of the vestibule on which it used to be. The statue of his son, Louis VIII., however survives (central bay). Louis IX., S. Louis, followed the example of his mother, Blanche of Castile, and, besides founding windows and chapels, he, 'by reason of his particular devotion to the Church of Notre-Dame, and for the saving of his soul and the souls of his forefathers,' to quote the words of a charter of the year 1259, caused the north porch to be completed. His statue is to be seen on the pier of the central bay.

The north porch, which was always in the Middle Ages dedicated to the Virgin, is peopled by 705 statues, who are the characters of a vast poem in stone. The subject of this poem is the 'Glorification of Mary.' 'It recounts,' says M. Bulteau, 'the carnal and spiritual genealogy of the Virgin, her prerogatives, her acquaintances, her virtues, her occupations, her life, death, assumption and crowning in heaven.' Then come the personages and the biblical scenes which have foreshadowed the Messiah and His Mother; S. John the Baptist and S. Peter, who inaugurated the Christian era; and to connect this vast whole with the Church of Chartres, S. Potentian, S. Modesta and the donors of the porch, S. Louis at their head. The Creation, the Earth, the Sea and the Heavens, Time also, and its seasons, assist at this glorification of the Mother of God, and appear to render her respectful homage.

We have had occasion to notice before (p. 27) the prominent position which S. Anne is allotted in the iconography of this Cathedral, and we have explained that the reason is that Chartres possessed a precious relic of that saint. For, after the sack of Constantinople in 1204, the Emperor Baldwin sent the head of S. Anne, the Virgin's mother, to Chartres, 'in order that the head of the mother might rest in the house of the daughter.' Departing, therefore, from the almost invariable custom by which the Virgin is represented on the pier between the two sections of the central door, the sculptors have here given us a colossal statue of S. Anne carrying the little Mary in her arms. Beneath her feet are the remains of a group in which S. Joachim, feeding his sheep, was depicted receiving from the angel Gabriel the announcement of the future birth of Mary.

Ranged on either side of this central doorway are ten large statues, beneath canopies and wearing haloes. They are the personages of the Old Testament who have prefigured the birth of Jesus Christ, His passion, His death, His resurrection and His eternal priesthood. They emphasise once more the parallelism of the Old Testament and the New; the New hidden in the Old; the Old made manifest in the New. The same thought is symbolised by the figurative image of the Son which the five statues on the left carry, and the effigy of our Lord which is borne by those on the right. For thereby the prophecy and its accomplishment is symbolised. The cathedrals of Paris, Amiens, Rouen, Sens, Bourges, Senlis and Reims, and all the great cathedrals of the thirteenth century, in fact, show the same persons surrounding the Virgin.

And at Reims several of the statues would seem to be from the same chisel as those at Chartres. The characters represented are Melchizedek, Abraham, Moses, Samuel and David on the left, and on the right, Isaiah, Jeremiah, Simeon, S. John the Baptist and S. Peter. S. John is introduced as the link between the old and the new, the prophecy and its fulfilment. He stands close to S. Peter, for he was the immediate precursor of Christ and S. Peter, shown here in the garb of a thirteenth century Pope, the immediate successor.

Melchizedek is the first and one of the best statues. He wears a priestly garment bound at the waist by a knotted girdle, and on his head a Papal tiara of the thirteenth century, the lower part suggestive of a crown, for both as king and priest he prefigures Christ.

In one hand he holds a censer, in the other the bread which he offered to Abraham. His grave features and absorbed mysterious gaze admirably shadow forth that most enigmatic personage, Melchizedek, King of Salem, the Priest of the Most High God, who met Abraham returning after the slaughter of the kings, and blessed him, to whom also Abraham gave tithes; Melchizedek, the King of Righteousness as his name implies, and the King of Peace also, without father, without mother, without descent, having neither beginning of days nor end of life, who was the forerunner and prototype of Jesus 'made an high priest for ever after the order of Melchizedek.'

Christ, as the Son offered by the Father and the sacrificial Ram, is prefigured in the neighbouring statue of Abraham with his son Isaac, whom he holds ready bound for the sacrifice. Beneath his feet is the ram caught in the bush. His face, which, with its flowing beard and prolonged nose, is distinctly of the Jewish type, is averted, for he is looking up at the angel who bade him stay his hand. Moses, trampling on the golden calf and carrying in his left hand the table of the law and a column about which the brazen serpent entwines, stands next to Abraham, and likewise symbolises Christ, the Deliverer and the Law-Giver. His right hand points to the serpent and suggests the words of our Lord himself, 'Even as Moses lifted up the serpent in the wilderness even so must the Son of Man be lifted up, that whosoever believeth in Him should not perish but have eternal life.' Next comes Samuel, clad in a garment which resembles the *taled* of the Jews, preparing to sacrifice and to anoint Saul, who is represented by the small kneeling figure beneath. This statue illustrates 1 Samuel ix. Lastly David, crowned in royal majesty, carries the lance and crown of thorns, instruments of that passion which he had so minutely prophesied in the Psalms. The lion at the base alludes to David's answer to Saul when he beheld Goliath, or else is the ramping and roaring lion of the Messianic psalms. Equally with David, Isaiah foretold in detail the events of the Gospels, and he, clad, like most of the other personages that remain, in a long robe and mantle, occupies the niche of the right bay facing David. The stem which was to come forth from Jesse rises at his feet, and the prophet points to the flower which should grow from that root.

Jeremiah is at his side, the sublime chanter of lamentations, bearing a beautifully-wrought Greek cross and recalling to mind his own words, 'Is it nothing to you all ye who pass by? behold and see if there be any sorrow like unto my sorrow.'

Next to him the aged Simeon caresses the young Christ whose sufferings he had foreseen.

S. John the Baptist, the prince of monks, is the link between these forerunners of Christ and His Apostles. His ascetic figure is revealed beneath his rough raiment of skins, for, in accordance to the usual practice of the Middle Ages, but not of former or more recent times, he is represented in the Apostolic costume of tunic and mantle, and as with the Apostles his feet are bare. He tramples under foot a dragon which typifies Vice, not a locust as some suppose. The extraordinary tenderness with which he clasps to his breast the lamb, which is Jesus, the lively expression of his worn and wrinkled countenance and his emaciated body, proclaim this to be one of the finest statues of the Cathedral porches. Lastly comes S. Peter, as we have described him above. He stands upon a rock in reference to the words of our Lord, 'Thou art Peter, and on this rock will I build My Church.'

All the details, the costumes and ornaments of these statues are wrought with extraordinary skill and minuteness, so that, like that of the western porch, the work might almost seem that of a jeweller, not a mason.

To the right of Melchizedek and to the left of S. Peter are two large figures which are related to the scheme of the central doorway. For they are Elijah and Elisha, who were the types of the ascension and the resurrection of Jesus Christ. Elijah is shown mounting to heaven in his chariot of fire; Elisha, promising to the Shunamite the son whom he afterwards raised from the dead.

In the tympanum of the doorway we have the Death, the Resurrection and the Crowning of the Blessed Mary, a subject which has received its most perfect treatment at Reims. It will be noticed that the Virgin is represented as quite young, for, as Michelangelo finely explained, when he had painted his Lady of the Seven Sorrows, virtue confers an eternal youth. Above are angels censing. The figures have been sadly mutilated. In the splay of the vaulting the first row contains a multitude of angels with halos, bearing censers, torches, books and palms, witnesses of the triumph of the Virgin. The next four rows exhibit the ancestors of Mary according to the flesh and according to the spirit—the prophets, that is, who announced her. Together they form a tree of Jesse growing from between the feet of Jesse below on the left. Compare it with the tree in the twelfth-century Jesse window of the Porte Royale and you will see that, though it follows the same order, the stone tree is even more complete. It includes the greater and minor prophets, with Judith, Esther and Deborah, and, beginning from the fourth row, the twenty-eight ancestors of the Virgin, mostly as described in the first chapter of the Gospel of S. Matthew. The last two rows translate into stone the first chapter of Genesis, giving the story of the Creation of the World and of Adam and Eve in the Garden of Eden in a series of admirable tableaux which explain themselves sufficiently. In the gable is Christ surrounded by angels.

Large statues of benefactors of the Cathedral and of the prophets Jephthah and Zachariah adorn the piers in front. The first two on the left are Philippe Hurepel, Count of Boulogne, and his wife Mahaut. The statue of the latter is particularly beautiful, the expression full of life and grace, the costume of striking simplicity. Next to these two there used to be, before the Revolution, statues of Philippe-Auguste, King of France, and Richard Cœur-de-Lion, rivals in the field but united here in their generous devotion to Notre-Dame de Chartres. The decoration of the plinths of these two piers is different from that of the others; it is Anglo-Norman in character, and the name RŌBIR cut hereon is probably that of the Norman sculptor who made them under the patronage of Richard in Normandy.

The brackets of these four statues are storied with incidents from the life of David—(1) a group representing the young shepherd being anointed by Saul, (2) David chasing away the melancholy of Saul, (3) David armed before Saul, (4) David and Goliath, (5) David triumphing over Goliath. The armour of Goliath is extremely curious.

On the right is a prophet in the Jewish Schimla, who may be Jephthah or perhaps Ezekiel, and next to him Louis VIII. and Isabella, his daughter, pious Sister of S. Louis. She is habited as a nun, for she founded the Convent of Longchamps, and died there, its abbess.

Zachariah, father of S. John the Baptist, comes next, and on the brackets beneath are six exquisite scenes from the life of Samuel. The prophet is shown with Hannah and Elkanah taking a lamb to Eli, serving in the Temple, beholding a vision. The remaining scenes are those of the capture of the Ark by the Philistines, the fall of Dagon, and the return of the Ark.

The second part of the north porch is the left bay, and it is consecrated to the life and virtues of the Virgin. On the splays of the porch wall are represented on either side the Annunciation and the Visitation, whilst on the left is Isaiah, the prophet of the Incarnation, on the right Daniel. The heads of Isaiah and Gabriel are broken, and indeed most of this bay is in a deplorable state. Of the surviving figures those of Mary, of Elizabeth and Daniel are rightly considered masterpieces. They are beautiful in pose, and their draperies are skilfully arranged, distinctly Greek in feeling. About them there seems to blow the wind that comes before the dawn of the Renaissance.

The tympanum is filled with the familiar scenes of the first Christmastide, the birth of Christ, the Announcement to the Shepherds, the Adoration of the three Magi, traditionally named Gaspar, Melchior and Balthasar, and their gifts of gold for the King, incense for the God, and myrrh for the Man who should die for men. Lastly comes the scene of their warning in a dream. These scenes are lit by a row of torch-bearing angels. The second and part of the third row of the vaulting contains the ten virgins of the parable, on the left the five foolish, with elegant garments and worldly, licentious faces, and lamps turned upside down; the five wise on the right, modest and veiled, hold their flaming lamps upright. The rest of the third row represents the battle of the Vices and the Virtues; Wisdom carrying an open book, and at her feet Folly nude and eating a stone; Justice with her sword and a balance, which the Injustice whom she tramples on vainly endeavours to disturb; Christian Strength in full armour, with Cowardice, a terror-stricken soldier, grovelling before her; Temperance caressing a dove, and at her feet Luxury, the abandoned courtesan. On the right hand, after these cardinal virtues, are the three theological virtues, Faith, Hope and Charity, and also Humility, with their corresponding vices. Faith catches in a chalice the blood of a lamb upon the altar, whilst Infidelity, with bandaged eyes, cowers below; the hands of Hope are clasped and she gazes heavenward, but Despair lies at her feet and has plunged a sword into her breast; Charity gives her garment to clothe the naked, but Avarice plays with pieces of gold and hides them about her person; Humility holds in her hand a dove, which is her symbol, and at her feet Pride has fallen. These Virtues and Vices are succeeded by a row of twelve queenly figures, which symbolise the Fruits of the Spirit. They are a translation of the passage in Galatians (v. 22) in which S. Paul enumerates them.

More remarkable still and more charming are the statuettes which fill the fifth row and which translate the doctrine of the mediæval theologians with regard to the active life and the contemplative life. These, according to S. Gregory, were typified by the two wives of Jacob, Leah and Rachel,[81] and again by Martha and Mary. Here, on the left, the active life is portrayed with extraordinary vividness and delicacy in the character of the virtuous woman described in the last chapter of the Book of Proverbs. 'She seeketh wool and flax and worketh willingly with her hands ... she layeth her hands to the spindle and her hands hold the distaff.' The six degrees of the contemplative life are shown on the right-hand side in the form of a veiled woman praying before reading, opening her book to read, reading in her book of hours, closing it immediately, comprehending the lesson she has learnt, and thereafter rapt in ecstasy.

At the ends of the moulding of the vaulting are two statuettes which seem to be connected with the subject of the active and the contemplative life; they are, a cobbler cutting leather and a monk reading.

In the last and outermost row were sculptured, for the first and only time, the fourteen Heavenly Beatitudes first described by S. Anselm, 'In heaven the bodies of the just shall enjoy the seven beatitudes, which are Beauty, Swiftness, Strength, Liberty, Health, Pleasure, Longevity; and likewise the souls of the just shall receive the seven beatitudes, which are Wisdom, Friendship, Concord, Honour, Power, Security and Joy.'

Two statues personifying the Synagogue and the Church were in front of this bay till 1793, and on the pedestals of these and the two other statues which were on these piers, but of which one only, that of Philippe III. le Hardi, remains, traces of a series of Virtues trampling the Vices underfoot are still visible.

On the wall of the right-hand bay, which is devoted to the persons of the Old Testament who prefigured and foretold the Messiah and His

Mother, are six splendid statues representing Balaam, the Queen of Sheba and Solomon on the left, and, on the right, Jesus, son of Sirach, Judith and Joseph. Each of these statues and the figures on which they rest demand careful study, but especially the statue of Joseph, the precursor of Christ in his persecution, his selling into captivity, and his deliverance of the people. A beardless figure with curling hair and a simple, open countenance, with Pharaoh's ring upon his finger and the sceptre of authority in his hand, and about him a robe of fine linen, he treads underfoot the bronzed dragon who is pouring into the eager ear of Potiphar's wife his foul suggestions. With extraordinary delicacy and reserve the artist has succeeded in making every line of this portrait—for a portrait it must be—express all the innocence and charm, all the passionate purity of youth.

In the tympanum, over the door, is, first, Job on his hearth, with a demon, for the trials and patience of Job foreshadowed the agony and triumph of Christ, and, second, the Judgment of Solomon, the prototype of Him who is called the Sun of Justice. The vaulting above contains twelve angels doing homage to Christ, then, on the left, the story of Samson, the story of Esther, and, on the right, the story of Gideon and that of Judith. The fourth row tells the story of Tobias, and on the outer edge are the twelve months of the year with the corresponding signs of the Zodiac and the allegorical representations of summer and winter, which should be compared with those of the western porch (*see* p. 130).

Four large statues on the arcade outside this bay represent Ferdinand, King of Castile, a great benefactor of the Cathedral, who was canonised 1671, two hundred years after his death, and whose body is

***Interior North Porch.***
***Facing Page 221.***

preserved at Seville. He is accompanied by a Judge of Israel, Barak, M. Bulteau suggests. On the right pier Tobias accompanies S. Louis. The beautiful and appropriate portrait of that devoted patron of Notre-Dame was fashioned in all probability shortly after the pilgrimage which he made to Chartres in 1260, walking, in spite of extreme fatigue, barefoot all the way from Nogent-le-Roi. He is represented, it will be noticed, with bare feet here, either in allusion to this pilgrimage, or to his annual practice of visiting barefoot, and in penitential garb, all the churches of any town in which he might be on Good Friday. But there is another incident in his life to which reference may be intended. In 1239 he and his brother Robert carried barefoot into Paris the instruments of the Passion which he had redeemed from Venice.

On the graceful supports of these four statues are allegorical representations of the arts and sciences: Agriculture, personified by Adam, Abel and Cain; Music, by Jubal, with his lyre; Metalwork, by Tubal-Cain; Medicine, by Hippocrates; Geometry and Architecture, by Archimedes; Painting, by Apelles; Philosophy, by Aristotle; Magic, by a wizard and a dragon. These, it will be seen, unlike those of the western porch, are not merely representations of the seven liberal arts taught since the sixth century. The artist of S. Louis's day is breaking away from the old tradition. He invents new types; he is looking for a new system. Lastly, on the western side of the porch, are two very beautiful statues, the one of S. Potentian, the other of S. Modesta (*see* p. 18). Below the former is a scene in which he, together with SS. Altin and Eodald are baptizing a neophyte, and another in which the Roman Governor, Quirinus, in spite of the intercession of his daughter Modesta, condemns him to be cast into chains. Below the graceful and impressive figure of Modesta are several bas-reliefs of incidents in her life. They are much worn and mutilated, but you can discern an angel rising from the Well of the Martyrs, the martyrdom of Modesta, and a pair of angels carrying her soul up to heaven.

We will now walk round to the south side of the Cathedral, turning, as it were, the last leaf of the Bible of Chartres. And, indeed, the south porch[82] may well be regarded as a postscript to the story of the windows and the porches; not only because it is later in date—it was begun under Philippe-Auguste, at the expense of Pierre Mauclerc, Count of Dreux, and only finished in the reign of Philippe le Bel—but also because the subject of it is a variant of that of the Porte Royale. It is the Glorification of our Lord again, but here in His office as Supreme Judge and in the presence of His saints and elect.

Like the northern one, the south porch is evidently an afterthought, and, like it, it consists of three open porticoes, corresponding to the doors of the transept, and supported in front by six piers, which are treated with amazing originality and skill. Enormous lintels of Berchères stone connect the vestibule with the doorway. These have had to be strengthened, as on the other side, by iron ties. Though only a couple of yards or so broader than the north porch, the south porch, thanks to the open space in which it stands, and to its advantageous position on top of seventeen steps, appears much larger and more imposing. The bays and the vestibule are peopled by 783 figures, in which the visitor will note the advance in art made by the sculptors since they took in hand the statuary of the western and, again, of the northern porch. The anatomy of these figures and the treatment of their drapery are infinitely more correct; the pose is more probable, the work more polished, the whole undoubtedly much more beautiful according to all the canons of classical art. But quite as undoubtedly there has been a loss of charm as well as a gain in the technique. The figures, if they are less crude, are also less expressive. The superb Christ of the central bay, classic in its calm and regularity, is not so convincing, so unforgettable as the Christ surrounded by the winged beasts of the western façade. Even the magnificent effigies of S. Theodore and S. George have not the same haunting loveliness as the earlier nameless kings and queens, which are ill-drawn, and unknown indeed, but alive for ever in their human simplicity.

The majestic statue of Christ, trampling under foot a lion and dragon, which I have mentioned, is on the face of the central bay, and holds the place of honour as the Master in the midst of His Apostles. On His right is the bay of the martyrs, whose strength He is, and He is the Light of the confessors in the bay on His left. His divine kingship is suggested by the representation of Him in the upper part of the central bay, judging the living and the dead.

Beneath the central statue are the figures of Pierre Mauclerc, Count of Dreux, and Alice, his wife, who spent some 10,000,000 francs upon this porch and the rose window above. They are represented in two scenes, praying and being married, but in both giving bread to the poor.

The Christ is surrounded by His Apostles. On His right, S. Peter, with a cross and two keys, tramples under foot Simon the magician. Next to S. Peter comes S. Andrew, his brother, clasping the cross of his martyrdom to his breast, and, beneath his feet, the proconsul who condemned him to death; S. Philip, with a sword, and, beneath, the King of Hierapolis, who crucified him; S. Thomas, with the sword of his martyrdom, standing upon the Indian King who gave him to the priests to be cut in twain; and similarly with swords, and trampling on their persecutors, S. Matthew and S. Simon. Opposite are S. Paul and the beardless John, the former holding and pointing to the sword of his martyrdom, and trampling down Nero, the latter with the (broken) palm of his martyrdom and the book of his Gospel, and, beneath him, Aristodemus, priest of Diana, offering to him a vase of poisonous snakes; S. James, the brother of John, comes next, and, below him, is Herod Agrippa, who put him to the sword; then S. James the Less, and the Jew who slew him with a club, S. Bartholomew and S. Jude and their persecutors beneath. All these statues are of great beauty and in the grand manner, varied in pose and movement, and correct in design.

Above them, in the tympanum of the bay, is Christ enthroned as the Judge, on the great and dreadful day of the Lord, the Virgin and S. John on either side of Him intercede for sinners, and around Him six angels bear the instruments of the Passion. Below are two scenes—S. Michael weighing a soul, and the separation of the just from the unjust. On the right of the archangel is the glorious army of the elect, clad in long robes, and wearing an expression of serene happiness. They are being led by guardian angels to the abodes of everlasting joy. On the continuation of the lintel are several types of the elect being led to Abraham's bosom. On the left of S. Michael is a lively picture of the fate of the wicked, the condemned of every class are being dragged by horrible demons to the mouth of hell, a dragon with flaming jaws, and on the continuation of the lintel also various types of sinners are meeting with a like fate.

On either side of the central figure of Christ the second row represents the Resurrection of the Dead, and, above this, are nine choirs of angels, then twenty-eight pairs of statuettes, representing the prophets of the Old Testament; and, lastly, fourteen admirable figures of Christian virgins who have fought the good fight of chastity, and carry in their hands, as symbols of their purity, fleurs-de-lis.

The Virgin Mother, holding the child Jesus on her knees, sits enthroned in a niche of the gable, whilst two archangels cense. The square pillars continue the main thesis, and carry on one side the twenty-four elders of the Apocalypse and their instruments of music, and, on the other side, the twelve Vices and twelve corresponding Virtues, in accordance with which the Last Judgment is decided. Here, then, we have once more, as on the north porch, Faith and her cross opposed to Idolatry and her idol, Hope to Despair, Charity to Avarice; Chastity, with her curious symbol, the Phœnix, confronts Luxury, Prudence, Folly, Humility, Pride. These appear on the western and southern sides of the left pillar; the series is continued on the one opposite. Docility, with an ox, faces, on the south side, Intractability, Mildness, Anger, Strength, Cowardice; and, on the east face, Perseverance, Inconstancy, Temperance with a camel, Drunkenness, Concord, Discord.

The left or western bay is entirely concerned with the noble army of martyrs, of whom the eight most honoured at Chartres, resting on storied bases, and beneath rich canopies of the kind called heavenly Jerusalem, adorn the walls. They are, on the left, S. Laurence, S. Clement, S. Stephen, and S. Theodore. The latter is clad in a coat of mail, of the time of S. Louis and the Crusaders. The statue is beautifully modelled and splendidly wrought, and forms a noble counterpart to the magnificent portrait of S. George opposite, who, likewise accoutred for battle, is trampling on the wheel of his martyrdom. The other martyrs on the right-hand wall are S. Vincent, S. Denis, and the S. Piat of whom we have spoken above (p. 44), and the outside of whose chapel, with the beautiful staircase connecting it with the main body of the Cathedral, we can see beyond the apse on our right.

**S. GEORGE**
*(From the South Porch)*

The story of S. Stephen is retold in the tympanum and the first row of the vaulting; in the next five rows are twenty-eight statuettes, representing the hierarchy of martyrs; in the sixth, the parable of the wise and foolish virgins reappears, and in the gable is S. Anne seated, holding a vase, in which is a lily, the symbol of purity.

The square pillar on the left hand, which helps to support the vaulting, gives us twenty-four scenes from the Golden Legend of the deaths of martyrs. On the east face, at the top, is S. Thomas of Canterbury, whose secretary and friend, John of Salisbury, one of the most attractive characters and typical minds of the Middle Ages, was Bishop of Chartres the last three years of his life. Among the other martyrs are several whose names occur in the story of Chartres—S. Blaise, S. Leger, S. Vincent, S. Laurence, S. Chéron; on the south face, S. John the Baptist, S. Denys of Athens, S. Saturnin, S. Piat, S. Procopius, S. Symphorian; on the west face, S. Calixtus, S. Cyprian, S. Ignatius, S. Theodore, S. Eustace, S. Gervais and S. Protais;

on the north, S. Clement, S. Potentian, S. Lambert, S. Vitus and S. Modesta, S. Bacchus and S. Quentin.

The right-hand bay is devoted to the confessors, and corresponds in arrangement to that of the one we have just left. Eight large statues fill the walls; on the west, S. Nicholas, S. Ambrose, S. Léon and S. Laumer (the latter a fourteenth-century insertion); and on the right or east, S. Martin of Tours, S. Jerome, S. Gregory the Great, S. Avitus (also fourteenth century). The tympanum gives the story of the lives of S. Martin and S. Nicholas. In the vaulting above S. Léon the legend of S. Giles is told, and in the outermost row of the vaulting are ten of the Apostles, crowning five rows in which is represented the whole hierarchy of confessors—warriors, monks, laymen, priests, abbots, bishops, archbishops, kings, emperors and popes, all wearing the halo of sanctity. In the gable the Blessed Mary is seated holding a book, supported by Gabriel and another archangel.

The pier on the right gives various incidents from the lives of confessors: on the west face, S. Léon praying at the tomb of S. Peter; S. Martin blessing a man who has threatened to strike him; S. Lubin (p. 36) giving extreme unction to S. Calétric; S. Avit, Abbot of Micey, reposing; S. Anthony reading the Scriptures and a devil appearing; S. Benedict seated and reading. On the south face is S. Gregory the Great writing his commentaries, inspired by the Holy Spirit in the form of a dove, and his secretary Peter behind a thick curtain; S. Remi consecrating and S. Solemnis blessing Chlovis; S. Laumer healing the Abbess Ulfrade; S. Calais or Karilef digging (the cloak in which, whilst he was working in his vineyard, a wren nested and laid an egg, is suspended from a neighbouring tree); S. Hilarion visiting S. Anthony. On the east face, S. Sylvester baptizing Constantin; S. Martin restoring a child to life near Chartres; S. Calétric visiting S. Lubin; S. Benedict blessing the poisoned cup (appearing thus for the second time on this pier, first as a hermit in the Cave of Subiaco, and now as Abbot of Vico-Varo, where the monks objecting to his strict rule vainly endeavoured to poison him); S. Lié or Lœtus of Pithiviers seated, and at his feet the owner of the forest to which the holy priest retired, and which afterwards became the site of the village Saint-Lié, in the department of Loiret. The gift of this forest to the saint as a dwelling-place is symbolised by the faggot which the owner is depositing; S. Armel exorcising a dragon; a Breton saint, born in Great Britain 482, and founder of the monastery at Plouarzel.

On the north face of the pier, S. Ambrose converting S. Augustine; S. Martin healing a deaf mute at Chartres; S. Marcel of Paris leading a dragon in his stole; S. Giles casting out a devil from a man at Athens; S. Jerome translating the Holy Scriptures; S. Martinien, the hermit of Cæsarea, with the penitent courtesan Zoe.

Above the porch, in the Gallery of the Kings of Judah, are eighteen life-size statues arrayed in the royal vestments of the time of S. Louis. They are the ancestors of Christ, and that was the only merit of some of them, as their history is given us in the Books of Chronicles and Kings. Varied in age and pose but similar in costume, they are, where they stand, sufficiently decorative, but they cannot compare with the kings and queens of the western porch.

Regarded merely as works of art, a large proportion of the two thousand odd statues in the porches of Chartres deserve almost as much praise as they excite interest. But when we consider the intentions of the artists who made them, and remember the conditions under which they were wrought, as they have been suggested in the previous chapters, we shall be able to appreciate them with a more perfect sympathy and to judge them with a broader understanding. The sculptors of the thirteenth century did not aim exclusively at sensuous beauty or at anatomical perfection, and they did not attain it. They were concerned with psychology as well as and even more than anatomy, and they strove to give by their art not only pleasure but instruction also. The perfection of the human body was not so obvious to them as the imperfection of the human soul. For them the flesh was only desirable when it exhaled the odour of virtue, when it was inspired by the sympathetic sadness which springs from the consciousness of frailty and resignation to the burdens of this life, combined with a burning desire for the eternal life to come, or when it was rendered sweet by the holy joyousness of spirit which springs from peace, pity and love. They added, then, to the science of art, the science of ideas. And if, therefore, mediæval sculpture never rose to the height of artistic perfection achieved by a Phidias or Praxiteles, yet their work remains fulfilled with a quality not possessed by any Apollo, the charm of a spiritual intelligence.

DIMENSIONS OF THE CATHEDRAL.

|   |   | ft. | ins. |
|---|---|---|---|
| 1. Total Length— | Exterior, | 506 | 4 |
|  | Interior, | 426 | 5 |

This is less than that of the Cathedrals of Le Mans, Reims, Amiens, Bordeaux and Rouen.

| 2. Length of Nave, | 240 | 4 |
|---|---|---|

| | | |
|---|---:|---:|
| 3. Length of Choir, | 121 | 5 |
| 4. Length of Transept (largest in France), | 211 | 6 |
| 5. Width of West Front, | 156 | 0 |
| 6. Width of Nave (largest in France), | 53 | 6 |
| 7. Length of Crypt, | 366 | 6 |
| 8. Width of Crypt, | 18 | 0 |
| 9. Height of Vaulting of Nave, | 122 | 3 |
| 10. Height of Vaulting in Aisles, | 45 | 6 |
| 11. North Tower (Clocher Neuf), | 377 | 4 |
| 12. South Tower (Clocher Vieux), | 349 | 6 |
| 13. Diameter of the three large Rose Windows, | 44 | 0 |

# CHAPTER VIII

# The Birth of the Bourgeoisie and the English Occupation

'Servanti Civem querna corona datur.'
*Town Motto.*[83]

WHILST the Cathedral was a-building, events had happened at Chartres which serve to indicate the importance of the position attained by the town in feudal France by virtue of the power of its Counts, the greatness of its Bishops and the prosperity of its commerce. The legate, Pierre Léon, who was afterwards to become the anti-pope Anaclete, held a council here and, in 1130, the legitimate Pope sought refuge at Chartres, where Henry the First of England came to prostrate himself before him. As to the Counts, their greatness had been increased by the inheritance of the County of Champagne. They were not chary of using their strength to advance their own importance. Thibault the Great, son of Adèle, Countess of Chartres and daughter of William the Conqueror, allied himself with the King of England and waged continual warfare with the King of France. When his foreign ally died, Thibault's brother Stephen ascended the English throne, and he himself became Duke of Normandy.

*Gable of the Old Hôtel de Ville*

His eldest son, Henry, was one of those who took the Cross when S. Bernard came to Chartres, preaching the Crusade of 1145. On that memorable occasion the Abbot of Clairvaux was elected, by acclaim in the

Cathedral, Generalissimo of the Christian forces. But with the example of the disastrous leadership of Peter the Hermit before his eyes, S. Bernard wisely declined. 'Who am I,' he wrote to the Pope, 'that I should order the lines of battle, and go out before the faces of armed men, or what is more remote from my profession?' Count Henry gained great renown in the Holy Land, and when at last, after fifty years of opposition to his King, the old Count died, he left to his valorous eldest son the County of Champagne, and Chartres and Blois passed to his second son, Thibault, owing homage to Henry. This Thibault, surnamed Le Bon, aided the King against Henry Plantagenet, and was rewarded by being made Seneschal of France. The amicable relations which were now at last established between the race of Thibault and the throne were still further strengthened by the marriage of Louis-le-Jeune with Alice of Champagne, the sister of Thibault, and mother, by this marriage, of Philippe-Auguste. Thibault himself, through the good offices of the Queen, obtained the hand of the King's daughter by his first wife. The alliance thus consolidated bore fruit for the King when he took the offensive against the King of England in 1167. For the troops of Chartres and of Champagne followed the royal standard on that occasion. A few years before, a younger brother of Count Thibault, William of the White Hands, had succeeded Robert-le-Breton as Bishop of Chartres, and he soon became the adviser of the princes whose relative he was. Philippe-Auguste used to speak of him as 'the watchful eye of his Council.' Together with Count Henry and the King, he received the exiled Thomas of Canterbury with open arms, and succeeded in effecting a reconciliation between him and the English King, whose imperious will he had thwarted. The reconciliation was hollow. Before long France was filled with horror at the news of the murder of À Becket. Louis demanded vengeance from the Pope: Count Thibault wrote to the Roman pontiff that the 'dogs of the Court had spilled the blood of the just'; the Bishop of Chartres excommunicated all the Continental possessions of the King of England.

But it was not till three years later that hostilities broke out between France and England, when the three sons of Henry Plantagenet—Henry, Geoffrey and Richard Cœur-de-Lion—united with Louis and the Princes of Champagne against their father. That redoubtable coalition of Frenchmen, Chartrains, Champenois and Angevins was, however, no match for the English King. Beaten near Verneuil, Louis was obliged to make terms with his enemy in the following year (1174).

The blood of the martyred À Becket had sprinkled his friend and secretary, John of Salisbury. 'By the grace of God and the merits of the martyr, S. Thomas,' as he himself expresses it, he was called to succeed William *aux Blanches-Mains* in the bishopric of Chartres. The life of the great writer was nearly over when he came there, bringing with him, as a gift to the treasure of the Cathedral, a phial containing some drops of the blood of the master whom he had so faithfully served at Canterbury and followed in exile, and the dagger with which that master had been murdered. But, short as was his tenure of the See, he left his mark upon the history of Chartres. He overthrew the exorbitant pretensions of the secular lords who claimed as *choses* of their domain all serfs set free by the Church, and thus rendered illusory the enfranchisement of ecclesiastical serfs, and he obtained for clerks brought to justice that they should henceforth not be condemned to undergo trial by ordeal, whether of duel, hot iron, or hot or cold water.

Philosopher and man of affairs, secretary of Archbishop Theobald, intimate friend of Nicholas Breakspear (the only Englishman who has ever filled the chair of S. Peter), and the devoted adherent of Thomas à Becket, John was born at Salisbury, but his enthusiasm for culture he owed to his training as a youth under Abelard at Paris, and in the school of Chartres. For that school still maintained the reputation which it had acquired under Fulbert. In his book *Metalogicus*, John, who has been termed the 'central figure of English learning' in his time, has left us a lively account of the method of teaching practised by Bernard Sylvester, 'the old man of Chartres, the most fruitful source of letters in all France,' and by his successors. The breadth of view, the sound common sense, and the lack of pedantry which characterise John of Salisbury's contributions to logic and to political thought are due, we may believe, not only to his practical training in the Archbishop's household at Canterbury, but also to the 'humane' teaching of Bernard and his school. John of Salisbury died in 1180, and was buried in the Monastery of S. Marie-de-Josaphat, now destroyed (*see* p. 98). His books he left to the Cathedral library. He was succeeded by his friend Pierre, Abbot of Celles, and afterwards of S. Remy, at Reims, with whom he had passed a great part of his exile, when the exquisite *chevet* there, one of the earliest bits of pointed architecture, was being built. This excellent bishop spent the two years of his episcopate in the execution of public works, the abolition of vexatious feudal customs, and the distribution of alms. At his own charges he constructed the town walls from the Porte des Épars to the Church of S. Foy, and repaved the streets. He obtained from the Count a modification in the exercise of the right of Banvin. For, according to usage, it was forbidden to sell wine during a period of time called the ban, in order to give the lord an opportunity of selling his wine without competition. Thibault consented to abolish this custom, whilst exacting a small toll from those who sold wine in inns during the ban. And the charity of Pierre de Celles was so abounding that, at his funeral, the crowd flung itself upon his coffin and embraced his corpse. His successor was Renaud de Mouçon, under whom the Cathedral was built. He, like Thibault, had taken the Cross in 1189, but, unlike the Count, returned home alive and well.

The thirteenth century saw yet another Count of Chartres lay down his life in battle with the Infidels. For Louis, who had been made King of Bithynia by the Emperor Baldwin after the sack of Constantinople (1204), was attacked by the Bulgarians before Andrinople and perished heroically. Jean de Friaize, seeing that he had been twice severely wounded, exhorted him to retire. 'Nay,' he cried. 'Leave me to fight and die. God grant that I may never be reproached with having fled the battle!' His son took part in the crusade against the Moors and also in that other holy war, more popular because less distant, which Simon de Montfort conducted. Following their Count and their Bishop, thousands marched south to massacre the Albigenses, because they entertained the heresy of the Manichæans, which admits the existence of two gods, identified with the principles of good and evil.

Meantime, whilst bishops and counts were warring against Turks, Moors and Albigenses, Chartres was left in the hands of the Countess Catherine, in whose name a marshal of her palace and a provost of the town administered justice. The jealousy between the Count's men and the *protégés* of the Chapter which was always smouldering broke out in a startling fashion about this time. The outbreak is worth mentioning, for it throws light upon the growing power and self-assertion of the people. Speaking generally, the tendency at this period was for the notable citizens of the town to become, under the title of *Avoués*, vassals or *protégés* of the Chapter, but the trades and corporations, revolting against the oppression of the *Avoués*, who tried to exact from them all the taxes and impositions laid upon the town, strove to secure their liberties and customs by rallying to the Count. On the pretext, then, of some injury done to a serf of the Countess by the Dean William, the people burst suddenly into the cloister and laid siege to the house of the Dean.

The Chapter demanded the intervention of the marshal and the provost, but those officers, instead of stopping the riot, incited the mob to break down the doors and smash the windows of the house. The Dean from the first had wisely taken refuge in the Cathedral, but his retainers, barricading themselves, returned the assaults of the rioters with a rain of tiles and faggots. Maddened by this resistance, the mob procured a heavy waggon, and using it as a battering-ram burst open the main entrance and sacked the house, hurling all the furniture out of windows.

Next day the outraged Chapter excommunicated the town and *banlieue*. No services were held; the altar of Notre-Dame was stripped of its ornaments; and even the curfew bell was not allowed to ring. Every day from the top of the jubé a priest pronounced the terrible curse known as 'the great excommunication, the anathema and fulmination.' At this solemn moment the candles were lit and the bells rung confusedly, and, as the priest finished his malediction, all became silent again and the candles were extinguished. But this demonstration, usually so effective, was received with shouts of laughter and screams of abuse.

However, a fire which destroyed the lower streets on the banks of the Eure filled the rioters with fear. The revolutionists, thinking that they beheld the finger of God, were ready to submit, but the Dean and Chapter had already summoned the King, who came incontinent to Chartres, and after inquiry ordered the Count's people to make *amende honorable* and to pay for the damage they had done. But the bishop returning from abroad was not satisfied, and at his request Phillippe-Auguste ordered the offenders to pay a heavy fine and to make *amende honorable* in full church, on a feast day, *nuds en chemise*, and bringing rods with which they were to be scourged before the altar of the Virgin. And this was actually done. Thus, says the chronicler, the Church by the aid of Heaven emerged from this tribulation.

But the quarrel between the two parties was not quenched. It broke out five years later, and was settled again to the disadvantage of the Counts. Later, in a collision between the *bourgeois* and the men attached to the Cathedral, two of the latter were killed. The murderers were pursued by some canons and protected by others. One canon was assassinated by his brethren. A new excommunication was pronounced upon the town. The synod appointed to judge the matter, not thinking itself safe in the presence of the growing power of the Third Estate, removed to Mantes. The banishment of the murderers and the intervention of S. Louis succeeded in producing an apparent calm. But the storm soon broke out afresh, and the people plundered and the Chapter excommunicated as vigorously as ever.

Troublesome as these perpetual conflicts between the rival authorities were, it is to be observed that the liberty of the cloister and the privileges of the clergy, which were in dispute, were institutions which led to the emancipation of some Chartrain families formerly subject to the Counts. The ecclesiastical corporations, in fact, set an example in this matter of enfranchisement which the Counts were slow to follow. And it was probably due to this antagonism that the feudal lords of Chartres delayed for so long the grants of a communal charter to the town.

It was not till the King Philippe-le-Bel bought the County of Chartres from Jeanne, the widow of S. Louis's son, Pierre de France, and gave it to his own brother, Charles de Valois (1293), that the dispute was finally closed. Three years later the town received its charter and the *Bourgeoisie* began to come into its own. The granting of the charter was a business transaction. The need of money was great in France. The differences of the King with the Pope, with England and the Flemings, rendered it imperative that he should prepare for war. Under the new conditions, when the King's domain included

**Courtyard in the Old Hotel de Ville**

two-thirds of all France and the days of feudalism had passed away, it was necessary both to maintain a fleet and to pay mercenaries. Philip, whose short-sighted methods of raising money had already got him into difficulties with Flanders and the Church, now sent his men through the 'good towns of France' to collect contributions. 'But,' says Souchet, the old historian of Chartres, 'the people of Paris, Rouen, Orleans and other cities rose and slew the commissioners who prosecuted their charge with more violence than was needful,' and the contemporary *Chronique de la Saint-Magloire* records:—

'En Normandie et en Chartrain
De ce suis je trestot certain
Que en France, que en Champaigne
Il n'y a nul qui ne s'en plaigne
Des coustumes qu'estoient levées
Sur blé, sur vin et sur denrées.'

In these circumstances, therefore, Count Charles of Valois, when he wished to raise money in Chartres to aid his royal brother, found that there was only one way of doing it and that was by granting to the citizens, who, as we have seen, had long been restive because they were subject to all kinds of feudal charges and services of which the surrounding towns had been freed, a kind of Charter of *Commune*. For a cash consideration of 12,000 *livres tournois*, he confirmed several usages which were already by tacit consent practised, and he compounded for the annual tribute paid to the Counts by the town. It would be interesting to quote this document in full, but I must be content to give a summary of it. Shortly, it provided that the citizens should in future be exempt from paying the Count the annual tribute of £400, and exempt also, unless in cases of pressing necessity, from *Taille*, *Ost* and *Chevauchée*; their horses were not to be impressed for the use of the Count, their personal liberty was to be respected and, for criminals, before their trial, bail allowed after a certain period of imprisonment. Lastly, the citizens were authorised to assemble and elect *Procureurs* or Governors for the needs and necessities of the town after the form and manner of the citizens of Orléans. The Count also undertook to make good the use and custom of the town by which contracting parties in case of dispute were judged exclusively by local courts.

Charters usually promised more than they gave. In spite of remonstrances, the citizens did have to supply considerable sums in tribute from time to time in the ensuing centuries. Whether under the name of loans, or advances, or *octrois*, Kings like François I. and Henry IV. bled the merchants freely, and, if they protested too loudly, quickly brought them to their senses by the threat of force. But, in the meantime, whilst Charles de Valois, with the aid of the Chartrain contribution, was asserting the rights of his wife to the throne of Constantinople, or earning, at Florence, a place in Dante's *Inferno*, the town of Chartres, profiting by his absence, was quietly organising and ameliorating its administration.

The development of the municipality and the subsequent absorption of the domain of Chartres by the Crown by no means diminished the loyalty of its citizens. A worthy reception was given to Philippe-le-Bel when he came with his son, the boy Prince Charles, after his victory over the Flemish at Mons-en-Puelle, to render thanks and offer his armour at the shrine of the Vierge-Noire. The King also founded in commemoration of his victory a service in honour of Notre-Dame-de-la-Victoire. Down to the year 1793 the martial ex-voto of the royal father and son was shown from the pulpit on each anniversary of the defeat of the Flemings. In that year, however, the rich armour was stripped of the precious metals with which it was adorned. The gold was sent to the mint in Paris. The remaining fragments, pieced together, may be seen in the town museum (*see* p. 317). The example of Philippe-le-Bel was followed some years later by Philippe de Valois after his similar victory at Cassel. Fully armed, he rode into the Cathedral, knelt before the ancient statue, and left a thousand pounds to redeem the armour and steel which he had dedicated to the Virgin.

It was at this period that Chartres may be said to have reached the zenith of its prosperity. From this time forward we have to trace the process of its decay. For not only was Chartres, like all provincial towns, destined to suffer from the centralising tendency of the new era which succeeded that of feudalism, but it was also condemned by its position at the gates of Paris not to escape any of the catastrophes attendant upon the political and social developments of the day. Its history, however, becomes on that account more rather than less interesting. It was taken and retaken in the fifteenth century by the Armagnacs and the Burgundians, the English and the French, twice besieged in the sixteenth century by the Huguenots of the Prince de Condé and of Henry IV., and torn asunder by the passions of the Fronde in the seventeenth.

With the fourteenth century France entered upon a period of disaster and defeat. To the terrible ravages of the Black Death were added the horrors of famine, and the shame and devastation of the Hundred Years' War. The odds in that war, brought on by the continual intervention of the French King on behalf of Scotland and his obstinacy in the matter of Guienne, must have seemed at the first enormously in favour of France. But the vast superiority of the French in numbers and wealth was to prove useless in the face of the English yeomen. Crécy and Poitiers revealed the fact, bewildering to feudalism, that the superb bravery of French knighthood was futile when confronted with the English unmounted churl shooting his cloth-yard shaft. A cavalry charge in the face of those archers had no more chance of being successful than the charge of the Dervishes at Omdurman, or the later frontal attacks of our own infantry upon positions defended with magazine rifles. King John, taken prisoner at Poitiers, was carried captive to London, whilst in France, his routed soldiery turned into free companies of bandits, pillaged the country, and held the Chartrains prisoners for six months within their walls. The captive lords procured the sums needed for their ransom by extortion from the peasantry, who were driven by oppression and famine into frantic insurrection, butchering their lords and firing their castles. And Paris, impatient of the weakness and misrule of the Regency, rose in arms against the Crown.

Chartres in these days was compelled to strain every nerve to defend herself. A band of mercenaries was engaged to garrison the town. The Church of S. Saturnin, which was then in front of the Porte des Épars, and several convents, hospitals and mansions outside the walls, which might have given a foothold to the enemy, were destroyed. And in 1358 an order was issued that everyone should co-operate to fortify the town, 'which is the safety and salvation of all the people within and without.' Money for this purpose was raised by an extra tax upon beasts and skins. The ramparts of the town were now defended by a ditch and moat, and the gates, which had formerly been square and without ravelins, were modified and reconstructed in accordance with the more modern ideas of fortification, which the introduction of

*Porte Guillaume*

gunpowder and artillery had developed. Cannons were mounted on the walls. The Porte Drouaise, Porte S. Michel and the Porte des Épars have disappeared, but the Porte Guillaume remains to show us what they were like. This gate, named after the Vîdame Guillaume de Ferrières (1182), has been referred to the tenth century by local enthusiasts. But that date is too ambitious, except perhaps for the foundations. The inside of the gate, on the town side, and part of the vaulting belong to the year 1182, when the enlargement of the town *enceinte* took place and the perimeter of the walls and fortifications was extended, especially in the quarter between the Gates Châtelet, des Épars and S. Michel. But the outside of the Porte Guillaume, its façade very much as we have it now, was constructed after Poitiers. With its well-preserved crenellated parapet and machicoulis, and the openings for the play of the drawbridge, it presents a fine specimen of the military architecture of that period, and reminds one not a little of the contemporary towers of the Bastille at Paris (1369), a plan of which is in the town museum. The drawbridge used to connect the main towers of the gateway with an advanced fortification surrounded by the waters of the moat. The reader will gain a clear idea of the arrangement by referring to the old print reproduced on page 275. The strength of the Porte Guillaume was so great, that though dominated by the heights of S. Barthélémy and S. Chéron, it withstood all the assaults and batteries of besiegers, and the town was never taken from this side. Deservedly, therefore, it remains almost intact, though nearly all the rest of the fortifications of Chartres have been converted into boulevards and

'Its once grim bulwarks tamed to lover's walks
Look down unwatchful on the sliding Eure.'

Close under it, in old days, was a chapel dedicated to S. Fiacre, whither pilgrims afflicted by the distressing complaint known as Mal de S. Fiacre used to come in hopes of healing. But this has long since disappeared.

The new defences of Chartres were soon shown to be needed. Charles-le-Mauvais, a third competitor to the throne of France, plotted, but in vain, to surprise the town. Nor were his English allies more successful. For no sooner had the 'Jacquerie'[84] or peasant rising been crushed, than Edward again poured ravaging over the wasted lands of France, for the Dauphin refused to sanction the humiliating terms upon which the English King proposed to treat with the captive King John. The sufferings of the country around Chartres under the repeated ravages of the soldiery of all nations were now unspeakable. The enemy passed over the vineyards, the cornfields and the gardens of La Beauce like a storm, but they were only succeeded by the unpaid troops of the French. Plunder, indeed, was forbidden them, but plunder was their only means of living. 'Damoiselle Picorée' (Miss Plunder) 'sold me this' was the private soldier's proverbial explanation as he helped to accomplish the ruin of those he was supposed to defend. And at the inn, when the bill was being prepared, he would lay his sword with a clatter on the table and exclaim with intention, 'God send me no need of thee.' Whether there was need or no would depend usually upon the landlord's physical courage and capacity.

The bitter cry of France at this juncture is voiced by a document embodying a resolution of the canons.

'The persecution of the Church,' it is written, 'can only be compared to that of Jerusalem; there are no friends left to us, and those entrusted with our affairs do us more harm than our enemies. None dare quit the city: our houses are sacked, our property in the country burnt, our retainers killed or imprisoned. Our debtors do not pay their debts, and the voice of the Church is of no avail. Justice is departed from the land with the captive King. There is no more confidence in the royal safe-conduct, and that of the English is abhorred by the nobles and the people. We, therefore, the canons of Notre-Dame met in general assembly, decree that the fruits and emoluments of the prebends shall be shared in common among all the canons in order that each may have a morsel of bread to break; that each resident canon shall provide himself with arms, and maintain two knights and an armed page to resist the assaults of the enemy.'

But an event was shortly to happen which relieved France, for a while at least, from the presence of a foreign enemy. The misery of the land at last bent Charles to submission, and Edward III., weary of constant warfare in a famished country, at last concluded a peace. The incident which induced him to sign the Treaty of Brétigny was regarded by all his contemporaries as miraculous. The part which 'our Lady of Charters' played in this affair is recorded in the fascinating chronicles of Sir John Froissart. 'Edward,' he tells us, 'having put the realm of France into great tribulation, intended to lay siege to Paris after August and not to return again to England till he had France at his pleasure. Leaving garrisons, therefore, to make war in France, Champagne, Poictou, Ponthieu, Vexin, Normandy and all the realm of France, he came into "the good country of Beauce" with the idea of staying in Brittany till the vintage season. But he was led to change his mind.

'All this season the Duke of Normandy was at Paris, and his two brethren and the Duke of Orléans, their uncle, and their Counsels. They imagined well the courage of the King of England, and how that he and his men brought the realm of France into great poverty, and saw well how the realm could not long endure in that case, for the rents of the lords and of the churches were nigh lost in every part. As then there was a sage and discreet person Chancellor of France, called Sir William of Montague, Bishop of Terouenne, by whose counsel much of France was ruled, and good cause why, for ever his counsel was good and true, and with him there were two other clerks of great prudence, the Abbot of Cluny and the master of the Friars Preachers, called Sir Simon of Langres, a master in divinity; these two clerks, at the desire of the Duke of Normandy and of the whole Council of France, departed from Paris with certain articles of peace, and Sir Hugh of Geneve, Lord of Autun, in their company, and they went to the King of England, who rode in Beauce towards Galardon. These two clerks and two knights spake with the King and began to fall in treaty for a peace, to be had of him and his allies; to the which treaty the Prince of Wales, the Duke of Lancaster and the Earl of March were called. This treaty was not as then concluded, for it was long a-driving and always the King went forward. These ambassadors would not so leave the King, but still sued and followed on their purpose, for they saw how the French King was in so poor estate that the realm was likely to be in a great jeopardy, if the war continued a summer longer. And on the other side, the King of England required so great things and so prejudicial to the realm of France, that the lords would not agree thereto for their honours, so that all their treaty (the which endured a seventeen days, still following the King) they sent ever their process daily to the Duke of Normandy, to the city of Paris, ever desiring to have again answer what they should do farther, the which process was secretly and sufficiently examined in the Regent's chamber at

Paris, and answer was sent again by writing to them what they should do and what they should offer; and so these ambassadors were oftentimes with the King, as he went forward toward the city of Chartres, as in other places, and great offers they made to come to a conclusion of the war and to have a peace. To the which offers the King of England was hard hearted to agree unto, for his intention was to be King of France and to die in that estate. For if the Duke of Lancaster, his cousin, had not counselled him to have peace he would not have agreed thereunto. But he said to the King, "Sir, this war that ye make in the realm of France is right marvellous and right favourable for you: your men win great riches and ye lose your time, all things considered, or ye come to your intent, ye may hap to make war all the days of your life. Sir, I would counsel you (sith ye may leave the war to your honour and profit) accept the offers that ben made unto you, for, sir, you might lose more in a day than we have won in twenty years." Such fair and subtle words that the Duke of Lancaster said in good intention, and for weal of the King and all his subjects, converted the King by the grace of the Holy Ghost, who was chief worker in that case. For on a day, as the King was before Charters, there fell a case that greatly humbled the King's courage. For while these ambassadors were treating for this peace and had none agreeable answer, there fell suddenly such a tempest of thunder, lightning, rain and hail in the King's oost, that it seemed that the world should have ended: there fell from heaven such great stones that it slew men and horses, so that the most hardiest were abashed.

'Then the King of England beheld the Church of our Lady of Charters, and avowed devoutly to our Lady to agree to the peace, and, as it was said, he was as then confessed, and lodged in a village near to Charters, called Brétigny. And there were made certain compositions of peace, upon certain articles after ordained; and, the more firmly to be concluded by their ambassadors, and by the King of England and his Council, there was ordained, by good deliberation and advice, a letter called the Charter of Peace' (1360).

By this treaty the English King waived his claims on the crown of France and on the Duchy of Normandy; but, on the other hand, his Duchy of Aquitaine was not only restored to him, but freed from its obligations as a French fief, and granted in full sovereignty with Ponthieu, as well as Guisnes, and the new conquest of Calais.

The captive King, Jean-le-Bon, was ransomed and released, and he, like his captor Edward, and the Black Prince before him, made a pilgrimage to Notre-Dame, and passed piously beneath the Holy Chest, which it was deemed safe at last to bring forth from its hiding-place in the Chapel of S. Lubin.

A period of comparative quiet ensued under the administration of Charles the Wise, who summoned the States-General to meet at Chartres, and entrusted the patriotism of this and other principal towns with the task of raising forces to deal with the roving bands of freebooters which, under the name of *grandes compagnies*, swarmed over the country. The campaigns conducted by Duguesclin against the English in the south left Chartres undisturbed. She devoted herself to the restoration of order, the enforcement of law, and the strengthening of her wall. One little incident will show the progress which, in spite of war, and impositions of every sort, had been made since the high days of feudalism.

The house of one Guillaume Morhier, knight and seigneur of S. Piat, was forcibly entered by some bailiffs, who were charged to distrain upon him for the benefit of a horse-dealer. Morhier's daughter, when the chief official was preparing to read his warrant to her, snatched the paper out of his hands, and for this offence was roughly seized and, in spite of her protests, dragged on her knees across the town, as though she had been a common thief or murderess, and committed to prison in the Tour-le-Roi. She was thrown into the cells used for women of loose life. It was with the utmost difficulty that the unfortunate girl regained her liberty, after two friends had appeared to go bail for her. Intense indignation was aroused by this high-handed behaviour on the part of the officials. For the Morhier family was one of the most important in the district. The bailiffs, after a formal investigation of the case, lasting over two years, were condemned to make full apology, and pay a heavy fine. But the mere fact that Morhier did not, without trial, hang then and there the servant of the law who had presumed to raise his hand against his high-born daughter is significant of the advance that had been made in the last two hundred years.

The next thing of importance that happened at Chartres was the curious episode of the *Paix Fourrée*. A terrible crime plunged France into all the horrors of civil war. The Duke of Burgundy, John the Fearless, jealous of the popularity of the Duke of Orléans, caused him to be assassinated (1407) at Paris. A year of struggle and recrimination passed before Charles VI. could bring the murderer and the son of his victim to make even a pretence of reconciliation. The Duke of Burgundy demanded, without desiring, pardon, which the Duke of Orléans, without forgiving, granted. Each swore aloud to live henceforth in peace with his cousin, and swore beneath his breath to slay him. The ceremony took place in the Cathedral of Notre-Dame. Armed men in battle array stood at the porches of the church, and within, seated on a throne near the crucifix, with the Queen and Dauphin, the Kings of Sicily and Navarre, dukes, cardinals, and other nobles and officials near at hand, Charles waited the arrival of John the

Fearless, who had left Gallardon that morning with six hundred men-at-arms.

Amidst profoundest silence the cruel conqueror of the Liégeois advanced down the nave and made his submission to the imbecile King, who had so feebly forgiven the murderer of his brother. Then again advancing towards his 'dear cousins,' the children of the murdered duke, he formally besought them to banish from their hearts all hatred and feelings of revenge, and to live in amity with him. At these words, and at the sight of their father's murderer, the young princes burst into tears. The Queen and Dauphin approached them, and begged them to forgive, and, at the command of the King, the young duke and his brother repeated the prescribed words of the treaty, and they and the Duke of Burgundy, and all the princes of royal blood, swore upon the Cross and the Gospels to obey the behest of the King in this matter. This done, John the Fearless, without taking bite or sup in Chartres, mounted his horse and rode away. Little wonder that John of Montagu, brother of the former Bishop of Chartres, in registering this pact, wrote beneath it these significant words, 'Pax, Pax; et non est Pax' (Peace, Peace; and it is not peace). So also thought the excellent Fool of the Duke of Burgundy, who, wrapping an ecclesiastical paten (*paix d'église*) in his fur mantle (*fourrure*), remarked that it was but a patched-up peace (Paix Fourrée).

The Fool's verdict was soon justified. John the Fearless went to Paris, and curried favour with the people of the market-place. His popularity and democratic tendencies provoked the displeasure of the Orleanists, who represented the old feudal party. In the civil war which ensued between the Armagnacs, as the Orleanists were called, and the Burgundians, Chartres, lying very much in the centre of the operations, suffered almost equally from both sides.

The spirit of patriotism and the sense of unity were as yet scarce born in France. The example and exigencies of civil war were not calculated to promote their growth. Maddened by the assassination of the Duke of Burgundy in the very presence of the Dauphin, with whom he had come to confer, the Burgundians threw themselves into the hands of the English. After the Battle of Agincourt, where, against still greater odds, the English archers had inflicted a still more overwhelming defeat upon the French knighthood than at Crécy and Poitiers, Henry V. had been steadily reducing the province of Normandy. Now, by the aid of his new allies, he concluded with the maniac Charles VI. the Treaty of Troyes (1420), which handed over to England the crown of France and the whole kingdom. Chartres had been taken in 1417[85] by John the Fearless, and converted into his capital. Every citizen suspected of favouring the Armagnacs had been expelled from the city. The capital of the Burgundians was therefore not unnaturally one of the first towns to recognise Henry V. in his new *rôle* of heir to the French crown. The Dauphin, indeed, marched from Blois to take vengeance upon the rebellious city, but he promptly raised the siege when Henry, leaving Paris, advanced to relieve it.

Henry took Dreux, and remained there a month. Then he returned to Chartres as a pilgrim, with bare feet, and a candle in his hand. Rich gifts were bestowed upon Notre-Dame by the English soldiery, amongst which is mentioned a magnificent *ostensoir* that disappeared during the Revolution. The high bourgeoisie and clergy, captivated by the favours of the English King, were now all addicted to *Anglescherie* (Anglomania), a fault which they, with the rest of Europe, have since managed to correct. Thus, whereas formerly a Bishop of Chartres had equipped himself as a knight and gone to die at Agincourt in battle with the enemy, the Bishop now could only maintain his See by devoting himself to the English cause. This Jean de Frétigny did with success. As a rival of Orléans and Châteaudun also, Chartres naturally favoured Henry in days when centralisation and patriotism, that higher form of selfishness, were almost unknown, as the tragic history of the Maid of Orléans was shortly to show. Her brother, we may mention, was for a while captain of Chartres.

One year after Joan of Arc, the patriot before her time, had been put to death by a judicial murder at Rouen without one word of protest from her countrymen or the Church, Chartres was retaken by the French. The manner of its taking was on this wise.

Two merchants of the town, Guillaume Bouffineau and Jean Lesueur by name, who traded in salt, wine and corn with the people of Blois and Orléans, were won over by the governor of the latter city to the side of the French King, Charles VII. At his instigation they prepared a plan for surprising the town, which took effect on the 11th of April. On that day Bouffineau and Lesueur, accompanied by some soldiers disguised as waggoners, arrived early in the morning at the gate S. Michel with several loads of what they said was salt. They demanded admittance; and as they had the reputation of being the best possible of citizens, the guards lowered the drawbridge. Two waggons passed safely in; the third was purposely upset on the bridge. Profiting from the confusion caused by this accident, the conspirators attacked the guards, slew them, and rushed into the town shouting, 'La Paix, Ville Gagnée!' Two strong French detachments, commanded by Longueville, Dunois, Boussicault and La Hire,[86] who had been lying in ambush near at hand, now arrived, reinforced the assailants, and occupied the principal thoroughfares. The English party was taken completely unawares, and was slow to rally; for not only were the cries of the assailants confusing, but the eloquence of a confederate monk was enthralling. He had assembled the people at the other end of the town to hear him preach, and their interest in his sermon prevented them from realising their danger till too late.

The Anglicising Bishop Frétigny, however, when he heard of the affair, rushed to arms and fell fighting at the head of his men. The town was taken. The conspiring bourgeois were rewarded with money and office. Charles VII. achieved the pacification of Chartres with letters of pardon and confirmation. A strong force of French troops garrisoned it against any attempt of the English to retake it, and used it as a convenient spot from which to make marauding expeditions against the neighbouring English territory. It was, indeed, for a while a frontier fort, guarding the French marches. Night and day, from the towers of Notre-Dame, men watched the plains of La Beauce, ready to give the alarm when the English, moving from their quarters in Normandy, threatened this district. In 1491 the Chartrain garrison moved out and laid siege to Gallardon, which was still held by the English. Talbot, marching on the Ile-de-France, relieved his fellow-countrymen. But next year Gallardon fell into the hands of the Chartrains. Gradually the English were driven out of France, and the people of Chartres began to make a desperate effort to restore their ruined commerce by developing the

**CHARTRES IN 1500**
*(from an old engraving)*

navigation of their river Eure. Thereby they involved themselves in continual and expensive litigation with the owners of riparian rights and the jealous merchants of neighbouring towns.

Relieved from the pressure of a foreign enemy, the quarrels between the Bishop and the Chapter broke out with renewed vigour. The disgraceful and ridiculous scenes of the last century were repeated. Then the esteem in which the clergy were held had been damaged by the exhibition of the Bishop and the Chapter quarrelling over the question of authority, excommunicating each other and continuing to say Mass. Apart from deeds of violence—and these were not few—it was a sufficiently deplorable object-lesson for the people. Canons in the Cathedral made such a clatter with their chairs that the proclamations of the Bishop could not be heard. Now, the Chapter, who refused to recognise the right of mandamus claimed by the Bishop, was involved in a similar quarrel with Miles d'Illiers. When he endeavoured to enforce his episcopal jurisdiction upon the canons of the cloister, they declared that he was violating the rights of the Holy See, to which alone they were responsible, and forthwith excommunicated him. Nothing daunted, he appeared in the choir of Notre-Dame. The canons rose from their stalls and made for the doors, as if to avoid all contact with a man who had been excommunicated. The Bishop, treating the matter as a jest, pronounced his blessing on the fugitives, 'to absolve them from the excommunication which they were afraid of sharing with him.' Then he ordered his chaplains to continue divine service without the canons. The violent and imperious temper of Miles d'Illiers brought him into conflict, not only with the Chapter of the Cathedral, but also with the abbeys and the town. He was usually in the wrong. Louis XI., who divided his time between Chartres, where his devotion held him, and Paris, whither the administration of his kingdom summoned him, invariably decided against him when the cases of his aggression were submitted to him. These affairs, endless litigation with reference to the navigation of the river, the plague, and benefactions from the King to the Cathedral, made up the history of Chartres till the end of the fifteenth century.

**ARMS OF THE TOWN**

# CHAPTER IX

## The Siege and the Breach, 1568

'Le canon battait nos murailles.
La Vierge, comme un bouclier,
Au choc terrible des batailles
Opposait son blanc tablier.

Le plomb, dans sa course rapide,
Devant la Vierge se courbait,
Et l'obus, au vol homicide,
Sans bruit, dans son giron tombait.'
L. JOLLIET.

PLAGUE and famine weighed heavily upon Chartres throughout the sixteenth century; not less heavily the wars of François I. and of Henry IV., and the continual contributions in money which she was called upon to make in order to enable them to be waged. Year by year, under the three curses of that age—plague, soldiers, and impositions—the exhaustion of the city increased. She was able, however, to receive with sufficient magnificence the occasional visits of kings and princes. Particularly splendid was the reception accorded to Mary Queen of Scots, when, at the age of six, she was brought here in state by the Constable de Montmorency and the Duc d'Aumale. And the period in which Jean de Beauce wrought the Clocher and the Clôture of the Cathedral cannot have been one of abject poverty.

Royal visits to the town were not altogether wasteful. Not only did they, in the ordinary course of things, stimulate trade, but they also served the cause of sanitation. For on such great occasions, and on such occasions only, the streets were cleaned. Street police was still quite in its infancy; hygiene an art scarce beginning to be practised. We find mention of an order in 1526 forbidding swineherds to allow the animals in their charge (*bêtes porchines de M. S. Antoine*) to wander about the streets. But this was an unpopular measure, and stood rather as a pious opinion of the more enlightened than as an effective piece of legislation. Things were but little better than they had been when the heir of Louis-le-Gros, riding in the Rue S. Jean in Paris, was thrown from his horse by an abbot's pig, and died of his injuries.

The vile odour that arose from the narrow, ill-paved, uncleansed passages called streets, filled with the rotting garbage which so tempted the pigs, is not pleasant even to imagine. Little wonder that here, as at Paris, where the same reign of mud and dirt obtained, the plague broke out again and again.

In one of these outbreaks Chartres lost no less than 8000 of its inhabitants. As in Paris, and later in London, the houses tainted by the plague were marked with a cross, and persons who were infected by it were obliged to carry a white wand in the streets. But people have always been curiously slow to learn the lessons of sanitation. The open sewer, the filthy water, the system of burial, the state of the dwelling-houses, the tradition of personal uncleanliness, these were all powerful friends of the pest in every mediæval town.

'You have,' Voltaire wrote later of Paris, 'slaughter-houses in back streets with no issue, which give out in summer a cadaverous odour capable of poisoning an entire quarter.' On this point at any rate Chartres was superior to Paris. For in the sixteenth century public slaughter-houses (massacre—the name still marks a section of the river) were erected in an appropriate place. But the butchers did not take kindly to them. In spite of frequent pains and penalties, it was long before the inveterate habit of slaughtering animals and throwing their blood into the streets was abandoned.

As to the streets, the authorities contented themselves for the most part with quite platonic aspirations that they should be watered and cleaned. But on great occasions, as I have said, cleaned they were, along with the roads, passages and bridges. Such an occasion was the visit of the King and Queen in 1550, with the Dauphin and his young *fiancée*, Mary Stuart.

The masters and companions of each trade and mystery, and the pages of honour to accompany the King on horse and foot were carefully selected; and costumes were as nicely chosen. The Lieutenant-General de Hérouad indeed issued an order calling upon the citizens, on pain of forfeit and arrest, to array themselves for the ceremony in velvet, satin, taffetas, and other rich garments. Triumphal arches were raised before the gates. At the cross roads scaffoldings were erected and decorated with tapestries and gilt, whereon plays and mysteries were to be performed.

These elaborate arrangements, however, ended in a lamentable fiasco. As the *cortège* wound its way out of the Porte Drouaise to meet the King and Queen a violent storm burst over them, and compelled them all, Lieutenant-General included, to seek refuge in the Church of S. Maurice and the neighbouring houses, in order to save their gala clothes from ruin. At the same moment, unfortunately, the King and Queen left the road of

Josaphat, which they were following, and made a short cut for the town, where they arrived without meeting a soul to welcome them.

As the key and granary of Paris, Chartres began to be the favourite garrison town of the French army, and was obliged to contribute accordingly to the expenses of huge masses of men quartered on her.

*Queen Berthy Tower.*

Meantime, the County of Chartres was raised to a Duchy in favour of Rénée, daughter of the late King Louis XII. and Anne de Bretaigne, on the occasion of her marriage with Hercules d'Éste, son of the Duke of Ferrara. A more profitable honour befell the town a few years later, when a judicial tribunal was set up here, a step which tended in some degree to lessen the excessive expenses and delays of the law. This was done in 1552, and in 1566 Charles IX. authorised the merchants and various trades, who were groaning under the exactions of the *procureurs* and the ruinous procedure of the *gens du baillage*, to choose a merchant judge and four colleagues (consuls) in the town of Chartres. This tribunal was intended to deal with business affairs. The bailiffs and attorneys, seeing in the creation of a Tribunal of Commerce a severe blow to their interests, did their utmost to frustrate it. But the Tribunal got itself established none the less in the House and Meeting-place of the Merchants, as they then called it; the Maison des Vieux-Consuls, as it came to be known later, after the consuls had transferred the scene of their labours elsewhere.

The 'House of the Old Consuls' in the Rue des Écuyers, facing the entrance of the Rue de la Petite-Boucherie de Bourg, is not in itself remarkable, save as the seat and cradle of municipal justice in Chartres. For that purpose it was well placed, being in the centre of the steep old streets of the lower town and near the river, round which, as we have seen, clustered numerous industries. The site was originally just within the old walls of the ninth century, and it is possible that the house was part of the old Tour du Roy. But it was completely rebuilt in the seventeenth century, and were it not for the fifteenth-century entrance, and the extremely picturesque circular staircase with its elegant and curious carving (early sixteenth century), it would be of no account. This staircase is known as the *Escalier de la Reine Berthe*—Queen Bertha's Staircase. The name apparently is quite modern, and there is no explanation of it which can claim to be certainly correct.

The Queen Bertha indicated may be either the wife of Eudes I., Count of Chartres, who afterwards married King Robert, and who, when he was forced to repudiate her, came to live in the old castle at Chartres, where she ended her days striving to forget her ephemeral greatness and succouring the poor; or, and this seems more likely, it may be Bertha, sister of Count Thibault III., widow of the Duke of Aquitaine, who spent her widowhood at Chartres in this quarter of the town, a fact which has survived in tradition and is confirmed by a document of 1069. For there is mention of the house of the Countess between the Tour du and the Porte Cendreuse (*camera comitissa inter Turrim et portam Cinerosam*).

**Old Dormer Window from Maison du Saumon**

Of other old wooden houses in Chartres the most famous for its carving and its picturesqueness is the Maison du Saumon in the Place de la

Poissonnerie, No. 10, so called from the huge salmon which is carved upon one of the beams, and recalls the fact that Poissonnerie means Fish-market. And No. 49 Rue des Changes is also distinguished by its carving. The Étape-au-vin we have already mentioned.

The sixteenth century in France was an epoch of confusion and distress, but from the chaos that then prevailed modern civilisation sprang. Two great historic facts dominate that epoch: the Renaissance of art and letters and the religious Reformation. They were naturally not wholly disconnected. Gutenberg was the forerunner of Luther. The revival of interest in the intellectual treasures of antiquity introduced into a society formed by Catholicism and feudalism a new comparison. The languages, politics, art, philosophy and religious beliefs of Rome and Athens were contrasted for the first time in the light of history with those of an organisation already exhausted by the length of its duration and the poison of its own vices. To this extent the intellectual awakening of the sixteenth century, with its new study of things old, led up to and aided the Reformation. But the idea of reform was not new. It had appeared and been repressed many times and in many countries from the twelfth century onwards. The authority of the Councils and the rigour of the punishments directed against it had succeeded in choking the movement hitherto, for it is one of the most inaccurate of commonplaces which asserts that persecution only succeeds in promoting the cause it endeavours to check. The Reformation was for hundreds of years quite successfully checked by persecution. But it came at last when, in the fulness of time, the minds of men were enlightened by the new spirit of discovery, inquiry and learning, and when the authority of the Church was weakened by the schisms and depravity of its representatives. The country which had invented the printing press, that powerful engine for the dissemination of ideas, sent forth also Luther. The shock of the revolt inaugurated by him struck France at a moment when, in the person of François I., the prerogatives of the Crown were almost without limit, and the regal splendour in which the King delighted dazzled every eye. François did not at first perceive the political tendencies of the Reformation, and he allowed the Protestant doctrines to be cherished even at his own Court. Marguerite de Valois, his sister, openly encouraged Protestantism, and Clément Marot, his favourite poet, translated for the use of the Reformers the Psalms into French. That charming poet and witty epigrammatist had started in life with the intention of never giving offence or rousing inconvenient opposition. Like Rabelais, he was ready to espouse a cause with an enthusiasm that was warm indeed but stopped short of burning point (jusqu'au feu exclusivement).

'Tant de brouillis qu'en justice on tolère
Je l'écrirois, mais je crains la colère,
L'oisiveté des prêtres et cagots
Je la dirois, *mais gare les fagots*;
Et des abus dont l'Église est fourrée,
J'en parlerois, mais gare la bourrée.'

So he had written. But his zeal or his art soon outran his discretion. He provoked the enmity which he deprecated. Pursued by the hatred of the Lady of Annet, Diane de Poitiers, of the poet Sagon and the inquisitor Jean Bouchard, the satirist was imprisoned more than once, and at last banished in poverty.

Chartres was the last place in which Calvinism was likely to be popular. Marot, there, was as unwelcome as his Psalms. He was seized and imprisoned in the Tour de Roy. The courts recently established in the town were active in the suppression of heresy, and burnt their first victims at the stake in 1553, '*qui ne se voulurent jamais confesser ny reconnoistre nostre bon Dieu et sauveur Jesus, ny la benoiste vierge Marie.*' As time went on the inquisitions grew more exacting. Their increasing severity drew forth increasing resistance on the part of the Protestants. More Huguenots were burnt and hundreds were banished from the town. A bishop, suspected of favouring their cause, was quickly denounced and cited to Rome. He departed amidst popular execration. Chartres remained enthusiastically Catholic of the Catholics. The Church festivals were celebrated with renewed pomp in the Cathedral, and the Mystery of Abraham was performed with impressive solemnity.

From the commencement of the religious wars, Louis, Prince of Condé, head of the Protestant League, 'for the maintenance of the pure worship of God and the due observance of the edicts,' turned his attention to the country of the Orléanais in order to facilitate his communications with the South. Hoping to avenge the catastrophe of Rouen, he made a bold movement from Orléans upon Paris. But after meeting with a severe check at Corbeil, he was obliged to fall back upon Normandy, devastating and burning La Beauce on his way. He had vainly called upon Chartres to open her gates to him. 'Never,' was the bold reply he received from the governor. 'I hold the town for the King, and if your army attacks this place it will prove their cemetery!' Condé continued to retire northwards. The Royal army engaged him under the walls of Dreux, and there the first pitched battle of the war was fought. It resulted, after an arduous struggle, in a hard-won victory for the Catholics. Eight thousand corpses strewed the plain, and whilst Montmorency remained prisoner in the hands of the Protestants, Condé himself was a captive to the Royalists. The pacific arrangement which was made shortly afterwards was not of long duration.

The fierce persecution commenced by the Duke of Alva against their brethren in the Netherlands roused, not without reason, the apprehension as well as the indignation of the French Reformers. The Huguenots rose and moved upon Paris. A drawn battle was fought in the plain of S. Denis.

Chartres had but a moment's respite. It was employed with feverish activity in making preparations for defence. The inhabitants were commanded to lay in provisions for two months. The watchmen installed in the Clocher Neuf were instructed to make the following signals:—On the first appearance of the enemy three strokes of the bell, three more if the enemy advanced towards the town. If they were cavalry a tapering banner was to be flown, if infantry a square one, and if the Huguenots tried to rush upon the suburbs the tocsin was to be rung. A bell was placed at each gate to correspond with that of the watch, and to summon the quarter to arms. Urgent appeals were sent to the King for aid, who replied by despatching some troops with Jean de Bourdeilles, Baron d'Ardelay, to superintend, in conjunction with Antoine de Linières and his garrison, the defence of the town. They busied themselves with placing some artillery in position, and establishing a bullet manufactory. The church bells were melted to supply the forge.

On the approach of the enemy the bridges over the Eure outside the town were destroyed. On the last day of February, 1568, the Huguenot army, commanded by the gallant Condé himself, encamped at Lèves and Josaphat, and in the suburbs about the gates Drouaise, Guillaume, Morard and S. Michel. Their numbers are given variously at 10,000 and 45,000 men. Their artillery consisted of only five siege pieces and four small culverins. The first four days of March were employed by the enemy in fortifying their positions, and by the Catholic Chartrains in skirmishing about the environs and setting fire to the suburbs of the town. M. de Linières, their vigorous leader, who was afterwards to meet his death on the battlefield of Jarnac, destroyed, as a necessary measure of war, Mainvilliers, and the monasteries of the Franciscans (with its splendid library) and of S. John. The Huguenots, on the other hand, endeavoured to preserve some buildings which might afford them cover, but they destroyed the Churches of S. Chéron and S. Barthélemy, which could be of no use to them.

These preliminaries gave the inhabitants of Chartres time to complete an entrenchment stretching from the Monastery of S. Père to the Porte Morard, and to construct also a platform near the convent of the Sœurs-de-S.-Paul, on which was mounted a cannon named *La Huguenotte*, which had been taken from the enemy at the Battle of Dreux. This piece did such good service during the siege that it soon earned the name of 'The Good Catholic!'

On the 5th of March the German soldiers, the Reiters and Lanskenets of the enemy, took up a position at the entrance of S. Maurice and at the Filles-Dieu, and opened two batteries, one opposite the Porte Drouaise, masked by the walls of the house *Trois-Maures*, the other in the enclosure of the Filles-Dieu, intending to take the same gate on the flank. The bombardment began on the following day.

The householders had watched the forces of their enemy gathering from this side and that, and knew that at last the dreaded circle was complete. They knew that Condé was in command, and had sworn to ruin their Cathedral, to scatter the relics stored there, and to feed his horse at the high altar. They knew that his soldiers were eager to 'ruin and annihilate the most beautiful building in France that remained as yet undefiled by them, namely, this devout and excellent temple of the Church of Notre-Dame de Chartres, the terror and despair of the heretics.'[87] But in spite of this knowledge and preparation the opening cannonade took the people of Chartres, as two hundred years later it took the people of Paris, by surprise.[88] It was early in the day. A crowd of worshippers filled the Church of S. Foy (S. Faith, Rue d'Harleville), which was built partly on the ramparts. At the conclusion of the Mass the Sacrament was to be carried to a sick person. Touched by unusual devotion at this perilous time, the whole assembly rose to escort the procession on its way, passing out slowly, group after group, as if by mechanical instinct, the more reluctant led on by the general consent. At last the church was quite emptied, when, it is said, a shower of massy stones from the culverins or great cannon of the besiegers fell suddenly upon it, and the entire roof of the place sank into the empty space beneath.

The rebuilding of the little chapel rendered necessary by this disaster accounts for the Flamboyant style of architecture which it now represents. Originally it had been dedicated in the time of S. Fulbert, and was enlarged and raised to the dignity of a parish church in the days of S. Ives. It was horribly profaned during the Revolution, being converted into a *Salle de Spectacle* by a decree of the Municipal Council in 1794 on the motion of one Morin, an architect. It was not till 1857, on the same day as the Druidical Virgin, Notre-Dame-de-Sous-Terre, was restored to the traditional place in the crypt, that the church passed again by purchase into clerical hands and was carefully restored.

The changes and degradations which it has undergone have left little worth studying in what was once the parish church of the most populous quarter in the town.

Whatever damage it did elsewhere (and a few days later a neighbouring church was crushed like S. Foy, but with all its good people inside), the cannonade directed against the Porte Drouaise on two sides at once failed in its object. For the ravelin proved a sufficient protection for the besieged. It therefore

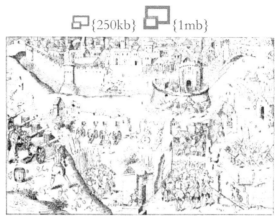

**CHARTRES BESIEGED BY M. LE PRINCE DE CONDE, MARCH 1568.**

A. *M. d'Andelot's regiment of from ten to twelve companies preparing to advance to the assault.*

B. *Four guns, belonging to M. Cassimir, leader of the Germans, on a ridge, firing as a rule into the town.*

C. *Regiment of Germans preparing to advance to the assault.*

D. *Breach of about 30 yards.*

E. *M. du Bordet, at the head of twenty-five or thirty soldiers and sappers who were to undermine the ravelin, was killed by a shot from an arquebus.*

F. *M. des Champs' regiment also making ready to advance to the assault.*

G. *A sortie made by the besieged against M. de Pille's troops.*

became necessary for the Huguenots to get possession of this advanced work. One of them, Du Bordet[89] by name, slipped with some pioneers into the ditch and began to sap, but being perceived by the defenders above, was shot down by an arquebus, and his men were unable to resist a sortie with which the arquebusiers followed up this success. On the same day the enemy were foiled in their endeavour to establish themselves near the suburb of S. Brice. But next morning the Huguenots, after a prolonged cannonade, effected a breach, and endeavoured to take by assault the ravelin from which they had been repulsed the night before. They were for a moment successful, but M. de Linières bravely recovered this important position. 'Incontinent,' wrote the contemporary historian, Simon de Gives, in his *Bref Discours du Siège mis devant la Ville de Chartres*,[90] 'Incontinent, the said seigneur began to pledge the captains who were near him, boldly resolute, with a heart not sad but joyful rather, drooping his head a little, and began to throw down planks to take the place of the bridge which the cannon had broken by force. These captains, wishing to show their generous courage and doing their duty marvellous well, entered the ravelin which the enemy had seized and held. Their own men, to recover it, engaged the Huguenots in a hand-to-hand fight, and being thus mixed together, the enemy were right manfully repulsed, and left many of their number dead within the ditch.'

At the same time the enemy had made an attack upon the ravelin of the Porte S. Michel, and were repulsed there also. But not without loss to the Chartrains. The brave D'Ardelay, colonel of the Gascons, received then a wound in the eye, of which he died some days later. Of his burial in the Cathedral and its sequel we have already spoken above.[91]

The failure of their efforts against the Porte Drouaise induced the Huguenots to direct their attention to the stretch of wall running from that gate to the Tower des Herses de Lethinière. And here it was that they established the breach so famous in the annals of Chartres. The whole of the 8th of March their batteries from the Clos-l'Évêque and the Filles-Dieu played upon the wall, and by two o'clock on the following afternoon a breach thirty feet wide had been made. The capable and energetic governor of the town, M. de Linières, had taken every possible measure of precaution to forestall the ill effects of the bombardment. As the breach widened a strong entrenchment was disclosed constructed of earth and bags of wool. A thousand workmen, soldiers and civilians, worked unceasingly at the task of throwing it up and strengthening it. Under pain of cord and gibbet, the inhabitants were impressed for the work. Night and day they toiled, and their toil was crowned with success. The Huguenots, seeing that there was no chance of delivering an assault with success, contented themselves with firing some salvoes on the 10th and 11th, and then shifted their artillery opposite the Porte Morard. There they began to endeavour, by destroying a large dam, to divert the course of the river, which ran through the lower town, and supplied the forces of the water-mills. This move, in spite of the wind-mills which M. de Linières had made at once, would very likely have been attended with serious results, had not rumours of peace begun to reach the ears of the belligerents. A truce, preliminary to the Peace of Longjumeau, was proclaimed. The Huguenots made haste to quit the town they had so unsuccessfully besieged. They removed their artillery on the 14th, and next day saw the last of their battalions disappear down the roads of Bonneval and Illiers.

'Thus, after fourteen days of struggle and vain assault,' exclaims our triumphant chronicler Rouillard, 'the enemy were compelled to retire with great loss and slaughter, and to give once more occasion for the name *des Reculés* (*see* p. 47), to the quarter in the midst of which they had proudly raised their accursed tents.' Disappointed of the plunder of the Cathedral treasure and of the pillage of the town upon which they had counted—for Condé himself had sold beforehand the lead of the Cathedral roof—they retired discomfited, to conclude the Peace of Longjumeau—*La Paix boiteuse et mal assise*, as it was called, because one of the negotiators was named Malassise, and the other was lame.

In memory of this deliverance it was decreed at Chartres that a solemn annual procession should take place on the 15th of March; that part of the street S. André should take the name of Rue de la Brèche, and that a commemorative inscription should be graven on the reconstructed wall.

In connection with the procession referred to we must mention the *Tour de Ville*, as it is called, or *La Chandelle du Tour*, or *Le Tour de cire*. This was a huge yellow wax candle, rolled on a wooden cylinder, and weighing as much as 220 pounds. 'From time immemorial,' the archives record, 'the town of Chartres has been wont to maintain this candle before the Black Virgin of the pillar in front of the jubé. It was instituted originally by the community of the said town as an oblation for the safety of the town, and was to burn before the said image.' Every day a piece was cut off and burnt on the town candlestick. For many years the *Tour de la Ville* was presented at one or other of the Church festivals indifferently, very often on the 17th of October, the Feast of the Dedication of the Cathedral. But in the seventeenth century it was decided that the presentation should take place on the 15th of March, the anniversary of the deliverance of the town from the siege of the Huguenots. The ceremony was very popular. All the officials of the town attended. Before the procession started the Mayor (for he had come into existence by that time), or, occasionally, some great man who happened to be the guest of the town at the time, lit the first candle before the shrine of the Black Virgin. Thereafter the *Tour de Ville* was carried in the procession to the breach. This custom lasted on to the days of the Revolution.

You can imagine the procession winding its way from the Cathedral down the steep curves of the Rue Muret towards the Place Drouaise and the Pont Neuf where once was the Porte Drouaise. Those who took part in it would pause, perhaps, and read the inscription let into the ramparts and engraved on two stones six feet long by three high which recorded the events of the siege in the Latin tongue for the instruction and example of posterity. One of the stones is, I gather, still preserved in the garden belonging to Madame Tillionbois de Valeuil and may be seen from the Pont Neuf. Pursuing their way up the Rue de la Brèche, the procession would next arrive at the Chapel of Notre-Dame-de-la-Brèche on their left. Let the reader enter this tiny chapel, after noticing the arms sculptured above the window, and he will find himself face to face with a statue of the Virgin which rests on the keystone of the old chapel erected in 1599 in memory of this event, and near the site of the famous breach.

About the altar are numerous cannon-balls of stone which are relics of the siege. Entering the large annex on the right the visitor will now perceive a still more curious relic of the siege—the fourteenth or fifteenth-century statue of Notre-Dame-de-la-Brèche, whose name was graven on the keystone above mentioned. And if he inquire how that name was earned he will be told that this is the very statue which was set over the Porte Drouaise and, by a miraculous intervention, saved the town. For the contemporary chronicler Duparc informs us that 'For all that the chiefs of the Huguenot army were esteemed the greatest soldiers in Europe, yet were they miraculously blinded by a manifest miracle. And the miracle was on this wise. There was on the Porte Drouaise an image of Our Lady against which the enemy fired many shots from cannon and arquebus alike, but without being able to hit it. And to show that many shots were fired at the said gate on which was the said image, the bridge of that gate was broken and cut in twain by the cannon-balls, and all round the image up to a few inches of it the marks of many bullets may still be seen. But it was hit by never a one, and it remained therefore whole and intact; in spite of the efforts of the enemy to destroy that image, it was never struck by a single shot. I know well,' he adds, 'that the heretics and some others laugh at this, but Herod also mocked at Christ when he beheld Him.'

Another version of this miracle is given by Chaline (b. 1596) in his old *Histoire de Chartres*. 'The Huguenots,' he says, 'having drawn near on the 9th of March to enter the town by the breach which they had made, it happened that there appeared on the said breach opposite to them a tall lady holding a child in her arms, against whom they fell to firing and to hurling volleys of abuse, without being able to reach or strike her in any way *terribilis ut castrorum acies ordinata*. On the contrary, the bullets which they fired fell harmless, without effect or force, at the foot of the wall, and they, thinking to enter, found themselves repulsed. The Chartrains perceiving this, and knowing that it was the Holy Virgin who, with her Son, was thus visibly taking the defence of the town into her own hands, the ecclesiastics and women turned to pray, and the men of war and all capable of bearing arms made a sortie upon the besiegers and vigorously repelled them.'

By a further development, the popular tradition of the country, so prettily expressed in the verses of M. Jolliet which I have put at the head of this chapter, now maintains that the Virgin caught the bullets in the folds of her mantle.

The chapel founded in 1599 was destroyed during the Revolution and rebuilt in 1843. Leaving this chapel and pursuing its way along the street, the procession would next arrive at the Parish Church of S. André and the adjoining Chapel of S. Nicholas, and then, after singing an anthem there before the bas-relief which commemorated events of the siege, would make its way up the steep ascents back to the Cathedral.

The Church of S. André, as seen in its ruins and desecration to-day, presents one of the most offensive examples of callous profanation in France. When you have mastered your disgust with the disastrous and discreditable fact that this once magnificent building is used as a municipal lumber-room, you begin to perceive that its remains are still beautiful, and you regret the more keenly the fire which, when it was an army forage store in 1865, completed the damage begun by the Revolutionists. Take first the extremely beautiful and interesting west front, which presents, as it were, an epitome of mediæval architecture—the Norman or Romanesque arch, the Gothic beginning and the Flamboyant decadence are all represented. For the lower portion is composed of three round-headed arches, the soffits of which are ornamented with round mouldings and zigzag work, and rest on columns with curious capitals formed of acanthus leaves from which grotesque heads peep out. Above these three round arches are three pointed windows. The transition character of these is emphasised by the mouldings in the soffits being continuations of those in the side piers. The windows rest on a simple cornice, carried by corbels, also grotesque. Above them was a Flamboyant rose, demolished after the fire in 1865.

*Tower of S<sup>t</sup> André*

The church was founded in 1108 by the great Bishop of Chartres, S. Ives, and was at once a collegiate and parochial institution in one of the most populous parishes of Chartres. A massive square tower flanks the south side of the transept; the spire which it once supported was destroyed during the Revolution. At the east end there was a curious feature. An arch was thrown out into the Eure in the thirteenth century, and was made to carry the annexed choir and sanctuary. This portion of the church was rebuilt in the Flamboyant style by Jehan de Beauce in the sixteenth century; and in 1612 a second arch, in continuation of the earlier one, completed the span of the river and connected the church with the right bank. The apsidal chapel built thereon was dedicated to the Holy Virgin. Vauban called the attention of Louis Quatorze to the excellence of these arches, but some picturesque traces only of them can be seen from the riverside to-day, for the arches collapsed and were removed in 1805.

The interior is in the simple Romanesque manner, and, in spite of base uses to which the place is now put, it remains impressive by virtue of the sixteen massive piers which support the nave and aisles, which have been simple always, and remain grand in their ruin.

Two early square crypts under the transepts are worth seeing. For the rest, of what once was, I need only mention the wooden jubé, carved by P. Courtier, on which Jehan de Beauce had also done some work. Among the carvings, it is said, was one which represented a pig churning butter—an epigram in stone against notorious heretics, for Calvin is frequently treated as a pig in this sort of imagery.

# CHAPTER X

## Mathurin Regnier and the Renaissance at Chartres

'J'ai vécu sans nul pensement
Me laissant aller doucement
A la bonne loi naturelle;
Et si m'étonne fort pourquoi
La Mort daigna penser à moi
Qui ne pensai jamais à elle.'
*Epitaph of Régnier.*

UNLIKE the English, who, in public, prefer to ignore genius, the French provincials, when they have any great men born within the borders of their town, are not ashamed to honour them. They erect monuments easily, and it even occurs to them to call their streets after the names of great writers. In Chartres you have the Rue Félibien[92] and the Rue Régnier,[93] with the house in which Mathurin Régnier was born.

God has made the men of La Beauce in the image of the soil whence they have sprung. They have the regularity, the monotony and the hardness of their native land. They are without passion or imagination, cold and avaricious, and their women are like them. Their wit, when they have any, is of the kind that delights in carping, ironical raillery. Their minds, when they are developed, are cast in a logical and scientific mould. Therefore it is that the representative writers of the sixteenth and seventeenth centuries at Chartres are Pierre Nicole, the moralist and theologian of the Port Royal School (*Essais de Morale*); Michel Félibien, the critical and scientific historian of Paris (*Histoire de la Ville de Paris*); the cold, but elegant, courtier poet, Philippe Desportes, and his nephew, Mathurin Régnier, the creator of French satire (1573-1613).

The School of Chartres had, we know, long been famous. When, at the end of the fifteenth century, the new movement in literature, philosophy and art began to be felt through France, the successors of Fulbert were not unaffected by it. They welcomed the new learning. The discussions of the schoolmen yielded place to the new appreciation of Greek and Latin, art and literature. Nor were the Chartrains slow to apply the new discovery of the art of printing. Twelve years after the introduction of Gutenberg's invention into France, Pierre Plume, a learned canon of Notre-Dame, caused to be printed, at his own expense, in his house in the cloister, and by the printer Jean Dupré, a magnificent folio missal for the use of the diocese (1482). A fine copy of this missal (*Missale Secundum usum ecclesiæ Carnotensis*) is in the town library.

In the architecture of this period the same tendency towards the adoption or imitation of classical models, as interpreted by the Italian artists, is evident. Jean de Beauce abandoned the Flamboyant style in which he had hitherto so triumphantly wrought, and built the Renaissance clock tower of the Cathedral; and a certain doctor, Claude Huvé by name (1501-1559), in his enthusiasm for the revival of the old classical style, erected the house in the Rue du Grand Cerf (number

**Courtyard Maison du Medecin**

8), which still goes by the name of the *Maison du Médecin*. The Renaissance façade and court of this house contrast strikingly with the narrow, mediæval streets and Gothic style of the old town. They speak with strange distinctness of the intellectual and artistic awakening of the world after the slumber of the Dark Ages. And, as you read the inscription on the front of the house—

SIC CONSTRUXIT CLAUDI HW'
IAT ΠΟΣ DECORI URBIS
AC POSTERITATI CONSULENS,[94]

—you sympathise at once in the pride and delight which this child of the new era must have taken in the new birth of old things revealed to him by the Italian artists of the Renaissance. The front of this house may be compared with the entrance of the Château d'Anet, built by Philip Delorme at the same period (1548), and now preserved in L'École des Beaux Arts at Paris.

About the same time, in the domain of literature, the satiric turn of mind which we have noted as typical of his countrymen, was illustrated by a young poet of good Chartrain family, named Laurent des Moulins. He wrote a long poetical satire, which is, however, really only a sermon in verse, entitled *Le Catholicon des mal advisés*. It is an allegorical vision, written after the manner of the *Roman de la Rose*. For Master Laurent, like all the poets of the fourteenth and fifteenth century, cast his verses in the mould of Guillaume de Loris and Jean de Meung. He turns a good verse out of that mould now and again, and he writes with a genuine moral intention, so that, in spite of his oddities, his tediousness and his prosaic view of life, he goes some way towards filling up, for the curious student of French letters, the dreary gap which separates Villon from Marot. He shows us the usual dreamer falling asleep, like William Langland, 'on a May morning on Malvern Hills,' and seeing troops of types in whom there is no good. And of them ('All I saw sleeping, as I shall you tell') he writes in several thousand lines, good, bad and indifferent,—

'Mêlant le vin rouge avec le vin blanc.'

Very different in style and in spirit from this sombre and unpolished poet was Philippe Desportes, Abbot of Tiron and Josaphat (1546-1606), the favourite poet, first, of Charles IX., who gave him ten thousand crowns for his *La Mort de Rodomont*, and afterwards of Henry III. and his *mignons*.

To them this most unclerical cleric, this courtier poet and successful diplomatist, wrote in his earlier days songs and sonnets of remarkable sweetness and grace, and was rewarded with poetic crowns and many abbacies. Devoid of the poetic passion and picturesque invention of his master, Ronsard, he was often content to translate or imitate an Italian celebration of an imaginary mistress, and to compensate by his gift of happy expression for his utter lack of sentiment or enthusiasm. Though the most prominent of Ronsard's own particular disciples, his style is so simple and correct that he seems to be rather a forerunner of Malherbe than a follower of the school which had endeavoured to introduce into French poetry curious words and a peculiar phraseology, and to substitute, for simplicity and directness of speech, ingenious periphrases.

The following *villanelle*, charming in its neatness of expression and polished elegance of style and form, is, I think, a good example of Desportes at his best in his lighter and more mundane manner. It was repeated, one may note, by Henri de Guise at Blois a few minutes before he fell by the dagger of an assassin.

'Rozette, pour un peu d'absence
Votre cœur vous avez changé
Et moi, sachant cette inconstance,

Le mien, autre part j'ai rangé.
Jamais plus beauté si légère
Sur moi tant de pouvoir n'aura.
Nous verrons, volage bergère,
Qui premier s'en repentira.

Tandis qu'en pleurs je me consume
Maudissant cet éloignement,
Vous, n'aimiez que par coutume
Caressiez un nouvel amant.
Jamais légère girouette
Au vent si tôt ne se vira.
Nous verrons, bergère Rozette,
Qui premier s'en repentira.

Où sont tant de promesses saintes,
Tant de pleurs versés en partant?
Est-il vrai que ces tristes plaintes
Sortissent d'un cœur inconstant?
Dieux, que vous êtes mensongère!
Maudit soit qui plus vous croira!
Nous verrons, volage bergère,
Qui premier s'en repentira.

Celui qui a gagné ma place
Ne vous peut aimer tant que moi;
Et celle que j'aime vous passe
De beauté, d'amour et de foi.
Gardé bien votre amitié neuve;
La mienne plus ne variera;
Et puis nous verrons à l'épreuve
Qui premier s'en repentira!'

Later, Desportes had other moods, more befitting his cloth, and under their influence he wrote devotional poems of considerable merit and somewhat feeble versions of the Psalms. Malherbe was quite justified in his criticism;—'Your soup is better than your Psalms.' For the table of the rich and sensual Abbot of Tiron, Bonport, Aurillac and other places was excellent, whilst the more edifying verses of his old age failed to acquire the bouquet of his wines.

Mathurin Régnier was born at Chartres in 1573. His mother was the sister of Desportes, and Mathurin, in spite of his father's protests, determined to follow in the footsteps of his uncle and to be a poet. So great was his natural talent that, notwithstanding his idleness and such indulgence in debauchery that his life was shortened by his excesses, he certainly succeeded. He holds a place unique in French literature. For he is, perhaps, the only French poet before the so-called classical period who has had the good fortune continuously to maintain his position. He attacked Malherbe, yet was praised by him. He was an ardent supporter of the Pléiade, that group of men who, with Ronsard, 'the prince of poets,' at their head, aimed at the reformation of the French language and literature by means of the study and imitation of ancient, classical models. His defence of the Ronsardising tradition secured him, later, the approval of the first Romantics. But he earned also the admiration of Boileau. And the praise of Boileau, who said that he was the French writer, before Molière, who best knew human nature, made his reputation safe during the eighteenth century.

Of his life we do not know much: what we do know is chiefly discreditable. His father was a citizen of position, and he wisely desired for his son the ecclesiastical but not the poetical eminence of his brother-in-law, Desportes. Mathurin, therefore, was tonsured at the age of eleven. For himself he had no hesitation. His uncle's example was too alluring. He began to write early, and he never wholly shook off the tradition of the school which his uncle represented and Malherbe with excessive bitterness and pedantry attacked. As he says himself in his Ninth Satire, wherein he so vigorously criticises the critics of the Pléiade:—

'Je vais le grand chemin que mon oncle m'apprit
Laissant là ces Docteurs que les Muses instruisent
En des arts tout nouveaux; et s'ils font, comme ils disent,
De ses fautes un livre aussi gros que le sien,
Telles je les croirai quand ils auront du bien,
Et que leur belle muse, à mordre si cuisante,
Leur donra, comme à lui, dix mil écus de rente.'

His father, so he tells us, had endeavoured to keep him from following the paths of poetry by instancing the present troubles of the country and the troubles that threatened. Poetry, he said, like many another father since, with as good reason and with as little effect, would not pay. His uncle's good fortune was exceptional and misleading.

'La muse est inutile, et si ton oncle a su
S'avancer par cet art, tu t'y verras deçu.

Un même astre toujours n'éclaire en cette terre;
Mars tout ardent de feu nous menace de guerre,
Tout le monde fremit et ces grande mouvements
Couvent en leurs fureurs de piteux changements;
Penses-tu que le luth et la lyre des poëtes
S'accordent d'harmonie avec les trompettes,
Les fifres, les tambours, le canon et le fer
Concert extravagant des musiques d'enfer.'
Sat. IV.

The clatter of drums and cannons, however, was destined soon to cease, and the voice of Régnier's muse was before long to be heard in the land. Régnier was a true child of the Renaissance in that he not only imitated, like his uncle, the Italian poets of his day, but he also based his satire on a close study of the classical writers. For he knew his Ovid thoroughly; like Ronsard, he modelled himself on Juvenal, and, like Joachim du Bellay, he recalls the manner of Horace. But apart from the knowledge and appreciation of great models, Régnier enjoyed also the genuine inspiration of a poet. He tells us how, in his youth, he would wander in the woods dreaming of fame and fortune, and learning the mysteries of the Muse:—

'Rêveur je m'égarai tout seul par les détours
Des antres et des bois affreux et solitaires,
Où la Muse, en dormant, m'enseignait ses mystères,
M'apprenait des secrets, et m'échauffant le sein
De gloire et de renom relevait mon dessein.'
Sat. IV.

This and other passages are enough to show that Régnier had the imagination as well as the temperament of the true poet. Therefore, in spite of his free imitation of the ancients, he remains original—a great poet of the order of Clément Marot. What he borrows he makes his own, and in adapting passages from the Roman writers to the Gallic manners of his own day he not infrequently improves them. And apart from his satires, he reveals in his lyrics, to a high degree, the same poetical sensibility, and he describes with a melodious melancholy the poet's regret for the days that are no more:—

'Un regret pensif et confus
D'avoir été et n'être plus
Rend mon âme aux douleurs ouverte;
A mes dépens, las! je vois bien

Qu'un bonheur comme était le mien
Ne se cognait que par la perte.'

    Mathurin was relieved from the restraints of paternal authority in 1591. For in that year his father was thrown into prison, under circumstances typical of the time. Philippe Desportes had chosen Jacques Régnier to farm one of his benefices, the Abbey of Josaphat, but he, instead of devoting himself wholly to the peaceful cultivation of the land, exerted himself politically on the side of the Chartrain *Ligueurs*. The good King Henry, whose habit it was to draw less blood than money from rebellious citizens, fined him sixteen hundred crowns, and, when he failed to pay, threw him into prison at Chartres. There he remained some months. His son, meanwhile, who had already got himself into trouble by writing lampoons on the inhabitants of his native town, and repeating them to the frequenters of a tennis-court which his father had built, took this opportunity of slipping away to Paris. There his uncle, Desportes, recommended him to the Cardinal-Archbishop of Toulouse, François de Joyeuse, and he took part in that prelate's embassy to Rome. At the same time he was presented with the small priory of Bouzancourt. Thus one fine morning he,

'Vif de courage abandonna la France.'

He seemed to be on the high road to fortune. But though a better poet he was a worse courtier than his uncle. In ten years spent with Joyeuse and his successor, the young secretary earned nothing except experience. Of that and its fruits he earned more than enough. He indulged without restraint in the careless joy of living, and he suffered, like so many of his contemporaries, from the intense delight in life and the feverish gratification of the pleasures of the flesh which marked the Renaissance movement. For men were encouraged to give free reign to the *bonne loi naturelle* by the whole spirit of an age which was a revolt from the gloomy monasticism of the Middle Ages. Of the results, in his own case, of such indulgence and of his sufferings, which had nothing in common with those of the saints, Mathurin Régnier tells us in some of his passages more than we care to know.

    They taught him at any rate a certain philosophy of a not very exalted sort, which he expounds to us in one of his satires. It is a kind of epicurean pococurantism, summed up in the words of Swinburne, 'Hope thou not much and fear thou not at all,' and expressed by the poet himself:—

'N'avoir crainte de rien et ne rien espérer
Ami, c'est ce qui peut les hommes bien-heurer.'

The best comment on it, perhaps, is that implied in the epitaph on himself which heads this chapter.

Régnier returned from Italy, then, with an ample provision of memories, and perhaps with those poems which are based on the works of the Italian satirists. He took up his abode in his uncle's house at Paris, and there, as in Rome, he noted in the intervals of dissipations the manners and the characters of men. He saw and knew the high personages who frequented the house of Desportes, and whose names occur in his poems. And not being a time-server himself,

'Instruit par le temps à la fin j'ai connu
Que la fidélité n'est pas grand revenu,'

he was content to draw with biting irony the portrait of a courtier bard, who,

'Ambitieux, pour les vers qu'il compose,
Quelque bon benefice en l'esprit se propose,
Et dessus un cheval comme un singe attaché
Meditant un sonnet, medite un evesché.'
*Sat. II.*

Or of the vain beggar poets who

'L'œil farouche et troublé, l'esprit à l'abandon
Vous viennent accoster comme personnes yvres,
Et disent pour bon-jour "Monsieur, je fais des livres,
On les vend au Palais, et les doctes du temps,
A les lire amusez, n'ont autre passe-temps." '
*Sat. II.*

***Renaissance***
***Oriel Rue de la Corroierie***

Or, again, he marks down a courtier with a vigour and point which Molière could not surpass:—

'Laissons-le discourir,
Dire cent et cent fois: Il en faudrait mourir;
Sa barbe pinçoter, cageoller la science,
Relever ses cheveux, dire; En ma conscience;
Faire la belle main, mordre un bout de ses gants,
Rire hors de propos, monstrer ses belles dents,
Se carrer sur un pied, faire arser son épée,
Et s'adoucir les yeux ainsi qu'une poupée.'
*Sat. VIII.*

A dozen other examples might be quoted to show with what satiric acid he can etch a portrait. Régnier can paint a scene, too, with same unerring detail and bitter accuracy, as, for instance, 'Le Souper Ridicule' and the less savoury 'Mauvais Gîte.' The latter poem is indeed the only one which deserves the imputation conveyed by Boileau's phrase about the author's *rimes cyniques*. Régnier is essentially a moral writer, for he makes vice, even when he describes it openly, the reverse of attractive. The worst that can and may be said of him is that, like Juvenal, he attacks vice with arms that make virtue blush. He says himself:—

'Je croirai qu'il n'est rien au monde qui guarisse
Un homme vicieux comme son propre vice,'

and certainly the sincere and vigorous pictures he draws will prove a temptation to no one, though they may inspire, like his habit of calling a spade a spade, feelings of repugnance and disgust. But this is the aim, as these are the means of all genuine satirists. Régnier's comment on his own failings is pathetic, but does not condone them. It reminds one of Ovid's words, '*Video meliora proboque. Deteriora sequor.*'

'Étant homme, on ne peut
Ni vivre comme on doit, ni vivre comme on veut.'

For, happily, the consequences of his loose living had wrought in him a tardy repentance. His conversion was as late and as sincere as that of La Fontaine—and not less needed. As he left politics alone, and attacked not individuals but social types, he made no enemies. For most men group others in classes but not themselves, or at any rate suppose themselves to be free from the vices of the class to which they belong. So they called our satirist Bon Régnier, as later they spoke of Bon la Fontaine, and the *bonhomie* implied by their nickname had the same seasoning of malice. But it was not rewarded with any great share in the goods of this world. His uncle, dying in 1606, left him only a legacy of 2000 *livres* on the Abbey *des Vaus de Cernay*. Henry IV., by conferring this request, gained the friendship of the poet, who expressed his gratitude in the admirable verses of his first satire. In 1608, the year in which his works were first published, he was presented with a stall in the Cathedral of Chartres. But only five years later he left Royaumont, the abbey of the Bishop of Chartres, who always made him welcome, and found his way to Rouen. There he consulted a quack doctor, a famous empiric, Le Sonneur by name, who promised to heal him of all his diseases. But he died after dining with this too encouraging physician.

I have spoken of Régnier as the creator of French satire, and so, in a sense, he was. But the phrase requires qualification. His satires are not indeed absolutely the first of their kind in France. They had been preceded by the terrific invectives of D'Aubigné, the vigorous outbursts of Jean de la Taille, and the less vehement but more polished satirical portraits of Vauquelin de Fresnaye. But in breadth and technical merit he far surpassed all his predecessors, and, in force, all except D'Aubigné. The longest, the best known, and undoubtedly the best of his sixteen satires, is the thirteenth. There, under the title of Macette, he describes an old woman who hides vice under a mask of hypocrisy, and corrupts youth with her evil philosophy of the world and its ways. The type is not new, but Régnier's description of it is original and vigorous in the extreme. His Macette, in fact, is the grandmother of Molière's Tartuffe.

'Loin du monde elle fait sa demeure et son giste
Son œil tout penitent ne pleure qu'eau beniste.
Enfin c'est un exemple, en ce siècle tortu
D'amour, de charité, d'honneur et de vertu.
Pour beate partout le peuple la renomme,
Et la gazette même a déja dit à Rome,
La voyant aimer Dieu et la chair maîtriser
Qu'on n'attend que sa mort pour la canoniser.'

Clearly the style of comedy had been found when a man could write like that, and Molière, fifty years later, had only to choose among the lines of Régnier when he wished to draw the character of Tartuffe.

'Le péché que l'on cache est demi-pardonné,'

becomes in Tartuffe

'Et ce n'est point pécher que pécher en silence.'

And in many other instances our Chartrain poet has supplied the great comedian with lines and hints, which Molière, true to his principle, *Je prends mon bien où je le trouve*, has appropriated as unblushingly and as successfully as a Vergil. This, apart from his other merits, and in spite of his faults, is in itself enough to justify the existence of the *rimes cyniques* of Mathurin Régnier.

# CHAPTER XI

## The Coronation of Henri Quatre

WHEN Henri III. fell beneath the dagger of the assassin, Jacques Clément, the King of Navarre was hailed King of France at S. Cloud. But the fair realm which was one day to be his

'Et par droit de naissance
Et par droit de conquête,'

was far from being prepared as yet to accept Henri Quatre as its ruler. The throne of S. Louis could not, in the eyes of a large section of the nation, belong to a heretic, and Henri de Béarn was a Huguenot. Paris, which was devoted to the Catholic League, closed its gates to him, and Chartres, equally enthusiastic in the same cause, refused to admit him. Resolved to make himself master of a town which was regarded as a boulevard of the capital, Henri had forced the rest of the Duchy to recognise him by the end of 1590, but Chartres was still stubborn. He sent, therefore, Marshal de Biron to lay siege to the town, and he began operations on the 12th February. But, contrary to the expectations of Henri, who was in communication with many of the citizens, the resistance offered by the Catholic city was vigorous and prolonged. Instead of a few days the siege lasted two months, and the defence was conducted with such energy and skill that M. de Réclainville, who had been summoned to their aid, with some troops of the Ligue, complimented the citizens on their bravery and resource. He had taken a part, he said, in many an affair, but never had he seen a finer struggle than the siege of Chartres.

The first few days were taken up with skirmishes in the suburbs and sorties by the garrison, who endeavoured, too late, to destroy the cover which the outlying buildings afforded the enemy. On the 15th of the month the King himself arrived, and the Royalists thereupon constructed a barricade, facing the ravelin of the Porte Drouaise, and opened a trench in the Pig Market, under cover of a battery masked by the ruined houses, and directed against the ravelin of the Porte des Épars. The latter point was chosen because there the walls of the ravelin being incomplete, gave greater scope for the effective play of the artillery.

But before commencing hostilities Henri resolved to try more peaceable means of gaining possession of the town. He had no wish to be involved in the expense and delay of an unnecessary siege. A trumpeter and herald were sent therefore on the 16th, the day after his arrival, to summon the Chartrains to surrender. But Suireau, the mayor, and La Bourdaisière, the military governor, rivalled one another in the vehemence of their refusal to open the gates so long as the King remained a heretic. Their vehemence was probably stimulated by the suspicion which had recently been thrown on their sincerity. For an epigram had recently been pasted on the walls of the town accusing them of treacherous intentions—

'Écoutez, Messieurs de Chartres
Si ne mettez bien tôt en chartres
La Bourdaisière et Suireau
Ils vous mettront tous au tombeau.'

Whether there was any truth in the accusation or not, their answer now was uncompromising enough. The Royalists retorted by pushing their trench and mines up to the ravelin of the Porte des Épars, whilst, on their side, the besieged prepared counter-mines. Meanwhile, they dealt successfully with the barricade which threatened the Porte Drouaise. Three heavy pieces of artillery were brought up, the feint of a sortie was made to distract the attention of the enemy, and when this had been successfully accomplished, the cannon were unmasked, and a few rounds 'poured into their nest quickly turned the birds out,' as a contemporary puts it.[95] The Chartrains completely destroyed the barricades during the ensuing night. But the besiegers quickly opened another trench, and began to run other mines against the counterscarp of the ditch between the Porte Châtelet and the Porte S. Jean. In order, if possible, to destroy the barricade which protected this trench a gun-platform was hastily erected, and some heavy pieces placed in position.

The King, who had a large number of supporters among the better class of citizens, had expected to take Chartres at the first attempt. Before beginning the bombardment he again summoned the town to surrender, and so anxious was he not to be drawn into the trouble of a siege that he engaged in still further parleyings with the governor and mayor. But it was all to no purpose. The people were determined to resist, and they cut short all attempts at negotiation.

On Ash Wednesday, therefore, February 27, the bombardment commenced. A battery of seven pieces established in the trench of the Pig Market, opened fire on the walls between S. Foy and the Porte des Épars. A furious cannonade was maintained at intervals during that day and the next, and made a serious impression upon the defences. Many houses also were levelled to the ground; the spire of S. Foy was knocked down; one cannon ball entered the room of the Bishop's Palace, in which Henri III. had been wont to assemble his Council, and in which, it is said, the Massacre of Blois was arranged; another ball lodged between the two spires of the Cathedral, and broke one of the figures in the Gallery of Kings. A third, weighing 42 pounds, entered the old spire; and a fourth crashed through a section of the western rose window and fell into the choir. After that, the Chapter decided to perform the service in the crypt.

The resistance of the besieged was desperate. But, none the less, the enemy succeeded in a few days in pushing their trenches and galleries right up to the walls of the ravelin of the Porte des Épars. The King decided that the moment had come to deliver an assault. On the 5th of March, accordingly, a terrific bombardment took place, which had the undesired effect of knocking some of the masonry of the gate into the breach—an accident which prompted Gramont to remark, that the King of Navarre had fired five hundred rounds and only succeeded in filling the breach, but that he would have to fire fifteen hundred more to open it again. Under cover of this bombardment, a party of soldiers massed themselves behind the barricade in preparation for the assault. But an officer of the garrison, who was on guard in the *Clocher Neuf* espied this movement, and informed La Bourdaisière of it. His warning saved the town. The besieged concentrated their forces to repel the attack when the enemy attempted to scale the breach of the ravelin. The struggle even so was long and desperate. It lasted from three in the afternoon till nightfall, when the Royalists were compelled to retire, leaving many of their number dead in the ditch. The Chartrains had also suffered heavily. Their losses included forty soldiers and twenty citizens. The gallant De Pescheray, one of the chief defenders of the town, was mortally wounded in this fight. But an important check had been given to the besiegers, who contented themselves for some days with driving their galleries and mines.

Ill with impatience, the King swore to make the citizens of Chartres pay dearly for the powder which they made him burn. But they, looking daily to be relieved by the Ligue from the quarter of Dreux or elsewhere, actively counter-mined the Royalist sappers, and when the fire of the arquebusiers had no effect upon them, they adopted Gramont's suggestion, and hurled bottles of burning oil and *fleurs de soufre* amongst the enemy.

And now the siege had lasted a month, when one morning—it was the 15th of March—Henri was amazed to hear all the bells of the town, *Marie* and *Gabrielle* and the rest, ring out in joyful peals. The streets, it was soon reported, were filled with processions of the inhabitants, who were celebrating with unwonted fervour and extraordinary pomp the anniversary of the deliverance of the town upon the investment of Condé. Yet, even as they did so, many shook their heads at the evil augury of the statue of the Virgin that had been set above the Porte Drouaise. Throughout the siege of

1568, it was pointed out, the cannon-balls of the Prince de Condé had never been able to touch it, but Henri's bombardment had succeeded in upsetting, though not in breaking it.

Struck by the devotion of the citizens, it is said, and charmed by the melody of the bells, Henri gave orders that no guns should be fired that day, in order that the harmony of the celebration should not be troubled.

If this story be true, the garrison acknowledged the courtesy of Henri in a scurvy fashion. For on the evening of this day Gramont exploded a counter-mine before the Porte des Épars. In so doing he not only destroyed the enemy's works, but also a large section of his own ravelin. The result might have been serious if an assault had been delivered at once. But, contrary to the King's directions, the citizens were given time to repair the damage.

Still there was no sign of immediate succour from without. Fair words from the Ligueurs at Dreux, and promises from the Duc de Mayenne came in abundance. But those in charge of the defence knew that unless aid came quickly or provisions were thrown into the town, it would be impossible to hold out long. Already they were dependent for their flour upon the little wind-mills set up in the town, one of which had just been discovered in the Clocher Neuf, where it had lain since the days when the English besieged Chartres.[96] Those in command of the garrison were indeed by this time quite ready to deliver up the town into the King's hands, but the inhabitants refused to entertain the idea of yielding to the heretic of Navarre. They therefore decided to gain time by any means. Negotiations were opened with this object. La Bourdaisière and Gramont held an interview with the King's representatives on the 19th, and again on the 26th. Biron and others, with a strong escort, came to the Porte S. Michel, when Gramont went forth to parley with them. But hardly had the conference begun when a cannon-shot, fired by mistake from the Royalist camp, ricochetted near them. The people of Chartres, thinking themselves betrayed, replied with a volley, which accounted for several soldiers of Biron's escort, and abruptly put an end to parleyings. Next day Gramont and others had an interview with the King in person at the Monastery of S. Lubin, and brought back terms which were promptly rejected by the Ligueurs, who were still in a majority in the Council. They would rather die, they said, than surrender to a Huguenot King. This reply provoked an assault from the enemy, but the Chartrains were still unshaken. They informed the King that they would recognise him when he returned to the bosom of the Church, and meanwhile proposed such terms of capitulation that Henri swore a *Mort Dieu*, instead of his usual *Ventre S. Gris*, and cried out that as soon as he had taken the town he would hang these mutinous rascals who made fun of him.

His next step was to shift all his batteries suddenly to the side of the bishop's palace, and, concentrating his fire on a small section of the wall in that quarter, speedily to effect a new breach. Every effort had been made by the defenders during the short respite allowed them to strengthen their position against the inevitable assault. And when the assault was delivered the defence was admirable. Six times the Royalist troops rushed to the breach; six times they were flung back by the desperate courage of the besieged. They retired finally at seven o'clock in the evening, after five hours' fighting. They had lost three hundred men. The trenches were filled with dead and dying. Among the Chartrains the losses were almost as heavy. After the fourth assault, not one of the defenders of the first entrenchment had remained unwounded. A truce for the removal of the dead was arranged, and during the following night the besieged filled up the gap in the walls with sacks and gabions. But a new trial was in store for them. The Royalists built a large wooden bridge, closed like a gallery, and this, on the night of the 7th, they rolled on barrels up to and over the moat. The garrison were filled with consternation when they woke to see it in position, and the soldiers within, safe from attack, engaged in pulling down the sacks and gabions with which the breach had just been built up. The discouragement was great. Many began openly to declare that further resistance was useless. In some cases the soldiers were only induced to enter the ravelin, which, they maintained, was now untenable, by the persuasion of their officers' swords. The King, hearing of the growing spirit of discouragement within the walls, made yet another attempt to bring about a surrender. But such was the suicidal intolerance and obstinacy of the leading Ligueurs, that in the proposals they submitted they still insisted on the absolute prohibition of the reformed cult, a governor of their own choice, and a long truce, to enable them to inform the Duke of Mayenne of what was being done. Henri, of course, tore up the paper on which these absurd conditions were written, and proceeded to impose his own terms. They were accepted on the 10th of April, and proved to be extraordinarily lenient.

Henri authorised the practice of the Catholic religion, and forbade that of the reformed cult in the town and suburbs; he confirmed the established government and offices, and promised to punish no one for an act of war. The Ligueurs were granted permission to retire from the town, and eight days were allowed in which to warn Mayenne. If within that time a relieving force of four hundred men or more succeeded in throwing themselves into the town, the capitulation should be regarded as not having taken place. Henri took care, of course, that no force should so find its way into the town. With the object of intercepting any relief that might arrive, he himself, it is said, rode unceasingly round the environs of the town, and so wore himself out with his excessive vigilance that one day, overwhelmed by fatigue, he dismounted, made his pages lie down side by side on the ground, and, stretching himself upon them, slept thus for some hours.

It was also provided that the professional soldiers who formed the garrison should be allowed to march out of the town with their arms and baggage, colours flying and drums beating, and that they should make arrangements, in which the King would aid them, for the care of their wounded.

The clergy were still firm in their refusal to treat with the heretic and held out hopes of a miracle. But La Bourdaisière and Gramont and the majority of responsible people declared that the age of miracles was past and the day of necessity was upon them.

No succour arrived, and on the 19th of April the garrison marched out through the Porte S. Michel between two rows of Royalist soldiery. They were accompanied by the principal Ligueurs among the citizens. It was arranged that next day all the clergy and communities of the town should present themselves at the same gate on the morrow to receive the King and conduct him in full procession to the Porte Royale of Notre-Dame, and that there the Bishop, De Thou, should pronounce an official harangue. The King arrived on horseback with his staff at the appointed hour and was presented with the keys of the city by the mayor. 'Sire,' he said, 'we are obliged to obey you both by human law and law divine.' 'You might add by *canon* law,' threw in the conqueror, with a laugh. Thereafter, beneath a canopy of blue velvet fringed with gold and silver, and supported by four aldermen, His Majesty went in triumphant procession across the city by the streets S. Michel and Des Changes until he came to the Cathedral. But then, instead of stopping opposite the western porch, he went on his way to the episcopal palace, without appearing to notice the Bishop and Chapter who awaited him on the steps. Not to be cheated of the opportunity of delivering their address, Bishop and Chapter cut across through the church and appeared beneath the northern porch in time to stop the King, make the harangue and receive a gracious reply.

Henri Quatre made arrangements for converting the Porte S. Michel into a citadel and for levying a large sum of money from the citizens, and then, after attending the Protestant meeting-house, he left Chartres.

For the moment it must have seemed that the obstinate defence of the town had done little except add to the lustre of its arms. For the Catholic city was held now by the Protestant troops and became, next to Tours, the most important place in the hands of the Huguenot King. Henri, indeed, soon made it his seat of government. He summoned the Parliament, the Cour des Aides and the Council of State to meet here, and here they sat till the year 1594. It was in that year that he took the 'perilous leap,' as he termed it, which was, however, nothing more or less than a step of the highest political wisdom. He put a stop to the civil war, which was plunging France into anarchy and ruin, by reconciling himself with the Church of Rome. Amongst those prelates, before whom at S. Denis he solemnly abjured his Calvinistic errors and made profession of the Catholic, Roman and Apostolic faith, was Nicholas de Thou, Bishop of Chartres. And from that same bishop, whom he had flouted three years before, he received the royal consecration in the Cathedral of Chartres. For to prove the sincerity of his conversion, which was still much doubted, he demanded of the Church the Holy Unction which consecrates the kings. And Reims, the proper place of coronation for the French kings, being still occupied by the troops of Mayenne, Henri chose the 'town of his good council' as the scene of this august ceremony. 'He was moved to make this choice,' says a writer of his day, 'by reason of the peculiar devotion entertained for Notre-Dame by the Dukes of Vendôme, his ancestors, and also because that magnificent temple is the most ancient in Christendom.' But whatever the cause, it may well have seemed to the Bishop and Chapter of Notre-Dame on this occasion that the conqueror was conquered and felt his captive's charms, that 'her arts victorious triumphed o'er his arms.'

The occupation of Reims by the enemy rendered it impossible for the sacred vessel of oil to be used for Henri's consecration, but as the monks of Marmoutiers possessed a phial of miraculous oil, the King sent a deputation to ask them to send it to be used for his coronation. The precious relic arrived in the capital of La Beauce on February 19, 1594, brought by three brethren, monks and officials of the monastery, and escorted by De Souvré, the King's deputy, the Bishop of Angers and a great number of gentlemen, presidents and councillors. The Bishop of Chartres had sent to meet them all the clergy of the parishes and monasteries of the town, who were joined by Guy Robert, the Provost of Chartres, and twelve notable burgesses, carrying torches decorated with the royal arms and those of the town. A huge concourse of citizens in festal garb accompanied them.

The relic was then carried in procession through the streets, which were hung with tapestry, and to the sound of peals of bells, till it reached the Abbey of S. Père. There it was entrusted to the care of Yves Gaudeau, the prior, and four other monks. On Sunday, the 27th, the Comtes de Cheverny, D'Halluin, De Lauzun and the Baron de Termes presented themselves at the abbey and begged Brother Giron and his comrades of Marmoutiers to bring the holy oil to Notre-Dame to anoint His Majesty withal. The monks acquiesced, but first exacted from the King's deputies an oath, which was given before notaries, to the effect that the said sacred vessel should be brought back in good faith to S. Père after the said consecration was performed. Then Brother Giron, mounted on a white hackney, bore the precious phial under a magnificent canopy of red damask, followed by the lords responsible for its safety, notable citizens and the multitude of the people. The bishop, Nicholas de Thou, received the sacred vessel from the hands of Brother Giron, and took the oath exacted from the deputies. Then commenced the ceremony of the coronation. Apart from its picturesqueness and the fact that it illustrates a really important moment in French history, the following account, drawn from a contemporary record, may prove of particular interest in this year of grace 1902. It will be not uninteresting to compare the ceremony with that which is to take place in Westminster Abbey in June. The choir of the Cathedral had been hung with rich tapestry. Two arm-chairs had been placed before the high altar, one for the King and one for the officiating Bishop. Behind these, seats were reserved for the peers spiritual and temporal, and for the seigneurs and magistrates invited to assist at the splendid ceremony, whilst the galleries of the choir and nave were expressly left for those who could find a place there through the good offices of those in charge.[97] The King, who had had to listen the previous evening to a preachment on the custom of anointing the kings of France, emerged from the episcopal palace clad in a *camisole* of crimson satin and a long robe of silver cloth. He entered the Cathedral by the Porte Royale, accompanied by the Bishops of Nantes and Maillezais and preceded by the archers of the Grand Provost, the clergy, the Swiss Guards, heralds, Knights of the Holy Spirit, the Scots Guards, and the Marshal de Matignon bearing the Constable's sword. Behind him came the Grand Chancellor of France, the Grand Master, the Lord Chamberlain and the First Gentleman of the Bedchamber. The King walked straight towards the altar, accompanied by the two bishops aforesaid, and deposited there as an offering a casket of silver gilt. Then he took the seat prepared for him at the foot of the altar steps. The Bishop of Chartres now took the sacred oil from the hands of the monks of Marmoutiers, showed it to the people and placed it on the high altar. Next, turning towards His Majesty, he said, 'We demand of you that you should grant unto each one of us, and to the churches whereof we have charge, the lawful and canonical privileges, rights and justice, and that you should defend us as a king in his kingdom should defend all the bishops and their churches.'

The King standing upright, his right hand on the Book of the Gospels, replied, 'I promise and grant you that I will preserve to you your canonical privileges and your churches, and that I will give you good laws and administer justice to you and defend you, by God's grace, according to my power, as a king in his kingdom should do by right and reason on behalf of the bishops and their churches.'

After he had made this response the Bishops of Nantes and Maillezais raised the King from his chair and asked those present whether they wished to accept him as king. Hailed as legitimate sovereign by the whole of that vast and magnificent assembly, Henri IV. then took the oath, his right hand resting on the Holy Book.

'I promise,' he said, 'in the name of Jesus Christ, three things to the Christians, my subjects. Firstly, I will take pains that the Christian people may live in peace with the Church of God. Further, I will strive that on all occasions robbery and injustice may cease. Further, I will command that in all judgments equity and pity be observed, to the end that God in His infinite mercy and pity may have pity upon me and upon you. Further, I will strive to my uttermost, in good faith, to chase from my jurisdiction and lands all heretics denounced by the Church, promising on oath to observe all that has been said, so may God and this His holy Gospel help me!'

The Bishop of Chartres, with the aid of the spiritual peers, then anointed Henri with the holy oil, and after the peers had been summoned by the Chancellor of France, taking the crown, and raising it above the head of the monarch, he gave it to the dukes and peers to hold, blessed it and placed it upon the brow of the King. Henri IV. was forthwith conducted by the Bishop and the great lords to the throne which had been erected on the Jubé, that all the people might behold him. The bishop officiating next bade the monarch be seated, and prayed to God 'to confirm him on his throne and to render him invincible and unshaken before those who strive unjustly to snatch from him the crown which has legitimately fallen to him.' Then he gave him the kiss of peace and cried aloud three times, 'Vive le Roi!' The cry was taken up and repeated by the peers and all the people. The sound of clarions, hautbois, trumpets, drums and other instruments of music echoed through the vaulting of the ancient Cathedral, whilst heralds threw amongst the crowd pieces of gold and silver 'marked with the effigy of the King and with the date of the day and the year of his anointing and coronation.' Mass was then celebrated, and the King, having received absolution from the bishop, partook of the communion with great humility. The service over, the bishops and lords escorted the monarch back to the episcopal palace. The Duke of Montbazon led the way, bearing the crown on a velvet cushion, whilst others accompanied him with the sceptre and the royal sword. The sacred vessel was taken back at once in procession to the Abbey of S. Père by the barons. They restored it to the safe keeping of the monks of Marmoutiers.

Meanwhile the King, clad in fresh robes of equal magnificence, 'sat at table under a canopy of beautiful stuff, in the great episcopal hall, which was adorned with rich tapestries.' On his right, at another table, were ranged the spiritual peers in pontifical garb; on the left, and at another table, the temporal peers in their coronation robes. Below the stage reserved for the King and these high personages, the ambassadors, the Chancellor, Knights of the Order and the principal officers of the realm took their place at yet another table. The banquet finished with a fanfare of trumpets, hautbois and clarions, and the King retired, preceded by the Marshal de Matignon, carrying before him the royal sword 'bared outright.'

In the evening there was another splendid banquet, after which grace was said and sung as the late King Henri III. had been wont to have it.

So closed that day of solemn pomp and of ceremonies not meaningless. For they impressed upon the people the reality of a conversion which was politically of almost as much importance to France as the conversion to Christianity of Clovis and his followers. The report of the consecration of the King at Chartres was followed almost immediately by the surrender of Paris, and Henri became in fact what he had so long been in name only, King of France.

I have endeavoured to illustrate each stage of this story of a French ecclesiastical town by the mention or description of some building, and to illumine each notable building by some historic episode connected with it or with the period at which it was constructed. There is little left of the walls and gates which he bombarded to remind us of the taking of the town by Henri Quatre. But if we go to the Municipal Museum and Library we shall find pictures of this siege[98] and of the unsuccessful siege laid by Condé, besides numerous old maps and plans which show us, with varying degrees of accuracy, the town as it was in those days of storm and stress.

The Hôtel de Ville,[99] in which the museum is lodged, is a fine building of red brick and stone, composed of three sections and a very handsome gateway. It is itself connected with the period under review; for, when Henri was besieging the place nearly half the town was in correspondence with the besiegers, and, among the rest, was the important family of Montescot. Montescot was a good courtier, and he was rewarded with a canon's stall in Notre-Dame. But he was also a good citizen, and he acted as intermediary between Chartres and the King in the matter of the pecuniary contributions levied from the town. He it was who built,[100] as a mansion for himself, the present *Hôtel de Ville* (1614), and in his character of good courtier he inscribed those words, 'HENRICO MAGNO,' over the principal entrance. The bust of Marie de Médici figures on the doorway of the right wing, the bust of Louis XIII. on that of the left. The old *Parloir aux Bourgeois*, or site of municipal administration, which had been in the hôtel known as the *Perron des Trois-Rois* in the *Rue des Changes* since 1571, was moved here in 1792. One wing of the building abuts on the *Place des Halles*, or market-place, at the corner of which is the Librairie Selleret (Petrot-

Garnier), the booksellers and publishers whose name is honourably connected with most of the publications of Chartres.

The municipal rooms, hung with tapestry, are on the ground floor; the library and museum above. The library is of exceptional interest, and it is admirably arranged. Unfortunately it is only open on Mondays, Wednesdays and Fridays from 12 to 3.30 p.m. But, if the hours are short, the visitor who may wish to study the extremely rich collection of books and manuscripts, which were removed here from the surrounding monasteries during the Revolution, will find every encouragement to do so. Without credentials or explanation I have read there myself many days, and it is with grateful pleasure that I take this opportunity of acknowledging the polite attention and the ready help proffered to me, a stranger, by the Librarian and his assistants. The collection includes over 100,000 volumes, and among the thousand manuscripts six hundred are earlier than the sixteenth century, and many beautifully illuminated.

The Museum, the entrance to which faces that of the Library, is open to the public on Thursdays and Sundays from 2 to 4 p.m. (gratuity). Catalogue, 1 franc, 50 centimes. I have referred already, in the course of my story, to most of the interesting things to

*Place de l'Hôtel de Ville*

be seen there. I have mentioned some of the Roman antiquities—the coins and pottery found in the neighbourhood—the armour of Philippe-le-Bel, and of Charles V., his son, offered to Notre-Dame after the battle of Mons-en-Puelle; and among the pictures, the numerous maps and pictures and portraits that relate to the history of Chartres.

It remains to call attention to the Layé collection of arms, armour, porcelain and medals, and, in the room above, what should on no account be missed, the magnificent pieces of Flemish tapestry (sixteenth century) which were brought here from the choir of the Cathedral. Five out of the original ten are to be seen in the Hôtel de Ville. The borders are rich and the work exquisite. They were presented originally to the church by that Bishop de Thou of whom we have spoken above. The designs of the five panels are based on those of the cartoons made by Raphael for the Vatican, and they represent incidents from the life of Moses.

A beautiful example of fourteenth-century French needlework should be noted in a triptych here.

# CHAPTER XII

## The Revolution—S. Père

THE events recorded in the last chapter, culminating in the coronation of Henri Quatre in the Cathedral of the town which, as the Huguenot King, he had besieged three years before, are the last in which Chartres played a part of real importance in the history of France. She suffered, indeed, during the troubles of the Fronde, both from the massing of troops that occurred continually about her borders, and from many serious attacks of plague and famine, for which they were doubtless, to a large extent, responsible. But the trials which she had undergone had damped her military ardour. Bitter experiences in the past had exhausted the vehemence of her enthusiasm. Henceforth she lays aside her militant character and devotes herself to the peaceful pursuit of a quiet municipal life. The part she takes in politics is distinguished by ecclesiastical sobriety and commercial prudence.

An excellent college, founded by a good merchant, Pocquet by name, sprang into prominence in the life of the town, whilst the citadel, established by Henri Quatre at the Port S. Michel, is declared to be no longer needed. It is handed over, in 1600, to the citizens, and converted again into a church. And the Huguenots, so much has the spirit of the age changed, are provided with a church, so that each may worship in peace according to his own conscience.

The year 1623 saw two changes which affected the nominal position of Chartres and continue still to affect it. In the first place the diocese of Chartres became in that year the first suffragan of the newly-created Archbishopric of Paris, and, in the second place, the Duchy of Chartres, definitely and officially united with the crown, passed to Gaston, Duke of Orléans, and has ever since remained in the house of Orléans. The Duchy, it will be remembered, had been created by François I. in favour of Renée, daughter of Louis XII. Louis XIII. now bought it back from the Duke of Nemours, and himself, Duke of Chartres, visited the town in October of the same year. (It was on a previous occasion that, as the historian Doyen narrates, he came to pay his devotions at the shrine of Notre-Dame, and thereafter was indulging in a game of tennis at the court in the market-place when he was informed that there was a certain woman there who played a strong game. He sent for her and played a set with her. But she beat him. *Cette femme prit un caleçon et gagna le roi, en jouant par-dessous la jambe.*) Three years later he presented his brother Gaston, on the occasion of his marriage and in exchange for the Duchy of Anjou, with the County of Blois and the Duchies of Orléans and Chartres. On the death of Gaston, the opponent of Mazarin, the Duchy of Chartres reverted to the Crown again, but Louis XIV., a few weeks afterwards, settled it, together with the Duchy of Orléans as an appanage, on his only brother, Philippe, on the occasion of the marriage of that prince with Henrietta of England. Since that time the title of Duke of Chartres has always been the appanage of the eldest son of the house of Orléans.

For the rest, Chartres passed more and more into the condition of a *Ville de Province*, where only the echoes of what is being said and done in Paris and France are to be heard.

The mystic heresy of the *Illuminisme*, propagated by the 'alumbrados' of Spain, appeared here in the first half of the seventeenth century, but was routed out before long. The method by which it was crushed is, however, significant. This heresy represented a revolt against the hierarchy of the Church. It rejected all dogmas and all ministers of religion. The chief exponent of it at Chartres was a hermit who took up his abode in the woods of Lèves, and soon secured a strong following among the unlettered classes. The heretics, in fact, began to make such progress in La Beauce and Picardie that Richelieu became alarmed. The Government gave orders that the sect was to be exterminated. The hermit of Chartres was therefore arrested and sent to Paris, where he recanted his errors.

He and his followers, in earlier days, would doubtless have been burnt at the stake without more ado. Now, such has been the growth of the central power, they were merely sent to Paris and converted. The punishment of heterodoxy had become generally much less severe. Very little hanging was now done for conscience's sake. We only come across one instance of a monk being hung at this time, and that was for celebrating Mass without having been ordained priest.

Throughout the succeeding centuries, then, the political action of Chartres is reduced to that of an ordinary commercial municipality. It suffered none the less in common with the rest of France from all those causes which had issue in the Revolution. The crash of 1789 was precipitated by the coincidence of two events—the imminent bankruptcy of the Government and the great famine which, following on one of the worst winters on record, produced universal rioting throughout the country and ended in pure anarchy. For the Government, having no money and no credit, could not feed the people. The people might bring the King from Versailles and sack the Bastille but that did not make bread cheaper. The Constituent Assembly was as helpless as the King. The pressure in Paris was worse in October than during the siege by the Prussians. These famine riots continued in Paris and all over the country till good harvests came. Then the country would have settled down. But the Revolution had been begun, and, under the extreme party, with the aid of the Jacobin clubs, was destined to bring in its train the Reign of Terror. The Girondins wished for war and that the country should not settle down.

The Government had been more or less insolvent since 1715, but since 1783 the share taken by France in the War of American Independence had rendered total failure inevitable. The wealth of the country was not small and it was rapidly increasing. But the Government had for years put an immense strain upon their preposterous financial system, and the ridiculous machine had now completely broken down. Since 1783, one Superintendent of Finance after another had declared that the only possible way to avert bankruptcy was to introduce a sweeping change in the system of taxation. As soon as they came to that conclusion they were dismissed, for Louis XVI., who half knew that they were right, could not stand against his Court. But in the year 1788 the fact became too obvious. The Superintendent Necker declared that, unless some reform were undertaken, bankruptcy, in a few months, was inevitable. Now, the National Debt was held almost entirely by the official class in France, to whom, therefore, even the loss of their privileges, which consisted to a large extent in not paying taxes, seemed better than the bankruptcy of the country. Necker advised the King to summon the States-General and to carry out reforms in connection with it.

The demand for it to be summoned was already loud. It was the old Parliament of France, but it had not met since 1614. Then it had consisted of three separate houses, the Nobles, the Clergy, and the Third Estate, each acting independently of each other and enjoying the right of presenting petitions to the King. How the Third Estate asserted itself and, after the States-General had been converted into the Constituent Assembly, proceeded to fulfil its Tennis-Court Oath and to give a Constitution to France we need not repeat here. What from the point of view of the story of Chartres requires to be noticed is that the new Constitution, which was gradually drawn up between the years 1789-1791, represented to a great extent the ideas implied in the list of grievances, *cahier des plaintes*, submitted to the Chartrain representatives of the Third Estate. They had had a sufficiently bitter experience in past years of the heavy and unjust incidence of taxation, and the congestion and confusion of the judicial system, which, together with the existence of the official class, were the real grievances of the age. The administrative arrangements of the new Constitution embodied the theories of Rousseau, who advocated extreme democratic decentralisation. For this was a panacea which the followers of Diderot and the Encyclopædists, believing that the correction of bad laws and bad government would produce the millennium, that, in fact, you can change the character of the whole by changing the arrangement of the units, imagined would cure all the evils of Society. Almost all real power, therefore, was taken from the King and placed in the hands of municipal and village Councils, of what Carlyle called 'forty thousand sovereign bodies.' One need not emphasise the grim comment passed by history upon these theories.

So far as Chartres was concerned they had their immediate and lasting effect in a decree of the National Assembly, dated January 15, 1790, which constituted our town Capital of the Department of Eure-et-Loir and gave it a departmental administration. The bishopric was preserved, and only a court of appeal was wanting. The assembly of citizens, some 1500 in number, met and elected the members of the new municipal body, which included a mayor, eleven municipal officers, twenty-four *notables*, and a *procureur de la commune*.

Besides drawing up a new Constitution, the Constituent Assembly had been busy promulgating a series of decrees, of which some, such as those bringing in a new financial system, proved inoperative, and others, such as that concerning seigneurial dues, were concerned with abolishing what had already ceased to exist. But their decrees concerning the Church had some effect, and that bad. In the first place, the whole property of the Church was confiscated and tithes were abolished. In the second place, under the civil constitution of the clergy, all beneficed clergy were, it was decided, to be beneficed by the State (July 12, 1790). Thirdly, all beneficed clergy were required to submit themselves to free election at the hands of laymen, and to undertake the discharge of their holy office only after swearing a solemn oath to obey the rules of the new Constitution. This decree was an immense blunder. It was offensive in the extreme to every good Roman Catholic, to whom the spectacle of a purely lay power interfering in questions of ecclesiastical discipline was unbearable.

The Pope intervened and forbade the bishops to take an oath which involved the renunciation of all Papal claims. The greater number of bishops and clergy obeyed the Papal order, and were supported by the majority of the lower orders in whom the love of the Church was still quite strong and deeply rooted. At Chartres, M. de Lubessac refused to take the oath, and the assembly of departmental electors met and appointed in his place Nicolas Boisnet, a doctor of theology and vicar of the parish of S. Michel. He was a worthy man who for forty years had offered an example of all the Christian virtues, and he only accepted the See of the civic episcopate on the express condition that he would render it to him who had abandoned it when he should see fit to come and take it again.

Meantime the revenues of the Church had been sequestrated, and the Chapter, yielding to force, had passed out of existence. It was after this fashion that religion, like the monarchy, was provided with a Constitution.

The Girondin Clubs had taken possession of Chartres as of the other towns. They soon had their way, and France was at war with Prussia and Austria. That war was entered into without any very definite plan or enthusiasm by the Allies, who expected a mere parade march to Paris and an opportunity of aggrandisement for themselves. But France, thinking that the victory of the Allies would mean the restoration of the old *régime*, took the war very seriously from the beginning. A voluntary movement of unequalled size and enthusiasm took place in the spring of 1792. Eure-et-Loir furnished several battalions of volunteers, and Chartres gave to France, as captain of their first battalion, the young and chivalrous Marceau. The vigour of this resistance surprised the Allies, who in the face of it would have been at a loss to know what to do if they had arrived at Paris. Instead of exerting themselves, therefore, they fell back upon the frontier. But their advance had proved fatal to Louis, who must have hoped for their success. As they advanced the panic in Paris had increased. The crisis came with the 10th of August, on which day a big mob rising, clearly engineered by the Girondins, drove the King to seek safety in the Assembly, whence he passed to spend his last sad hours in the Temple prison, and finally to meet death on the scaffold. Meanwhile, the Girondin leaders dictated three decrees to the Chamber. The King was suspended from his functions, the new Commune of Paris was recognised, and it was decided to summon an extraordinary National Convention, a single Chamber with powers to do what it pleased, elected by universal suffrage. To that celebrated Assembly Chartres contributed some very notable deputies. The upheaval of public opinion in the town is indicated by its representatives, for among them was Jérôme Pétion, Mayor of Paris in 1792 and President of the Convention, and Brissot de Warville. These men were Girondins, and when the party split in two they remained Girondins and suffered death in the following year at the hands of the extreme section, the Jacobins. As a Girondin town Chartres, then, was typical of the provincial towns of France. For while as to political theory Girondins and Jacobins were agreed in aiming at an ideally democratic Republic extremely decentralised, on the practical question of ways and means they differed. The Girondins insisted, in spite of the war, on carrying out their decentralising projects at once, but the Jacobins recognised that if Paris was to be defended at all in the ensuing campaign of '93, a strong central government, a dictatorship in fact, was absolutely necessary. The soul of the Jacobin party was Danton, the one man neither fanatic nor fool, and he saw not only the necessity for improvising a strong central government, but also how it could be done. It could be done by means of the organisation supplied by the political clubs scattered through France, and by terrorising the majority. For the numbers of the Jacobins were always small, but the audacity of their measures produced the illusion of power. Paris was cowed, the Girondin party crushed by force, and the Jacobin conquest of France, after the suppression of the risings in the Girondin provincial towns, for a while complete.

The Reign of Terror had begun and lasted till July 1794. It lasted, in other words, till the Jacobin party had done that side of its work, which was thoroughly national and popular, and, thanks to its conduct of the war, under Carnot, the danger on the frontier had ceased. Then the Jacobin Government fell at once. It was because they were doing their work with regard to the war, and no one else could do it, that France tolerated the policy of brigandage and butchery by which they governed;—for this reason, and because those most likely to resist were away at the frontier, and also through fear. For the Jacobins were an organised party, and the rest were a chaotic mass of individuals. Therefore they slew not less than thirty thousand men and women of all classes. A minority that had begun to rule by terror, they could not go back. They felt the weakness of their position, and went on increasing the pressure, themselves almost mad with terror. Individual zeal was required to make up for their lack of numbers. A scrutiny was held of their own members, and those who showed a lack of energy were expelled and guillotined. They executed also that they might confiscate, and thus provide the sinews of war. And an official theory, stated by the chiefs and formulated by Robespierre, was not lacking to justify their

***Rue des Béguines***

behaviour. Owing to centuries of despotic government, it was said, the mass of Frenchmen were corrupt and unfit for citizenship in the ideal Republic that was going to be established. They must wipe out the bad blood.

In this matter of wiping out bad blood a certain amount of moderation at any rate was observed at Chartres. But, short of bloodshed, every outrage and abomination conceivable by a horde of raging maniacs was solemnly proposed and perpetrated. The priceless treasure of the Cathedral was looted, and all the churches pillaged. The leaden roofs thereof, and the bells of the Cathedral, and all leaden tombs that could be found, were melted down to supply the army with money and with cannon. It was decreed that every statue within and without the Cathedral should be destroyed. The work of destruction had already begun on the north porch, when a member of the Convention, Sergent Marceau, raised his voice against the measure, and, in the interest of art, the decree was repealed. But next day, at a meeting of the Chartrain Club, a member arose, and, declaring that the Cathedral dominated this Republican city too much, proposed that it should be destroyed. The proposal was considered, and actually adopted.

But the Cathedral of Chartres was in the end allowed to stand. For a curious reason. It was found that the difficulty of getting rid of the vast masses of *débris* would be insuperable. No citizen would undertake to allow the fragments of the building to be cast upon his land, and, seeing that the town would be endlessly encumbered by them, it was decided that the Cathedral should not be destroyed.

But, if not destroyed, it must be profaned. Hideous orgies were prepared to celebrate the Feast of Reason. The group of the Assumption in the choir was converted into a group more conformable to the patriotic sentiments of the moment by setting a red cap on the head of the Virgin, and placing a pike in her hand. The marbles of the choir were inscribed with Republican maxims, and in the centre of the sanctuary a miniature mountain was raised. On the summit was reared a statue of Reason, leaning against an oak, on the highest branch of which was perched a cock holding in his beak a tricolour. The Temple of Reason was inaugurated by a sermon, in which the citizens were informed that they had recovered their liberty, and were once more men, pure as Nature herself. This discourse was followed by a musical drama, entitled *Reason Victorious over Fanaticism*, in which Watchfulness, in a robe sown with eyes, and Fanaticism in priestly garb figured, with Rousseau and Voltaire as acolytes of the former. Philosophy then engaged and easily vanquished with argument Fanaticism, who, seeing himself beaten, hurled himself, shrieking abuse, on Watchfulness. But the cry, 'To Arms!' was raised, and lo! the Republic, in the guise of a woman in a tricolour robe, rose from a cavern near and cast down Fanaticism, pierced him with a dart, broke the altars and trampled under foot a crucifix. Then a machine in the form of a cloud raised the Republic to the mountain top and set her beside the statue of Reason.

And M. Thirion, of the Convention, closed the proceedings with an address.

These profane and grotesque celebrations were followed up a month later (December 23, 1793) by a bonfire, which was lit in front of the Porte Royale on the day which would have been Sunday had not Sundays been abolished. Into this bonfire were hurled all ornaments of the Church which were not of precious metal—books and wooden crucifixes and statues. And with them was burnt the 'Druidical Statue,' Notre-Dame-de-Sous-Terre.

On the civil side, bread riots and brigandage were the order of the day at Chartres, but at last, under the Directory, comparative quiet began to be restored. The town, however, was accused of not supporting that highly centralised administration with sufficient warmth, and, indeed, Delarue, the deputy of the Five Hundred, made a report, in which he stated that the Chartrains 'had furnished arms and ammunition to five hundred brigands to suppress the liberty of the legislative body.' The municipal administration defended themselves vigorously against this charge. It was probably true enough that Chartres was not in favour of the Directory, which, from the beginning, rested on the support of the army, and thus began that process which was to end in the Consulate—when the army set up its own man. From this time forth the army is France. It had been enormously improved since 1792. Out of the unskilled rabble that had fled before the Allies without striking a blow it had been converted into an organised machine. Under Carnot, at the War Office, good men were coming to the front. In 1796 they took the offensive, and arranged a big triple advance upon Vienna. Jourdan was to advance from the Netherlands, Moreau from Alsace, Bonaparte through North Italy. The brilliant successes of the latter covered the failure of the other two, who were beaten back to the French frontier. But before their retirement the Battle of Altenkirchen had been fought, and there had fallen the young Chartrain, General Marceau—François Séverin Marceau-Degraviers—whose statue stands in the centre of the Place des Épars. He was only twenty-seven years of age at the time of his death. His praises were pronounced to the Council of the Five Hundred by his old friend and comrade in arms, Jourdan, who secured for his mother a handsome pension. Marceau represents to the Chartrains the ideal of that military ardour which is the keynote of modern France.

Nothing could be more eloquent of the difference between mediæval and modern France, of the change from the rule of Church and King to the domination of the established army, than the present state of the old Benedictine Abbey of S. Pierre, locally called S. Père, and its precincts. For the site of the old dormitory, refectory and cloisters is now used for cavalry barracks, and Chasseurs d'Afrique now stable their horses where once the cloistered monk tended his garden and fish ponds.

The church itself is one of the most remarkable in existence, and would doubtless be better known had Chartres no Cathedral. As it is, the magnificence of Notre-Dame obscures the excellence of the smaller church, and obliterates from the memory its striking characteristics. In any other town its glass alone would bring pilgrims from afar. For not only are the thirty-six great lancet windows of rare beauty, being filled, to a great extent, with thirteenth and fourteenth-century glass, but the impression which they give you on first entering the church is almost unique. The apse is ablaze with colour, the triforium of the choir glazed, chiefly in grisaille, and the delicate triforium of the nave is topped by huge lights of colour and grisaille, which are interrupted by hardly any framework of stone. It seems as if the whole of the upper part of the building were one continuous sheet of glass gloriously coloured. The effect, indeed, is scarce an illusion.

For the monks of S. Père have taken up the idea of the flying buttresses where the builders of the Cathedral had left it. We have seen (p. 189) how those builders had felt their way with the buttresses of the nave, and developed those later ones of the choir. In happy rivalry of the Cathedral, our monks now, it would appear, determined to show the full possibilities of the idea. They built a temple of glass and supported it with flying buttresses. Windows took the place of walls in their church, and the walls were set several yards outside the windows. That is the effect of this amazing *tour-de-force* as you look at it from the east or west. The line of buttresses show like the solid wall of the church without. Yet so cunningly were those buttresses arranged to carry the thrust of the building, that the church, windows and roof and all, still stands unimpaired.

Something of the history of this once large and famous abbey we have already given in the course of our extracts from the Chartulary of S. Pierre, which was written in great part by the monk Paul in the eleventh century. There is an old tradition, quite devoid of foundation, that a church was built at Chartres in honour of S. Peter, who then held the See of Rome, by S. Potentian and his disciples. This church, tradition further asserts, was connected with an abbey by Clovis, and endowed by Queen Clotilda on the death of her husband. However that may be, the church was certainly founded by the middle of the seventh century, and probably the monastery also. They grew and flourished exceedingly in spite of wars and sieges, burnings and bishops, and waxed in wealth and importance to such an extent as to provoke serious jealousy in the hearts of the clergy and adherents of Notre-Dame. Thus, even as early as the year 840, we find the monks asserting the rights of their constitution against the Bishop Hélie, and refusing to recognise the episcopal jurisdiction. The bishop did not hesitate to have recourse to arms. The very threshold of the Church of S. Père was stained with blood. The greater part of the monks were forced to flee from their monastery, whilst the prelate seized all the precious ornaments and property that belonged to them, and left but a bare sustenance for the small band of brethren who had dared to remain. The hand of the Northman completed, in 857 and 911, the ruin of the abbey thus begun by the bishop, and it was not till 930 that that 'noble, rich and virtuous prelate,' Aganon, built on the site of the ruins a vast monastery and great church, and restored to the brethren and canons thereof their confiscated vineyards and property. The work of the material and spiritual reformation of the monastery was continued by his successor, Ragenfroy. To this period must be referred the great square western tower, of which we have spoken as being contemporary with the Cathedral of Fulbert (*see* p. 66 ff.). It is even possible that it formed a part of the church reconstructed by the Bishop Aganon about the year 940. It is certainly much the oldest portion of the building. The rest, together with the monastic buildings, perished in the great fire which destroyed the town and damaged the Cathedral in 1134. After that disaster the monk Hilduard was entrusted by his abbot with the task of rebuilding the church of the monastery, and he began to work in the year 1150. After he had finished the choir, however, lack of funds brought matters to a standstill. A wall was built across the western end of the choir in order to enclose it. But whilst the foundations of this wall, which was meant to serve as a temporary west end, were being dug a discovery was made, the result of which was quickly to furnish the means needful for continuing the construction of the church. A small vaulted chamber was opened, in which was found the body of S. Gilduin. Miracles began to occur. The faithful flocked to the new shrine, bringing rich gifts, and about the year 1210 the building was again able to be taken in hand. The church was completed. But when this was done, either because they were not content with the choir of Hilduard, as being unworthy of the later nave, or because it was already in need of repair, the monks of S. Père rebuilt the choir towards the end of the reign of S. Louis. The apse was finished in or about the year 1310. The monks made it, as it were, almost one sheet of glass, and supported their beautiful, if daring, creation by a series of sixteen buttresses without, which are higher, lighter and more graceful than those of the nave. A beautiful thirteenth-century doorway on the north side of the church is the remaining feature of note on the exterior. But, in spite of the variety of dates to which the various portions of the building belong, it is, as a whole, singularly well proportioned and full of grace.

Within, since the Revolution, when the tombs of Fulbert and many other bishops were destroyed together with much valuable and artistic furniture, carved stalls and a Renaissance jubé, there are two main attractions—the windows and the Limousin enamels. But before speaking of them we must mention the epitaph of Robert, son of Richard, first Duke of Normandy, who was *not* Archbishop of Rouen, as the inscription which is in the aisle states. Also the very rich and graceful triforium of the nave, and the later and still more delicate triforium of the choir, cannot fail to please.

The unique gallery of fourteenth-century glass presented by the windows of S. Père is, as M. l'Abbé Bulteau remarked, arranged methodically in a carefully-considered combination and not according to the whims of the various founders, as was to a large extent the case with the thirteenth-century lights of the Cathedral. On the left-hand side of the nave are represented the Apostles and episodes from the Gospel story; on the right, the Confessors and incidents drawn from the lives of the martyrs; in the choir, martyrs, prophets and saints group round our Saviour, who, as a little child, is borne on His mother's arm, and as a grown man hangs upon the tree of the Cross.

All the windows of the church, therefore, viewed thus, seem to converge towards a common centre, which is Jesus Christ our Lord.

The scheme of the majority of windows is the presentation of large single figures of stained glass surrounded by broad bands of grisaille.

On the north or left-hand side, beginning from the west end, next the old tower, are two Apostles, set in a broad frame of grisaille.

These two Apostles are S. James the Less and S. Matthias. The next window gives S. Jude and S. Barnabas, and the next two tell the story of S. John the Baptist—(*a*) Baptizing Jesus; the daughter of Herodias demanding his head and presenting his head in a charger to her mother; John showing the Divine Lamb to his disciples. (*b*) The announcement to Zacharias; his childhood, preaching, and answering Herod. The fifth window shows S. Andrew (with a book) and S. John (with a book open). In the next S. Bartholomew holds a cutlass and S. James a book, whilst the seventh and eighth recount the history of S. Peter. For the seventh shows him with his disciples, healing a man born blind, preaching, and being delivered from prison by an angel. In the eighth S. Peter receives the keys, appears before Nero, confronts Simon, is crucified and taken up to heaven.

S. Thomas and S. Philip, S. Matthew and S. James fill the ninth and tenth windows. The eleventh and twelfth recount the chief incidents in the life of Jesus Christ. In the eleventh, the entry into Jerusalem, the Last Supper, the Betrayal, the Crucifixion, the Resurrection and the 'Touch me not' are represented, and in the twelfth the disciples of Emmaus, S. Thomas, the Ascension, Pentecost and Judgment. On the right-hand or south side of the nave we are shown the Confessors and incidents from ecclesiastical history. The first, next to the tower, gives S. Benedict and S.

Maur, for the Church of S. Père, it will be remembered, was the church of a Benedictine monastery. The second light gives S. Avitus and S. Laumer. The third relates the legend of S. Agnes; she repels the son of the Proconsul and her modesty is miraculously shielded; she is burnt at the stake and transferred. The story of S. Catherine, who disputed with the Emperor and converted the heathen philosophers and led them to martyrdom, is told in the fourth.

S. Malard and S. Solemnis, S. Lubin and S. Martin fill the fifth and sixth. The seventh and eighth, which are now in a deplorable condition, once illustrated the lives of S. Denis and S. Clement, the pope and martyr. S. Gregory and S. Sylvester fill the ninth, the Virgin and Child, with the donor kneeling below, the tenth.

The eleventh traces the history of the parents of the Virgin. Joachim and Anna are repelled by the priest, Anne by her servant. Joachim feeds his flocks; an angel appears to him and also to S. Anne, who goes out and meets her husband at the gates of Jerusalem. She gives birth to Mary, who presents herself at the Temple and marries Joseph.

The twelfth window portrays further scenes in the life of the Virgin— the Annunciation, Visitation, Birth of Christ, Adoration of the Magi, the Presentation and Death of Mary.

The windows of the choir, with the exception of those in the apse, are of thirteenth-century glass. In them the patriarchs, prophets and personages of the Old Testament are shown, to the number of forty, carrying palms in their hands, and speaking, apparently, to each other.

The six apsidal windows contain the most brilliant glass in the abbey. They are as remarkable, so M. l'Abbé Clerval observes, for elegance of design as for vivacity of colouring. Each of them holds four life-size figures of bishops or apostles surrounded with rich architectural ornamentation; whilst the heads, divided into three quatrefoils, give scenes of martyrdom and an angel bearing a crown for the martyred saints below.

The grisailles of the triforium were replaced in the early part of the nineteenth century by some glass painted in 1527 by Robert Pinaigrier, which had been saved from the adjacent Church of S. Hilaire, destroyed during the Revolution. Unfortunately they have been arranged with extraordinary indifference to their meaning, and pieces of glass have been stuck in pell-mell according as they happened to suit the shape of the window or convenience of the glazier. The result is that windows which, both in colouring and design, were quite exceptionally good have been deprived of all the charm of their design and much of the effect of their colour.

The lower series of windows of the church are for the most part modern. They represent chiefly scenes from the Gospel story of the life of Christ and come from the hand of M. Lorin, the glass-painter of Chartres, whose *atelier* is in the Rue de la Tannerie.

Leaving the study of the glass you should now go to the apsidal chapel dedicated to the Conception. This chapel has been restored and polychromed by M. Paul Durand, and contains a statue of the Virgin by Bridan and the tombstone of Simon de Beron, Canon of Chartres in the twelfth century. But it is the magnificent Limoges enamels of Leonard Limousin, 1547, which we wish to see. They are ranged round the walls of the chapel, and in order to see them you must ring the bell near the chapel railings and summon the attendant.

These enamels, which are of extraordinary beauty and size (24 x 10⅝), exquisite in colour and shading, and are in perfect preservation, come from the chapel of the famous Château d'Anet, which Diane de Poitiers built, *voulant une œuvre toute Française*, and of which Henri II. wrote to his Queen—

'S'il vous souvient, Madame, d'avoir lu
En quelque livre élégante et eslu
Le dessein rare et la description
De quelque lieu beau en perfection
Je vous supply imaginer et croire
Que c'est d'Annet le pourtraict et l'histoire.'

This magnificent château, the noblest type of the Renaissance in France, was destroyed to a large extent (1799-1810,) but was in great part restored by the late M. Moreau. Lying, as it does, on the Évreux line, it is quite worth stopping to see. But the tourist may be grateful for the information that it is 1½ kilomètres from the station, and is only shown on Thursdays and Sundays.

The beautiful enamels before us, so rich in their varied shades of blue, were presented by Henri II. to the lovely and accomplished mistress, who, in spite of her years, had won his heart when he was but a lad of thirteen.

They had been wrought for François I. by the famous Léonard Limousin,[101] after the designs of Michel Rochetel. The date (1547) and the initials and salamander of François bear witness to this fact, and the initials L. L. on the handle of the sword of S. Paul and beneath S. James the Less proclaim the artist.

The panels represent the twelve apostles, with their characteristic emblems, and each apostle is set in a framework of Renaissance ornament—genii and fantastic animals and garlands of flowers.

There is nothing else in S. Père of sufficient interest to detain us.

# CHAPTER XIII

## The Prussians at Chartres

'Je sais le plan de Trochu
Plan, plan, plan, plan, plan!
Mon Dieu! quel beau plan!
Je sais le plan de Trochu!'

ON the 26th of October 1901 a monument, standing at the entrance of the Promenade des Charbonniers, near the Place du Châtelet, and dedicated to the memory of the children of Eure-et-Loir, who laid down their lives for their fatherland, was unveiled by M. Caillaux, the Minister of Finance. The monument was designed by M. Nénot, and consists of a triumphal arch in the Classic style, crowned by a pediment bearing the arms of Chartres, Châteaudun, Dreux and Nogent-le-Rotrou. This is accompanied by three groups in bronze: on either side an artilleryman and a foot soldier of the *mobile*; in the centre, beneath the arch itself, the principal group, representing 'France calling to the defence.' It consists of a female figure, who personifies the Fatherland and the Republic, brandishing in one hand a flag tattered and torn with bullets, and pointing with the other in the direction of the enemy. And an officer at her feet fires a revolver in that direction.

To the France of to-day this monument is not a mere memorial of the past and useless valour of her sons, but a warning also, lest she should forget the coming of the Prussians in 1870, her own military unpreparedness, and, it should be, her own fatal political weakness. Something, too, it doubtless expresses of that thirst for revenge which threw her some years ago into the arms of Russia, and which that alliance was really certain to prevent her from gratifying.

It was on Friday, the 30th of September 1870, that the Prussian soldiers appeared for the first time near Chartres.[102] Three weeks later Châteaudun fell, after a desperate and heroic defence, for which that picturesque and ancient town paid the dear price of failure. Two days later the enemy marched in force upon Chartres. The *tirailleurs* and *mobiles* and troops of the National Guard, who endeavoured to defend the town, after vain marching and counter-marching, with the same generous ardour and utter ineffectiveness as had distinguished the movements of the other armies before the disasters of Wissembourg, Wörth and Sedan, returned exhausted. Without firing a shot they had been rendered incapable of fighting. Fighting in any case would have been useless. It was wisely decided to capitulate, and on the 21st the Mayor and Prefect of the Department drove out to Morancez to save the city and Cathedral, by surrendering them to General von Wittich, from the inevitable destruction of which Châteaudun had given them a terrible example. What they saw on their way of the French defence and the Prussian advance convinced civilians and military men alike that it was impossible to hope to defend Chartres. It was agreed that half the French garrison should evacuate the town, and that the Prussians should halt at the Three Bridges till half-past four, and then take possession. When the news of the capitulation was heard by the troops assembled on the Boulevard Chasles,[103] they protested, and

**Old Houses in the Rue Ste Même**

raised the cry of treason, which was the watchword of the whole war.

It had been expressly stipulated that the National Guard should be disarmed, and Colonel Heiduck, who conducted the negotiations at Morancez, had demanded the surrender of 2000 rifles. 'But,' replied M. Labiche, the prefect, 'there never have been more than 1300, and we really have not time to get any more to make up the 2000.' With such inadequate means of defence, and with the threat of immediate bombardment from the artillery, which was ranged in a semi-circle round the town on the south-west side, hanging over their heads, the representatives of Chartres behaved wisely in yielding at once. The stranger at least cannot regret that the Cathedral was preserved from the ordeal of a bombardment.

'The Prussian troops,' said the *Cologne Gazette*, 'entered Chartres with bands playing and saluted with enthusiastic cheers Prince Albert of Prussia, whom they marched past. Next morning presented a striking scene when these German warriors met in the famous crypt of the Cathedral, and visited by the light of the lamps every part of that splendid subterranean building.'

The occupation of Chartres lasted for five months—the place, of course, was important to hold during the siege of Paris—but the inhabitants would appear to have suffered very little, except from German music. This is how M. Caillot, the historian of the occupation, describes the behaviour of the Prussians on the morrow of their entry.

'Towards nine o'clock in the morning their infernal music, which they had had the indecency to parade through the town the night before, echoed through the Place des Épars. The officers, smart and pomaded like circus-clowns, strutted round the musicians and saluted each other with a stiffness that they seemed to have borrowed from the English. Out of the hotels and houses they poured in an endless stream, men of all colours, sizes and ages, stiff, proud and haughty, with all the airs of conquerors.'

Conquerors, after all, they were, but though, like all the French writers of the period, M. Caillot refers to the Germans as barbarians and savages, they seem to have done little that can honestly be called savage—unless leaving without paying their bill, which amounted to nearly half a million francs, can be considered so. The fact is that, according to the unanimous testimony of foreign observers who accompanied the army, the moderation of the German soldiers was as remarkable as their successes.

During the weary months that ensued, the Chartrains remained as ignorant of what was going on in the Department and round Paris as the beleaguered Parisians themselves. The same unfounded hopes and false rumours, the same invincible optimism and futile belief in the 'plan of Trochu,' in successful sorties from Paris or in the victories of the army of the Loire prevailed as in Paris itself. They are recorded in M. Caillot's little volume with something of the same pathos, but not with the same spirit that distinguishes Francisque Sarcey's *Le Siège de Paris*. There we learn how the Chartrains listened to the battle of Loigny raging in the distance, and thought that the sound of the Prussian artillery was that of the French guns till the arrival of 2400 French prisoners told them the bitter truth, and how they rejoiced at the lyrical proclamations of Gambetta, only to be reduced to despair at the news of the fall of Orléans.

They learnt on the 29th of January, with bitter grief and mortification, that Paris had been forced at last to capitulate, and from that time onwards they were busy with the payment of their share of the impositions and indemnities that were inflicted upon the conquered nation.

The Prussians left Chartres on the 16th of March 1871.

# CHAPTER XIV

## Itinerary and Expeditions

THE following scheme may perhaps prove of use to those who have but a few hours to spend in Chartres and wish to find their way quickly about the picturesque but tortuous streets of the old, lower town.

Leaving the station, go down the Rue Jean de Beauce, cross to the far corner of the Place Châtelet, go down the Rue Sainte Même, take the first turning to the left down the Rue du Cheval Blanc, and keeping up to the right, where the street divides, you come out opposite the west front of the Cathedral. Go down the Rue des Changes (opposite the south porch of the Cathedral), and turning to the left before reaching the Place Billard (the old site of the Castle of the Counts) reach the Place de la Poissonnerie (fish-market: Maison du Saumon). Pass on into the Rue S. Eman, and turning to the right pass Queen Bertha's staircase, which is in the Rue des Écuyers, opposite the Rue du Bourg. Bearing up the Rue des Écuyers, follow the Rue S. Pierre. You leave the Church of S. Aignan on your right and arrive at the old Abbey Church of S. Père. Leaving the Place S. Pierre by the Rue du Pont S. Hilaire at the eastern corner of it, cross the water and turn sharp to the left down the Rue Foulerie, which skirts the river with its picturesque tanneries and wash-houses. You pass on the right the street leading down to the Porte Guillaume. Continuing, the Rue de la Foulerie becomes the Rue de la Tannerie, and the Rue de la Tannerie the Rue Massacre. Cross the river and visit the ruined Church of S. André, then go down the Rue de la Brèche. The Chapel of Notre-Dame de la Brèche is on the right in this street, which runs into the Place Drouaise. Before reaching this take the turn to the left up the Rue Muret, which winds up into the Rue du Cardinal Pie (formerly called the Rue du Marché de Filasse), from which a picturesque archway leads through the old cloister buildings into the Rue S. Ives, which opens on the north porch of the Cathedral. The Bishop's Palace is now on your left.

The promenade[104] known as the Tour de la Ville, at the foot of the ancient ramparts and round the old moat of the town, should not be omitted. You will start naturally from the Place Châtelet, down the Promenade des Charbonniers, which brings you to the Place Drouaise, and so on across the Pont Neuf to the Porte Guillaume and the Boulevard de la Porte Morard. Hence the Rue du Pont de la Courtille leads to the Place S. Michel, and thence by the Boulevard Chasles to the Place des Epars.

The Rue Régnier leads from the Boulevard Chasles to the Place des Halles.

Some magnificent views of the Cathedral and the town, and 'bits' of the old walls and moat, will be obtained in the course of this circuit.

### EXPEDITIONS.

The Château de Maintenon (Duc de Noailles) lies on the line between Chartres and Paris, and, with its waterworks, is well worth a visit. Other châteaux in the neighbourhood are those of Villebon, near Courville, which belongs to the Marquis de Pontoi-Poncarré, and Éclimont, near Gallardon, the property of the Duc de La Rochefoucauld.

### DATES OF THE CHIEF FESTIVALS AT CHARTRES.

May 31.—Notre-Dame du Pilier.

August 15.—Feast of the Assumption.

September 8 and 15; December 8.—On September 15 and December 8 a magnificent procession through the Crypt takes place in the evening.

{487kb} {2mb}

# FOOTNOTES:

[1]

'Belsia, triste Solum, cui desunt bis tria tantum:
Fontes, prata, nemus, lapides, arbusta, racemus.'

The couplet has been neatly translated:—

'Le triste pays que la Beauce!
Car il ne baisse ni ne hausse;
Et de six choses de grand prix
Collines, fontaines, ombrages,
Vendanges, bois et pâturages
En Beauce il n'en manque ... que six!'

[2] In this connection, *see* the window, No. 6, in the clerestory of the nave of the Cathedral, north side, the subject of which is 'Tilling the Ground.'

[3] Un Athée serait mal à l'aise ici.

[4] September 15 and December 8.

[5] For a theory of the relation of their ceremonial to that of other primitive cults, *see* Mr. J. G. Fraser's fascinating book, *The Golden Bough* (2nd Edition), and Mr. Andrew Lang's criticism of that theory in his *Magic and Religion* (New Edition).

[6] Such Roman remains as have been found at Chartres together with these coins will be found in the Musée, Hôtel de Ville (Rue de la Mairie, Place des Halles).

[7] Tibullus, i. 8.

[8] *Acta SS. MM. Saviniani et Potentiani*, manuscripts edited by L'Abbé Hénault, Origines Chrétiennes de la Gaule Celtique.

[9] Representations of these early martyrdoms are to be found in the beautiful statue of Modesta, with bas-relief of the well, etc., and the statue of S. Potentian, with bas-relief of his martyrdom, on the western supports of the north porch (looking towards the new tower), and in the first window of the Chapel of the Sacred Heart.

[10] The monk Paul, who lived at Chartres towards the end of the eleventh century and wrote the *Cartulaire de Saint Père*, speaks of it as *Locus Fortis*.

[11] The crypt is open and free from 6 a.m. to 9 a.m., and shown to visitors by the concierge at certain hours throughout the day for a small fee. Apply to the lodge of the Maison des Clercs at the south-east corner of the church.

[12] Pintard MS.

[13] *See* pp. 23, 43, 64, 76.

[14] Notice in this connection the two beadwork belts dedicated by the chiefs of the Hurons, 1676, and Abnaqui Indians, 1700, which are now in the western recess, which is the Chapel of S. Savinian or the Saints Forts.

[15] Wisdom.

[16] The Rue des Changes, starting almost opposite the south porch of the Cathedral, leads in a direct line to the Place S. Aignan.

[17] The third window from the north-west corner is called the Bishop's Window, and contains figures of S. Aignan, S. Martin of Tours, S. Denis, and S. Nicholas.

[18] See him portrayed in the beautiful brown and yellow glass of the fifth window of the south clerestory of the Cathedral nave.

[19] Third window of the south clerestory of the nave.

[20] The episcopal palace as it now stands is a handsome eighteenth-century red brick building, and was built by the Bishop de Fleury in 1760. Vast and sumptuous, with its Italian portico and flights of steps, with its gardens of which you see but a small part through the *grille* which opens on the cloister near the north porch of the Cathedral, with its wing 'de la Duchesse,' as it was called after the Duchesse de Fleury, mother of the bishop, and the wing built in 1702, wherein are the immense reception-rooms, this palace, regal almost in its size and magnificence, suggests the temporal and spiritual power of the prelates who numbered among their vassals the highest barons of the realm and whose diocese was known at Rome as the Great Bishopric. But it is little in accord with the life or the means of the twentieth-century bishops, to whom, as to their Anglican brethren, the palaces they have to maintain are usually white elephants.

[21] There is a punning saying that this church has 'trois clochers et deux cents cloches' (deux *sans*).

[22] He figures in the Galerie des Rois, on the western façade of the Cathedral.

[23] As early as 680 the Episcopal schools of Chartres were held in repute.

[24] The story of this presentation is told in the glass of the Chapel of S. John the Baptist in the Church of Aix-la-Chapelle. Charles-le-Chauve caused it to be brought thence into France.

[25] S. Piat preached the Gospel to the Carnutes in the third century before going to gain the crown of martyrdom at Tours. He is the saint to be invoked by farmers for fair weather in the rainy years. See the chapel dedicated to him, built out beyond the apse of the Cathedral. This chapel was added in the fourteenth century, and is a good example of that period, the doorway at the foot of the staircase which gives access to it from the Cathedral being especially beautiful. In the tympanum of this doorway is a statue of the Virgin and the Christ-Child playing with a dove. The bracket of the tympanum of the doorway at the top of the staircase once supported a statue of S. Piat. It has been destroyed, but you may see a picture of the saint in the grisaille above this door. The glass belongs partly to the fourteenth and partly to the fifteenth century, and is good, though not so good as that of the rest of the Cathedral. It has suffered from an ignorant application of oil-colour some fifty years ago. The polychrome bosses in the roof and the rich capitals are full of detail, and skilfully wrought. The exterior, unlike the interior, is unprepossessing. Before the year 1793 it could boast a spire of lead and wood, which may have done something to relieve the present effect of heaviness. The staircase which connects the chapel with the Cathedral is, however, very beautiful.

[26] *Roman de Rou.*

[27] *Le livre des Miracles de Chartres* (translated into French verse from some Latin collection in the thirteenth century).

[28] *Cartulaire de S. Père.*

[29] It was outside the walls of that day. The New Gate was that which afterwards formed the gate of the cloister, opposite the Renaissance clock tower, north-west of the Cathedral, destroyed at the end of the eighteenth century. Two pillars of the gate then destroyed are still visible.

[30] Le Pré des Reculés.

[31] To visit the treasure, apply to the chaplain who guards the Chapel of Notre-Dame du Pilier. (Fee, half a franc.)

[32] *Cf.* the phrase in the Charter of King John (1356) 'quam-quidem ecclesiam ipsa virgo gloriosa elegit pro sua camera speciali.'

[33] *Cf.*

'Ne leissent en Chartrain et en Duneiz bordel,
Ne mezon en estant ki seit fors du chastel;
Ne leissent boef ne vaque, genice ni torel
Coc, capon, ne geline, ne viez chien ne chael.'
*Roman de Rou.*

[34] Compare the castles and cathedrals of Durham and Lincoln.

[35] This monastery, south of the town, like that of S. Martin-au-Val, formed part of the domain of the Counts.

[36] Fulbert's name in Chartres has been given to a street which runs parallel with the south-west corner of the Cathedral. A statue of the bishop, holding in his hand a scroll on which is incorrectly displayed a plan of the *present* Cathedral, is to be seen on the eastern extremity of the choir screen. A fresco portrait of him was discovered some years ago in the Church S. Hilaire at Poitiers. The curious portrait of him speaking to his people *within his Cathedral*, which is here reproduced, was painted on vellum by André de Mici in 1028, the year of Fulbert's death, and illustrates a *tombeau*, or panegyric, composed in his honour by his pupil, the musician, Sigo.

[37] *Migne's Patrology*, Vol. 141.

[38] *Cf.* York Minster.

[39] It was situated outside the walls, on the north side. Destroyed by the Huguenots in 1568, the site is still marked by the name of the Clos S. Jean, which is near the railway station, and upon which you look from the Butte des Charbonniers.

[40] Monographie de la Cathédrale de Chartres par l'Abbé Bulteau, 2nd edition, 1887-1891. Two vols.

[41] Henricus Rex hujus ecclesiæ lacunar construxit.

[42] Those who are curious on this subject will find some examples of his plain-song in a volume edited by M. Merlet and M. L'Abbé Clerval, and entitled *Un Manuscript Chartrain du XI^e. Siècle.*

[43] *Œuvres de Fulbert*, p. 177, 1608 edition.

[44] S. Eman of Cappadocia founded a small hermitage beneath the shadow of Notre-Dame, and this hermitage was afterwards turned into a

chapel, fragments of the walls of which still remain (Rue S. Eman). The apse was formerly supported by the old town wall of the ninth century.

[45] It is only fair to add that the *Cartulaire* of Notre-Dame speaks of this bishop (Abbot of Brêmes) in terms of the highest praise. Under Arrald, among many other benefactions, *William the Conqueror* (1070) caused 'a good, a precious' campanile to be erected over the central point of the transept of the Cathedral, 'for the repose of the soul of his daughter Adeliza,' piously observing that 'The gifts which we offer to God, and which we dedicate to His glory, are not for us loss or sacrifice, for thus we only preserve our riches and multiply them with the hope of eternal life.'

[46] The Pope had condemned the royal investiture by cross and ring as implying spiritual jurisdiction in the throne.

[47] Fresnay l'Évêque. The bishop's house may still be traced in the name of a farm, Château de l'Évêque.

[48] A *Bénitier* saved from it is to be found in the Cathedral crypt.

[49] Marquis, may the monks of Cluny make you their head or may you be Abbot of Cîteaux, since you have a heart so base as to prefer two oxen and a plough at Montferrat to being Emperor elsewhere.

[50] Stalls first, and then shops, were set up about the western porch as soon as it was built. Pilgrimages meant commerce. There was traffic not only in images of the Virgin, but also in the necessaries of life. Merchants found here a ready market, and one in which they were protected from the rapacity and exactions of the feudal lords.

[51] Lépinois's *Histoire de Chartres*, 2 vols., 1858.

[52] The present one is on a pivot, and serves as a weather-cock.

[53] The roodloft or gallery over the entrance into the choir is sometimes called the Jubé, from the words 'Jubé, Domine, benedicere,' pronounced from it. (Parker).

[54] Page 25.

[55] The south tower of the west front.

[56]

Clocher de Chartres, nef d'Amiens,
Chœur de Beauvais, Portail de Reims.

[57] The octagonal spire is made of the light stone of Marboué.

[58] 'The endless upward reach of the great west front, the clear silvery tone of its surface, the way three or four magnificent features are made to occupy its serene expanse, its simplicity, majesty and dignity—these things crowd upon one's sense with a force that makes the act of vision for the moment almost all of life. There is an inexpressible harmony in the façade of Chartres.'—HENRY JAMES—*Portraits of Places*.

[59] *Livre des Miracles*.

[60]

Mens hebes ad verum per materialia surgit
Et demersa prius hac visa luce resurgit.

[61] There were formerly five statues on the front of the south-west tower. The Ass is resting on two human heads that seem crushed by his weight. The Sow is much mutilated. A similar piece occurs on the façade of S. Pol-de-Léon (Finisterre). The motive of an ass playing a lyre is found in ancient Egyptian monuments; a dog playing a lyre occurs at Poitiers.

[62] The same legend is connected with the Imp of Lincoln and also with one of the churches at Rome.

[63] I drink—burn wood—prune vines—give grass—flowers—field sports—hay—harvest—vintage—sow corn—fatten swine on acorns—kill swine.

[64] Revelation, chaps. iv., v.

[65] *La Cathédrale*.

[66] 'Cui toto par nulla hodie splendescit in orbe.'—Book IV.

[67]

'La haute dame glorieuse
Qui voloit avoir merveilleuse
Iglise et haute et longue et lee
Si que sa per ne fu trouée
Son douz fils pria doucement
Que miracles apertement
En son iglise a Chartres feist
Que touz le peuples le veist
Si que de toutes pars venissent
Gens qui offerendes tant feissent
Que achevée fust siglise

Qui estoit a faire emprise.'
*Livre des Miracles*, p. 32.

[68]

'Lors vindrent gens de totes pars
Qui en charrestes et en chars
Grans dons a l'iglise aportoient
Qui a l'œuvre mestier avoient . . .
Tant y venoit de pelerins
Et par voïes et par chemins
Que c'estoit une grand merveille,
Chacune nuit fesoient veille
Et en avoit tant en l'iglise . . .
Si que li clerc qui a matines
De nuit a l'iglise venolent
Entrer ou cloitre ne poaient.'

[69] The window which recorded in a series of medallions many of these miracles has been sadly mutilated (south aisle).

[70] *Histoire de la Peinture sur verre d'après ses Monuments en France*, 2 Vols., folio, 1841. The coloured plates of this fine work give no idea, however, of the real richness of the colours of the glass. *Windows*, by Lewis Day, is the best English book upon stained glass.

[71] The strong iron bars supporting the glass are frequently bent to follow the outline of the medallions. This is only found in early glazing.

[72] The subject of the French apprentice is pleasantly expounded in Mr. Tighe Hopkins's *An Idler in Old France*. His German counterpart I have dealt with in my *Story of Nuremberg*.

[73] Henry James, *Portraits of Places*.

[74] A similar legend is told of the consecration of Westminster Abbey. 'One stormy Sunday night during the reign of King Sebert, the eve of the day fixed by Mellitus, Bishop of London, for the consecration of Sebert's newly-finished church at Thorney, it happened that one Edrie, a fisherman, was casting his nets into the Thames. His attention was arrested by a voice calling from the opposite shore at Lambeth. He crossed, and found there a venerable stranger in foreign garb, who desired to be ferried over to Thorney Isle. Edrie complied with the request. The stranger landed and went at once to the church. And while Edrie waited on the bank, suddenly the air grew bright with celestial splendours, there was no darkness more or shadow in the monastery, and choirs of angels he beheld

ascending and descending on a ladder which reached from heaven to earth, with song and flaming tapers and sweet odours of incense. The fisherman remained gazing at these wonders and caught nothing all night. At last the stranger returned and said unto Edrie, "I am Peter, keeper of the keys of Heaven. When Mellitus comes to-morrow, tell him all that you have seen, and show him that I, S. Peter, have consecrated my own Church of S. Peter, Westminster." '

[75] Rouillard, *Parthénie*.

[76]

'Quer tele fu sa destinée
Que dou seint feu fut alumée
Dont li martir ardant alument
Qui a seint Leu Fort acoustument
En la crote à Chartres venir
La ou la Dame fet fenir
Dedens ix jorz la maladie
Ou soit a mort ou soit a vie.'
JEHAN LE MARCHANT.

[77] *Cf.* Walter Pater, Gaston de Latour.

[78] *Introduction to the Study of Gothic Architecture.*

[79] Chartres.

[80] The choir is the largest in France, after that of Laon.

[81] Two large statues of Leah and Rachel were formerly on the piers here, but were destroyed in 1793.

[82] Restored 1901.

[83] First used on some *jettons d'argent* struck for distribution on January 1, 1775. It is, perhaps, an adaptation in elegiac verse of the 'Ob cives servatos' found on certain coins of Augustus.

[84] Jacques Bonhomme was the nickname of the French peasantry, and his cry had been

'Cessez, cessez, gens d'armes et piétons
De piller et manger le Bonhomme
Qui de long temps Jacques Bonhomme
Se nomme.'

[85] It was in this very year that Louis de Bourbon, Comte de Vendôme, in expiation of the vow which he had made when held prisoner by his brother, the Count of Marche, having come as a pilgrim to Chartres, began to build the Flamboyant chapel, in the south aisle of the Cathedral, which bears his name.

[86] Of this La Hire the following anecdote is told. He was marching to relieve Montargis, which was in dire straits after a long resistance to the besieging English. On his way he met a priest, from whom he demanded absolution. 'Confess your sins, then,' returned the priest. 'I have no time,' was the reply, 'for I am in a hurry to engage the English; and, besides, the tale of a soldier's sins is not a short one.' The priest somewhat hesitatingly pronounced the sentence of absolution. La Hire immediately knelt down by the wayside and prayed aloud, 'God, I pray Thee to do this day on La Hire's behalf what Thou wouldst that La Hire should do for Thee, supposing he was God and Thou wast La Hire.' His somewhat uncanonical prayer was granted. He attacked the English and obliged them to raise the siege of Montargis. I note a curious parallel between this prayer of his and the quaint old English epitaph of John Hildebrod,—

'Here lies the body of old John Hildebrod.
Have mercy on his soul, O God!
As he would do, if he were God,
And you were old John Hildebrod.'

[87] Contemporary MS. (Bibliothèque Municipale), Duparc, 1578.

[88] *Siège de Paris*, Francisque Sarcey.

[89] This incident is represented in the engraving by Perrissim, 1570, here reproduced. It will be noticed that the artist has ignored the river.

[90] Edited by M. L'Abbé Métais, 1895.

[91] (*See* p. 198).

[92] Left of the Place de la Gare.

[93] Connecting the Boulevard Chasles with the Rue des Bouchers.

[94] Thus built Claudius Huvé, physician, for the adornment of the city and the benefit of posterity.

[95] *Journal des Choses plus Mémorables Advenues à Chartres*, 1579-1592.

[96] *Histoire de Chartres*, Souchet.

[97] Cérémonies observées au sacre et couronement du très-chrestien et très valeureux Henry IV., etc.—Paris. Jamet Mettayer. 1594.

[98] No. 189, a picture of the Flemish school, represents Henri-Quatre surrounded by his staff and watching the effect of the bombardment of the town. The quarter of S. Jean is in flames. His soldiers are endeavouring to force their way through the breach at the Porte-Drouaise. The Cathedral, it will be observed, has here its third *flêche*. The towers in the fortifications are square.

[99] Starting from the Place des Épars, you reach the Place des Halles by the Rue du Bois Merrain, and enter the Hôtel de Ville by the Rue de la Mairie.

[100] On the window of the façade runs the following inscription:—'Atavitam Montescotiorum domum qua natus Cl. restituit an. 1614.' He built it, then, on the site of his old home.

[101] Leonard the Limousin, so called to distinguish him from Leonard the Engraver, was retained by Francois I., who gave him the post of one of his valets. He was the greatest enameller of his day, excelling chiefly in portraiture. His other work is unequal, being often inferior in colour and marred by the influence of the Italian school, the defects and absurdities of which, without its merits, he, in common with the decorators of Fontainebleau, too frequently reproduced.

[102] *Les Prussiens à Chartres*. Ernest Caillot. Petrot-Garnier, 1871.

[103] So called after M. Michel Chasles, the eminent geometrician, who was a Chartrain.

[104] Carriages may be hired by the *Course*, 75 centimes; by the hour, 1 franc 75 centimes. Outside the town the fare is 2 francs the hour.

Milton Keynes UK
Ingram Content Group UK Ltd.
UKHW042144281024
450365UK00010B/594